Pelican Books
OVERKILL: The Story of Modern Weap

The splitting of the atom is recognized as one of the major scientific achievements of the twentieth century, but what has it meant for us? So far we have not seen nuclear power harnessed to provide us with cheap and efficient heating and lighting for our homes, or energy to drive our factories and cars. Instead, we have seen two nuclear bombs used in war – together they killed a quarter of a million people. There is now an amazing variety of sophisticated ICBMs, MIRVs, LRCMs and SLBMs which could wipe us off the face of the earth: the threat of nuclear holocaust is ever present.

In *Overkill* Dr John Cox explains for the non-specialist the scientific and historical background of these modern weapons. He tells the story of the Hiroshima and Nagasaki bombs, and goes on to explain nuclear energy and how it is harnessed for weapons of destruction. He describes the current arms race and, in a chapter on how war might start, tells of incredible accidents involving nuclear weapons. Finally, in a few powerful and controversial chapters, he argues that only complete disarmament can make the world safe.

With a glossary of strategists' terms, informative photographs and simple scientific diagrams, and most of all with its widely informed yet clearly written text, *Overkill* offers a fascinating combination of history and science that should appeal to anyone interested in what is happening right now. It was published originally in 1977 and has made a big impression on the current generation of nuclear disarmament campaigners. This edition is updated with new material on cruise missiles, Trident submarines, the neutron bomb and Civil Defence, and has an additional chapter concerning the Campaign for Nuclear Disarmament (CND).

Dr John Cox was born in Cardiff in 1935, where he went to school before studying mathematics and chemical engineering at Imperial College, London. He works as a consultant engineer, though much of his spare time is spent lecturing on the dangers of the arms race. Currently he is Vice-Chairperson of CND (Chairperson for six years), having first been elected to the CND Executive in 1961. He lives with three generations of his family in Talywaun, Gwent.

John Cox

OVERKILL

The Story of Modern Weapons

With prefaces by
Professors Joseph Rotblat and Michael Pentz

Penguin Books

Dedicated to the memory of Betty England,
who died suddenly on 4 July 1981.
She campaigned for CND for over two decades
and never lost her faith in people.

Penguin Books Ltd, Harmondsworth, Middlesex, England
Penguin Books, 625 Madison Avenue, New York, New York 10022, U.S.A.
Penguin Books Australia Ltd, Ringwood, Victoria, Australia
Penguin Books Canada Ltd, 2801 John Street, Markham, Ontario, Canada L3R 1B4
Penguin Books (N.Z.) Ltd, 182–190 Wairau Road, Auckland 10, New Zealand

First published in Peacock Books 1977
Published simultaneously in hardback by Kestrel Books
Second edition published in the U.S.A. by T. Y. Crowell 1978
Third edition published in Pelican Books 1981

The diagrams were drawn by R. Sherrington and R. Paull

Filmset by Northumberland Press Ltd
Gateshead, Tyne and Wear
Printed in Great Britain by Richard Clay (The Chaucer Press) Ltd,
Bungay, Suffolk
Set in Monophoto Plantin

Contents

List of Plates   7

Acknowledgements   8

Preface to First Edition by Professor Joseph Rotblat   10

Preface to Third Edition by Professor Michael Pentz   12

1. The first atomic bombs   15

2. Nuclear energy – how it works   28

3. Nuclear war – what to expect   45

4. Many ways of killing   59

5. Weapons systems   71

6. The arms race   98

7. How war might start   117

8. Arms control   128

9. Disarmament   144

10. War as a way of life   154

11. How many more?   172

12. Concerning CND   189

Appendix   236

Book list   238

Films   241

Glossary of terms   242

Join CND   245

Index   247

List of Plates

I Alamogordo

II J. Robert Oppenheimer

III Hiroshima

IV Nagasaki

V *News Chronicle*, 7 August 1945

VI Bikini

VII Fishermen from the *Lucky Dragon*

VIII A fallout shelter

IX A napalm victim

X General Westmoreland

XI A nuclear submarine

XII A ground-launched cruise missile (GLCM)

XIII Palomares (sequence)

XIV Soviet missile

XV Effect of underground explosion

XVI Aerial photograph

XVII Eisenhower and Macmillan

XVIII Russell and Collins

XIX Aldermaston march, 1960

XX Committee of 100 sit-down, 1961

XXI For peace in Vietnam, 1969

XXII Crawley, 1970

XXIII Faslane, 1973

XXIV Newbury, 1980

XXV 26 October 1980, march

XXVI 26 October 1980, demonstration

Acknowledgements

The author and publishers would like to thank the following for their kind permission to reproduce extracts from copyright material: pp. 24, 25–6, *Nagasaki: The Forgotten Bomb* by F. W. Chinnock, copyright © 1969 by F. W. Chinnock, reprinted by permission of Allen & Unwin Ltd and The New American Library, Inc., New York; pp. 18–23, *Hiroshima Diary* by Michihiko Hachiya, copyright © 1958 by Michihiko Hachiya, reprinted by permission of Gollancz and Collins-Knowlton-Wing; p. 179, 'The Dangers of Leaving Defence Planning to "Experts"' by Mary Kaldor, reproduced from *The Times*, 29 October 1975, by permission; pp. 39–42, Frederick Muller Ltd, *The Voyage of the Lucky Dragon*, by Ralph E. Lapp, to the author; pp. 96–7, *The Essence of Security* by Robert S. McNamara, copyright © 1968 by Robert S. McNamara, by permission of Harper & Row, Publishers, Inc.; p. 156, 'Warfare is Only an Invention – Not a Biological Necessity' by Margaret Mead, from *Asia*, vol. 40, no. 8, 1940, pp. 402–5, to the author; p. 36, extract from the *Western Daily Press*, 20 July 1974, to the editor; pp. 212–14, extract by Michael Foot from *Voices in the Crowd; against the H bomb* edited by David Boulton, reprinted by permission of Peter Owen Ltd, London; p. 217, extract by Peter Fuller from *Time Out*.

The author and publishers would like to thank the following for their kind permission to reproduce illustrative material: ATOM Committee for pp. 131, 169, 199 and 207; Bill Mauldon/*Chicago Sun Times* for p. 128; *Guardian*/cartoons by Papas for p. 173, by Arthur Horner for pp. 125 and 127, by L. D. Gibbard for p. 176; New Science Publications for pp. 63, 66 and 68, the Grimbledon Down cartoons first appearing in *New Scientist*, London, the weekly review of science and technology; Express Newspapers for p. 194; HMSO for pp. 46–7 and 50–51, material from *Protect and Survive* reproduced with the permission of the Controller of Her Majesty's Stationery Office, and for pp. 109 and 112; *Labour Weekly*/cartoons by Murray Ball for title page and p. 114; Herb Lock © 1973 for p. 144; *New Statesman*/cartoon by Vicky, 1960 for p. 178; Penguin Books Ltd for pp. 57, 161 and 163; *Punch* for pp. 60 and 208; *Sanity* for pp. 118, 180 and 187; *Scientific American* from pp. 18–19 of 'The Great Test Ban Debate' by Herbert F. York, November 1972 issue, for p. 39/from pp. 19–21 of 'Missile Submarines and National Security' by Herbert Scoville Jr, June 1972 issue, for pp. 105 and 108/from p. 29 *top* of 'The Detection of Underground Explosions' by Sir Edward Bullard, July 1966 issue, for p. 135/from p. 15 of 'The Accuracy of Strategic Missiles' by Kosta Tsipis for p. 76; US Navy Department for p. 87; SIPRI for material redrawn on pp. 82–3, 84, 91, 99, 102, 130 and 164.

The author and publishers would like to thank the following for their kind permission to reproduce photographic material: US Defense Nuclear Agency for Plates I and IV; Associated Press Ltd for Plates II, VII and X; Keystone Press Agency for Plates III, VI, VIII, XVII, XVIII, XIX, XXI and XIII (left top and middle and top right); Associated Newspapers Ltd/British Museum Newspaper Library for Plate V; Pressen Bild Stockholm, Sweden for Plate IX; US Navy Department for Plate XI; Labour Party Library for Plates XII, XX and XXIV; Popperfoto for Plate XIII (bottom left and bottom right); Novosti Press Agency for Plate XIV; Lawrence Radiation Laboratory, Nevada, USA for Plate XV; RAF Photo/DOE © Crown copyright for Plate XVI; CND for Plates XXII, XXIII and XXV; *Morning Star* for Plate XXVI.

Preface to First Edition

About two thirds of the world population in 1976 were born *after* the bombs on Hiroshima and Nagasaki. For the pre-atomic generation the news in 1945 of the unleashing of a new, immensely powerful and awesome source of energy was a tremendous shock. Except for a small number of scientists, nobody suspected its coming, and its demonstration in such a spectacular and tragic manner made 6 August 1945 a turning point in the history of mankind: from then onwards the continued existence of the human species on this planet could no longer be taken for granted.

This cataclysmic perception of nuclear energy appears to be absent among the majority of people alive today. Having been born in the atomic age and having grown up with *the bomb*, they believe they can live with it, and give as evidence the fact that since Hiroshima and Nagasaki there has been no instance of nuclear weapons being used for military purposes. While everybody agrees that a nuclear war would be an unmitigated catastrophe, the attitude towards it is becoming similar to that of potential natural disasters, earthquakes, tornadoes, and other Acts of God: we know the threats exist, but there is nothing we can do about them.

This fatalistic attitude is, of course, fallacious and unrealistic. Unlike Acts of God, which by definition are unpredictable, the occurrence of a nuclear war is a predictable event; its probability is increasing with time. The so-called nuclear stalemate is not a static phenomenon; it is dynamic, and can only be described as a state of unstable equilibrium with a pre-determined outcome.

If, so far, we have managed to avoid a conflict in which nuclear weapons are to be used (although threats of their use have been made on several occasions) it is because no side has yet reached a position from which it can be sure of winning a war without incurring unacceptable damage itself. But they keep trying. This is the essence of the nuclear arms race, which goes on unabated and is accelerating in two dimensions: vertically and horizontally.

The vertical arms race, in which the main contestants – at the moment – are the USA and USSR, is the continuous attempt to gain numerical and technological superiority – more, faster, bigger and deadlier missiles; eventually this is bound to result in one side acquiring a first-strike capability. Already it has led to the mad state of affairs, known as overkill, in which the stockpiles of nuclear weapons are considerably more than enough to destroy every human being on the earth.

Perhaps even more dangerous is the horizontal arms race, in which more and more nations acquire the potential to produce nuclear weapons, or to procure them otherwise. The more nations 'go nuclear', the greater is the probability that these will include states with unstable governments or irresponsible leaders, who will not exercise the restraints so far shown by the nuclear powers. There are enough examples of such states at the present time to make this a most terrifying prospect.

If, at one time, it was perhaps conceivable to look at the nuclear arms race as a duel between the USA and USSR, from which other nations, particularly the large number of developing countries, could stay away, this is no longer the case. Nuclear power states now comprise more than half the world's population, and – unless drastic steps are taken – one can predict with certainty that the 'disease of nuclear armaments' will soon spread to the rest of the world. We are in a vicious circle. Many nations will not sign the Non-Proliferation Treaty as long as the nuclear powers do not fulfil their undertaking to implement effective disarmament measures. On the other hand, the USA and the USSR cannot stop the arms race, not only because they do not trust each other, but because they are beginning to feel threatened by the nuclear potential of other nations.

There appears to be only one way out: complete disarmament. All attempts at partial arms control measures – the step-by-step approach which has been tried over the past years – have failed. Our only hope of survival is a return to the earlier concept of bringing the arms race to an end, namely by general and complete disarmament. The arguments leading to this conclusion are lucidly and logically developed by Dr Cox. I hope that the book will be read and debated in many circles, particularly by the young generation.

Joseph Rotblat, May 1976
Professor of Physics in the University of London
at St Bartholomew's Hospital Medical College

Preface to Third Edition

In the five years that have passed since Professor Rotblat wrote the preface to the first edition of *Overkill*, the danger of nuclear annihilation has increased. Three developments in the nuclear arms race were threatened at that time:

1. the adoption of strategies in which nuclear weapons are to be *used*, to fight and win nuclear war;
2. the development of new, more accurate weapons systems, such as the cruise missile, which could, directly or indirectly, make the nuclear arms race irreversible by placing insurmountable obstacles in the way of Strategic Arms Limitation agreements;
3. the extremely dangerous implications of the intensive research then being done on anti-submarine warfare.'

The theories of limited nuclear warfare of five years ago have now taken a more precise form, in which the 'limitation' is intended to be primarily *geographical*, with Europe as the chosen arena for 'theatre nuclear war'. There is no doubt that present 'doctrines of counter-force and limited nuclear war' threaten imminent death for the entire population of Europe, East and West.

By 1978, the progress in anti-submarine warfare was already such that an analysis by SIPRI (the Stockholm International Peace Research Institute) of strategic anti-submarine warfare and its implications for a counterforce first strike reached the conclusion that although

the USA does not at this moment have the capability to eliminate Soviet sea-based missiles ... research and development is leading in this direction ... and Soviet decision makers have grounds for fearing such a capability ...

and the study ends with this sombre paragraph:

The situation as a whole demands urgent attention. If the USA achieves a first-strike capability against Soviet ICBMs [Intercontinental Ballistic Missiles], as appears to be one of the objectives of the MX programme, and if this is coupled with maintenance of the present lead in ASW, there are serious grounds to fear that the concept of mutually assured destruction, with all its faults, will be abandoned in favour of a war-fighting and war-winning strategy.

By 1980, Mr Paul Warnke, President Carter's first SALT negotiator and Director of the US Arms Control and Disarmament Agency, in an interview with Jonathan Steele (the *Guardian*, 27 October 1980), was underlining the present danger in these terms:

> In my opinion, the key to strategic stability, the key to security in a nuclear age, is survivable forces. What troubles me about modernizing our ICBMs with MX is that we seem to be emphasizing the counterforce capability (the ability to hit Soviet missile sites and not just their cities). You don't improve security by threatening the survivability of their forces ... The people that ought to be worried about survivable forces are the Soviets, not us, ... Submarines are much harder to target than land-based silos, and our submarine-launched nuclear forces are so much stronger than theirs.

We are confronted, in the next five years or so, with an escalation of the nuclear arms race which, both quantitatively and qualitatively, reduces all that has happened so far to insignificance. As has been the case for the past thirty years, the United States is leading the race, with three major programmes – MX, Trident and the cruise missiles – that will between them increase the total counterforce capacity of the US strategic nuclear forces more than a hundred-fold within a decade. For the first time, one side in this deadly game will acquire a credible first-strike capability.

It is inconceivable that the Soviet Union will do nothing in the face of such a threat. It would not be surprising if they follow the example set by the MX project and make their principal ICBMs mobile. This could complicate the problem of verification to such a degree as to make any further Strategic Arms Limitation agreements impossible. Coupled with the intrinsic problem of satellite surveillance of cruise missiles, these developments could easily amount to the 'last leap' in the nuclear arms race – the leap into what Earl Mountbatten called 'the final abyss'.

If the peoples of the world – and particularly the peoples of Europe – are to be able to pull back from the edge of the abyss, it is vitally important that they should be both informed and organized. The comprehensive revision and updating of Dr Cox's book could not be more timely. We are, fortunately, in the midst of a powerful upsurge of public concern about this race to oblivion. There is a new determination to act for peace, which cuts across all boundaries, of age, of politics, of religion. This movement needs tools for the complex task before it, and it needs weapons for the fight – a fight it cannot afford to lose, for it is a fight for survival. This book should be in the tool-kit – and the armoury – of everyone engaged in this historic struggle.

Michael Pentz, March 1981
Dean and Director of Studies,
Faculty of Science, The Open University

Murder: to kill unlawfully with malice aforethought

'Thou shalt not kill'

War: hostilities conducted by organized and premeditated force

'The world is wet with mutual bloodshed and homicide is a crime when individuals commit it but a virtue when many commit it. Not the reason of innocence but the magnitude of savagery assures impunity for crimes' (St Cyprian, 2nd Century AD)

Genocide: extermination of an entire population

The German Nazi leaders 'determined upon and carried out ruthless wars against countries and populations, in violation of the rules and customs of war, including ... the indiscriminate destruction of cities, towns and villages, and devastation not justified by military necessity' (Nuremberg War Crimes tribunal, 1946)

Overkill: the ability to exterminate a population more than once

'Both the US and the Soviet Union now possess nuclear stockpiles large enough to exterminate mankind three or four – some say ten – times over' (Philip Noel-Baker, Nobel Peace Prize winner, 1971)

Strategic superiority: more overkill than the opponent

'One of the questions we have to ask ourselves as a country is what in the name of God is strategic superiority? What do you do with it?' (Henry Kissinger, US Secretary of State, 1975)

1. The first atomic bombs

In some sort of crude sense which no vulgarity, no humor, no overstatement can quite extinguish, the physicists have known sin; and this is a knowledge which they cannot lose.

J. Robert Oppenheimer
Director of the first A-bomb project

Atomic weapons were born from the fear that Hitler's Germany would dominate the world with a monopoly of atomic bombs. The initiative for their development came from Dr Leo Szilard, a Hungarian-born refugee from fascism, who obtained the support of Albert Einstein. Einstein, a German-born Jew and a life-long opponent of German militarism, was then living in self-imposed exile in the United States of America. On 2 August 1939 he wrote to the President, Franklin D. Roosevelt, warning of the danger that Germany might develop the bomb:

Some recent work by E. Fermi and L. Szilard, which has been communicated to me in manuscript, leads me to expect that the element uranium may be turned into a new and important source of energy in the immediate future. Certain aspects of the situation seem to call for watchfulness and, if necessary, quick action on the part of the administration. I believe therefore that it is my duty to bring to your attention ... that extremely powerful bombs of a new type may ... be constructed. I understand that Germany has actually stopped the sale of uranium from the Czechoslovakian mines which she has taken over ...

The USA was not at that time at war and so Einstein's warning did not meet with an energetic response. On 7 March 1940 Einstein, again after an approach from Szilard, wrote a second and more urgent appeal. Preliminary work on bomb manufacture then started, shortly after this second appeal, and by the time they joined the war, US government and military officials knew that 'extremely powerful bombs of a new type' could be constructed in the way suggested by Szilard and Fermi. In fact the decision to go ahead and build an A-bomb was taken on 6 December 1941 – the day before the Japanese attack on Pearl Harbor which brought America into the war.

In the next four years the scientists worked feverishly to develop atomic weapons in advance of Germany. Enrico Fermi, Leo Szilard, Niels Bohr, Hans Bethe and Joseph Rotblat were among the many Europeans who worked for the project (despite the fact that some were not even American citizens). Several British nuclear scientists also participated. All were united in their fear of what might happen if Hitler were to get the atomic bomb first.

But by November 1944 it was clear that Germany was not in fact making such a bomb. In December 1944 Rotblat, who later became Professor of Physics at St Bartholomew's Hospital Medical College, London, left the project because it no longer seemed necessary. In the spring of 1945 Szilard and Einstein again wrote to Roosevelt, this time with a quite different purpose: to warn him of the dangers which would face the post-war world from the development of atomic energy.

Then, on 8 May 1945, the European war ended and it was confirmed that Germany had never seriously considered building an atomic bomb. The $2,000 million project need never have begun. And there no longer seemed any need to continue with it, since it was known that the Japanese, who were still fighting, had no uranium. At this time the scientists had not got as far as building even a prototype bomb.

Already the more far-seeing were becoming concerned about the long-term implications of atomic weapons. Einstein, Szilard and Bohr had all attempted in different ways to warn the politicians of the coming dangers. They felt that the bomb project could be abandoned and the emphasis switched to peaceful uses of nuclear energy.

After 8 May this feeling began to be shared by more and more of those who had worked to build the bomb. A poll of these atomic scientists was taken and only 15 per cent wholeheartedly favoured its military use against Japan.

Nonetheless, work on the bomb continued with renewed urgency.

Alamogordo (see Plates I and II)
The first atomic test was at Alamogordo in the New Mexico desert on 16 July 1945. According to one eye-witness from more than five miles away:

The whole country was lighted by a searing light with an intensity many times that of the midday sun ... Thirty seconds after the explosion came, first, the air blast pressing against the people and things, to be followed almost immediately by the strong, sustained, awesome roar which warned of doomsday and made us feel that we puny things were blasphemous to dare tamper with the forces heretofore reserved to the Almighty. Words are inadequate tools for the job of acquainting those not present with the physical, mental and psychological effects. It had to be witnessed to be realized.

Immediately following this test, many atomic scientists signed a petition – drafted by Szilard – urging that the bomb should not be used against Japan without prior demonstration and the opportunity to surrender. It also urged that the American government start immediately to study the possibility of securing international control of the new weapon. The official response to the petition was to declare its contents secret and it was not made public until after the end of the war.

Already there were differences between the United States and Britain on the one hand and their communist ally. The Soviet Union was about to join the war against Japan and the Allies feared that she might occupy Japan whilst American forces were still hundreds of miles away. Though the new weapon was mentioned casually to the Soviet leader Stalin, its full significance was not indicated. The true nature of the Alamogordo test was kept secret whilst preparations went forward to drop the bomb on the Japanese city of Hiroshima.

An Hiroshima Diary*

6 August 1945

The hour was early; the morning still, warm and beautiful. Shimmering leaves, reflecting sunlight from a cloudless sky, made a pleasant contrast with shadows in my garden as I gazed absently through wide-flung doors opening to the south.

Clad in vest and pants, I was sprawled on the living-room floor exhausted because I had just spent a sleepless night on duty as an air-raid warden in my hospital.

Suddenly, a strong flash of light startled me – and then another. So well does one recall little things that I remember vividly how a stone lantern in the garden became brilliantly lit and I debated whether this light was caused by a magnesium flare or sparks from a passing train.

Garden shadows disappeared. The view where a moment before all had been so bright and sunny was now dark and hazy. Through swirling dust I could barely discern a wooden column that had supported one corner of my house. It was leaning crazily and the roof sagged dangerously.

Moving instinctively, I tried to escape, but rubble and fallen timbers barred the way. By picking my way cautiously I managed to reach the roka and stepped down into my garden. A profound weakness overcame me, so I stopped to regain my strength. To my surprise I discovered that I was completely naked. How odd. Where were my vest and pants?

What had happened?

All over the right side of my body I was cut and bleeding. A large splinter was protruding from a mangled wound in my thigh, and something warm trickled into my mouth. My cheek was torn, I discovered, as I felt it gingerly, with the lower lip laid wide open. Embedded in my neck was a sizeable fragment of glass which I matter-of-factly dislodged, and with the detachment of one stunned and shocked I studied it and my blood-stained hand . . .

---

* From *Hiroshima Diary* by Michihiko Hachiya, Gollancz, 1955.

'We'll be all right,' I [told my wife.] 'Only let's get out of here as fast as we can.'

She nodded, and I motioned for her to follow me.

The shortest path to the street lay through the house next door so through the house we went – running, stumbling, falling, and then running again until in the headlong flight we tripped over something and fell sprawling into the street. Getting to my feet, I discovered that I had tripped over a man's head.

'Excuse me! Excuse me, please!' I cried hysterically.

There was no answer. The man was dead. The head had belonged to a young officer whose body was crushed beneath a massive gate ...

We stood in the street, uncertain and afraid, until a house across from us began to sway, and in a minute it, too, collapsed in a cloud of dust. Other buildings caved in or toppled. Fires sprang up and whipped by a vicious wind began to spread ...

7 August 1945
I must have slept soundly because when I opened my eyes a piercing

Hiroshima: part of a bustling shopping precinct, about 500 metres from the hypocentre

hot sun was shining in on me. There were no shutters or curtains to lessen the glare – and for that matter no windows ...

In the space of one night patients had become packed, like the rice in sushi, into every nook and cranny of the hospital. The majority were badly burned, a few severely injured. All were critically ill ... They came as an avalanche and overran the hospital ...

Mr Katsutani ... had come all the way from Jigozen to look for me, and now that he had found me, emotion overcame him.

He turned to Dr Sasada and said brokenly: 'Yesterday, it was impossible to enter Hiroshima, else I would have come. Even today fires are still burning in some places. You should see how the city has changed. When I reached the Misasa Bridge this morning, everything before me was gone, even the castle. These buildings here are the only ones left anywhere around. The Communications Bureau seemed to loom right in front of me long before I got anywhere near here.'

Mr Katsutani paused for a moment to catch his breath and went on: 'I *really* walked along the railway tracks to get here, but even they were littered with electric wires and broken railway cars, and the dead and wounded lay everywhere. When I reached the bridge, I saw a dreadful thing. It was unbelievable. There was a man, stone dead, sitting on his bicycle as it leaned against the bridge railing. It is hard to believe that such a thing could happen!'

He repeated himself two or three times as if to convince himself that what he said was true and then continued: 'It seems that most of the dead people were either on the bridge or beneath it. You could tell that many had gone down to the river to get a drink of water and had died where they lay. I saw a few live people still in the water, knocking against the dead as they floated down the river. There must have been hundreds and thousands who fled to the river to escape the fire and then drowned ...'

8 August 1945

During the day, an effort was made to sort and rearrange the patients according to the nature and severity of their injuries, and not a few dead were found among the living, though fewer than yesterday ... I felt that the dead should be moved with greater dispatch in order to make room for the living. This is another example of my changed outlook. People were dying so fast that I had begun to accept death as a matter of course and ceased to respect its awfulness. I considered a family lucky if it had not lost more than two of its members. How could I hold my head up among the citizens of Hiroshima with thoughts like that in my mind? . . .

Yaeko-san and I found beds near each other that were not too badly bent. Our sleeping mats were placed over the frames, and without further ado we were ready to resume life in our new quarters . . .

In all four walls were large casement windows which afforded a commanding view in every direction. There were no shutters, no curtains, nor even glass to impose the least obstruction to air or light. Looking east, south and west was an unobstructed view of Hiroshima, and in Hiroshima Bay we could see the island Ninoshima.

Near the centre of the city, some 1,500 metres distant, one could see the blackened ruins of the two largest buildings in Hiroshima, the Fukuya Department Store and the Chugoku Press Building. Hijiyama, the sacred and beautiful little mountain in the eastern sector of the city, looked almost close enough to touch. To our north no buildings remained.

For the first time, I could understand what my friends had meant when they said Hiroshima was destroyed. Nothing remained except a few buildings of reinforced concrete . . . For acres and acres the city was like a desert except for scattered piles of brick and roof tile. I had to revise my meaning of the word destruction or choose some other word to describe what I saw. Devastation may be a better word, but really I knew of no word or words to describe the view from my twisted iron bed in the fire-gutted ward of the Communications Hospital . . .

Towards evening, a light, southerly wind blowing across the city wafted to us an odour suggestive of burning sardines. I wondered what could cause such a smell until somebody, noticing it too, informed me that sanitation teams were cremating the remains of people who had been killed. Looking out, I could discern numerous fires scattered about the city. Previously I had assumed the fires were caused by burning rubble. Towards Nigitsu was an especially large fire where the dead were being burned by hundreds. Suddenly to realize that these fires were funeral pyres made me shudder, and I became a little nauseated.

9 August 1945
Now, I could state positively that I heard nothing like an explosion when we were bombed the other morning, nor did I remember any sound during my walk to the hospital as houses collapsed around me.

It was as though I walked through a gloomy, silent motion picture. Others whom I questioned had had the same experience.

Those who experienced the bombing from the outskirts of the city characterized it by the word: *pikadon* ...*

While I lay there brooding ... old Mrs Saeki came up quickly and stood by my bed. One look into her pale, careworn face and I knew what she had come to say. Her son was dead; her eldest son – her only child left in the world. She had been so hopeful yesterday when he was brought in, and now he was gone. Her son's wife and her second

* *Pika* means a glitter, sparkle or bright flash of light, like a flash of lightning. *Don* means a boom or loud sound. Together, the words came to mean to the people of Hiroshima an explosion characterized by a flash and a boom. Hence 'flash-boom'. Those who remember the flash only speak of the *pika*; those who were far enough from the hypocentre to experience both speak of the *pikadon*.

son had been killed on the day of the *pikadon*, and now no one was left. She put her hands over her eyes and cried, but her sobs were scarcely audible. I could not speak for a while because there was something in my throat . . .

Darkness came and still there were no lights except the lights from the fires where the dead were burned. And again, the smell of burning flesh. The hospital was quieter, but in the isolation ward, the stillness of the night was broken again and again by the little girl.

At least 75,000 people lost their lives at Hiroshima in the first hours after the bomb was dropped. Most were disintegrated immediately by the fireball; the others died shortly afterwards from burns, blast and shock. The eventual death toll was probably 200,000.

According to the American government, the bomb was used so that the war would end quickly and save lives. Yet the US military command saw no need for the attack. After the event the US Strategic Bombing Survey came to the following conclusion:

It seems clear that, even without the atomic bomb attacks, air supremacy over Japan could have exerted sufficient pressure to bring unconditional surrender and obviate the need for invasion . . . Based on a detailed investigation of all the facts and supported by the testimony of the surviving Japanese leaders involved, it is the survey's opinion that certainly prior to 31 December 1945, Japan would have surrendered even if the atomic bombs had not been dropped, even if Russia had not entered the war, and even if no invasion had been planned or contemplated.

Supreme Commander Eisenhower declared more succinctly, 'It wasn't necessary to hit them with that awful thing.'

If the intention was to save lives, a few days' grace would have been appropriate before dropping a second bomb. Communications with Tokyo were so disrupted that it took over a week for the Japanese government to appreciate the strength of the new weapons.

But the politicians were anxious, since Russia had now entered the war. The Russians had originally agreed with the Allies to attack Japan three months after the ending of the war in

Europe. Since Germany had surrendered on 8 May, the deadline for Russia's entry into the Japanese war was 8 August –
only two days after the bomb was dropped on Hiroshima. There
was therefore little time to ensure that Japan would be occu-
pied by America rather than Russia.

So the third atomic bomb was dropped on Nagasaki – on
9 August – even as Dr Hachiya continued to puzzle over the
Hiroshima *pikadon*.

Nagasaki (see Plate IV)

There is a spot in the upper Urakami river where nature has formed
a small pool. That morning a group of ten boys, in coloured loin-
cloths, was playing a game called 'find the bell'. One of the boys,
eleven-year-old Koichi Nakajima, had a little gilded bell. He would
throw it in the water, count to three and they would all dive after it.
The first to find it won the game.

Now Koichi held up the tiny bell and shouted, 'Here we go. One,
two, three.' There were ten splashes as the boys dived for the prize.
But the river had become oily, and no one found it.

Koichi began to get worried. He had taken the bell from his sister's
workbox without her permission. She would be very angry if he lost
it. He surfaced, took a deep breath, and eeled his way down to the
bottom.

Nine seconds later, the bomb exploded over his head. When Koichi
surfaced, he heard two of the boys screaming with pain. He stared
around in fright. There were bodies of his friends on the riverbank,
and beyond them he saw that all the houses had been knocked down.
What had been a beautiful city a moment before was now a wasteland
with a big, black cloud rising above it like smoke from a funeral pyre.
Though it was deadly hot, Koichi's teeth began to chatter.*

When the bomb exploded, heat, light, gamma radiation and
pressure were all released, burning many people beyond
recognition and simply obliterating others. Hundreds received
mass cremation and others died unrecorded after fleeing to the
country and mountains. The exact number killed at Nagasaki,

* From *Nagasaki: The Forgotten Bomb* by F. W. Chinnock, Allen & Unwin,
1970.

like Hiroshima, will never be known, but there were certainly more than 40,000 deaths in the first few seconds.

For three fifths of a mile nearly all unprotected living organisms – birds, insects, horses, cats, chickens – perished instantly. Flowers, trees and plants all shrivelled and died. Wood burst into flames. Metal beams and galvanized iron roofs began to bubble, and the soft gooey masses twisted into grotesque shapes. People within that doomed section neither knew nor felt anything.

Fewer were killed instantly at Nagasaki than at Hiroshima because the explosion took place within a valley. But, after the heat and blast, there came the third killer, radiation, the most frightening of all because it kills silently and invisibly. At the moment of the explosion, alpha, beta and gamma rays, X-rays and neutrons were all given off. And, following the explosion, fission products such as strontium-90 and caesium-137 were scattered everywhere; these gave off further atomic radiation and held an ever-present threat to those who had survived the heat and blast. It is thought that, even if heat and blast had been entirely absent, the number of deaths within 1,000 yards of the Hiroshima and Nagasaki bombs would still have been almost the same. The main difference would have been in the time it would have taken for the victims to die. Those who were killed instantly might instead have survived a few days whilst the radiation destroyed their white blood cells and bone marrow.

Even today the people of Hiroshima and Nagasaki are suffering from the after-effects of the atomic explosions. On average, more dead and deformed children are born to the survivors than elsewhere. Survival after an atomic attack can be worse than death.

But death, that day, was much more common. Little eight-year-old Matsuo was happy that morning. He was playing hide-and-seek with six other boys, around the Chinzei Junior High School on a hillside in the centre of the Urakami Valley. Although he had been 'it', the one who looks for the others, for the last three games, he didn't mind.

For this was the first time the slightly older boys had even allowed him to play with them.

Now Matsuo stood in the centre of the yard trying to spot the others hiding. When the bomb exploded some 400 yards behind him, he neither heard nor felt anything when the heat rays focused on him and obliterated him. The other boys, huddling in gullies, or crouching behind walls, were completely untouched by those same rays. Minutes later, they crept from their hiding places and walked to where the remains of little Matsuo's body lay on the ground. In horrified silence, they stared at each other. They were the lucky ones, or so they thought.

But once more the invisible killer was at work. Within one year, three of the six boys would be dead from radiation.*

Outside Japan, most people welcomed the news of the atomic bombs, as they seemed likely to end the war. Since then more and more people have come to agree with the words of Professor P. M. S. Blackett, the British physicist who won a Nobel Prize in 1948: 'the dropping of the atomic bombs was not so much the last military act of the Second World War, as the first act of the cold diplomatic war with Russia'. Thomas K. Finletter – who later became Chairman of the U S Air Policy Committee and head of the U S Marshall Plan mission in London – explained clearly (15 June 1946) why there had been no demonstration of the new weapon's power to the Japanese government before it was decided to drop the bombs:

There was not enough time between 16 July, when we knew at New Mexico that the bomb would work, and 8 August, the Russian deadline date, for us to have set up the very complicated machinery of a test atomic bombing involving time-consuming problems of area preparations, etc. ... No, any test would have been impossible if the purpose was to knock Japan out before Russia came in – or at least before Russia could make anything other than a token of participation prior to a Japanese collapse.

Most of the leading scientists who worked on the first atomic bombs later regretted their participation. Szilard, Bohr, Einstein and Rotblat became prominent in campaigns against nuclear weapons. In 1955 eleven prominent scientists, including nine Nobel Prizewinners, signed a manifesto call-

* From *Nagasaki: The Forgotten Bomb* by F. W. Chinnock.

ing upon scientists throughout the world to work for peace:

We are speaking on this occasion not as members of this or that nation, continent or creed, but as human beings, members of the species Man, whose continued existence is in doubt . . .

We have to learn to think in a new way. We have to learn to ask ourselves not what steps can be taken to give military victory to whatever group we prefer, for there no longer are such steps; the question we have to ask ourselves is: what steps can be taken to prevent a military contest of which the issue must be disastrous to all parties? . . . Shall we put an end to the human race; or shall mankind renounce war?*

Bertrand Russell	Albert Einstein
Max Born	P. W. Bridgman
Linus Pauling	H. J. Muller
J. F. Joliot-Curie	C. F. Powell
Joseph Rotblat	L. Infeld
	Hideki Yukawa

Following its publication the Manifesto was endorsed by hundreds of scientists and provided the impetus for an international conference to discuss the threat posed to the world by nuclear weapons. Out of the first conference of scientists, held at a small Canadian village called Pugwash, grew the Pugwash Movement. The conferences are now held regularly.

But, though the knowledge of the implications of nuclear energy has become more widespread, not all nuclear scientists have shown the concern of those in the Pugwash Movement. Making nuclear weapons has become a living for thousands of scientists, technologists and production workers in this, the nuclear age.

By 1949 Russia had exploded her first A-bomb and in 1953 Britain joined the 'nuclear club'. The scientists involved do not appear to have been concerned with the moral implications. Nor were the politicians: on 1 June 1953 British Prime Minister Winston Churchill reported: 'We had one and let it off – it went off beautifully.'

* From the Russell–Einstein Manifesto.

2. Nuclear energy – how it works

They shall beat their swords into plow-shares, and their spears into pruning hooks: nation shall not lift up sword against nation, neither shall they learn war any more.

Isaiah 2:4

The splash headlines of the *News Chronicle* for 7 August 1945 declared 'FORCE OF NATURE HARNESSED: ATOM BOMB ON JAPAN – Power equal to 20,000 tons of TNT' (see Plate V). A smaller heading on the same page said 'Next step is to control the force'. If we survive the twentieth century, the smaller article may prove the more significant. In it Sir John Anderson explained that the importance of the discovery of nuclear power

far transcends that of the discovery of electricity and makes steam something of the far past. It has opened a new door to physics which has hitherto defied all approach. It means that man has at last found the way to release the forces of the atom.

Nowadays most people know in general terms that an atom is the smallest particle of any element of matter – for example, iron, tin, aluminium – and that all atoms are composed of neutrons and protons surrounded by electrons. The neutrons and protons (together called nucleons) form the nucleus of the atom and are kept together by nuclear binding forces. Protons have a positive electric charge and the number present in an atomic nucleus determines its chemical properties. So each chemical has a unique number of protons (for example, hydrogen has 1, helium 2, lithium 3, etc.) but the number of neutrons may vary. For example, although the ordinary hydrogen nucleus consists simply of 1 proton, there are two other forms (or *isotopes*) of hydrogen, called deuterium and tritium, which have an additional 1 and 2 neutrons respectively. It is the 'force of the atom' which keeps these neutrons and protons together in the nucleus.

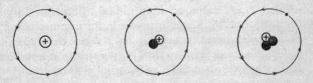

ORDINARY HYDROGEN   **DEUTERIUM**   **TRITIUM**

Atomic power

Nuclear energy is released when a heavy atom breaks into two (a process called *fission*) or when two light atoms join (*fusion*). Heavy atoms tend to be naturally unstable, because the nuclear binding forces find it difficult to keep the neutrons and protons together. Substances which are unstable in this way are *radioactive*. They emit radiations and are transformed into slightly different atoms. The rate of decay of a radioactive atom may be very low, sometimes it takes millions of years, but if such an atom is given an extra jolt, for example by being hit with a neutron, it will break up instantaneously into two parts. It

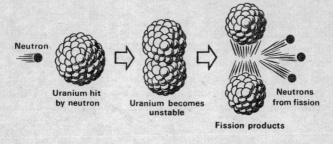

Neutron

Uranium hit
by neutron

Uranium becomes
unstable

Neutrons
from fission

Fission products

is this process of fission that can be used to make atomic bombs – like those dropped on Hiroshima and Nagasaki – or to produce electricity by nuclear power generation.

Uranium and plutonium were the chemicals used for the first atomic bombs. The nucleus of uranium contains 92 protons and, in its most common form (uranium-238), 146 neutrons. Uranium-238 (92 + 146 = 238) undergoes fission when hit by high-energy neutrons, but it can absorb low-energy neutrons without splitting. Another form of uranium, uranium-235, which has 143 neutrons, is much less stable. But natural uranium (i.e. that mined from the earth) contains only 0·7 per cent of U235. So the first step in the manufacture of an atomic bomb based on uranium, is to *enrich* the U235 component of natural uranium from 0·7 per cent to at least 70 per cent. When this is done, a self-sustaining *chain reaction* can occur in the uranium.

When the U235 atoms undergo fission they release energy as well as a few neutrons. These neutrons hit other atoms and in turn can cause these other atoms to undergo fission. On average 2·5 neutrons are given off from each uranium-235 atom and this opens up the possibility of a chain reaction. In effect, neutrons from one fission can induce fission in other atoms,

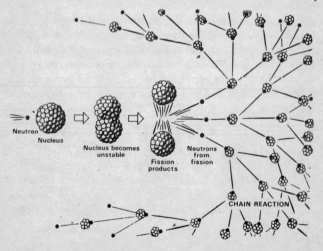

Neutron Nucleus Nucleus becomes unstable Fission products Neutrons from fission CHAIN REACTION

in turn producing more neutrons. These neutrons produce still more fission and still more neutrons. So long as there are plenty of U235 atoms near by, this can go on and on. Within milliseconds there is a tremendous release of heat.

This chain reaction continues only if there is sufficient uranium present. The amount needed for a self-sustaining reaction to take place is known as the *critical mass* (about fifteen kilogrammes in the case of U235). An A-bomb contains two or more lumps of radioactive material which are each smaller in size than the critical mass and are kept apart when the bomb is assembled. The atomic explosion takes place when these subcritical masses are brought together.

Fission is also used for nuclear power generation. In this case a slow, controlled, release of energy is needed and the composition of the uranium fuel is in most cases 1·5 to 5 per cent uranium-235, as opposed to the 70 per cent used in the atomic bomb. The amount of uranium is regulated so that the self-sustaining chain reaction does not 'take off'. This is, in effect, a controlled nuclear explosion, with the heat being removed to generate electricity in the same way as in coal-fired and oil-fired power stations. However, the *waste by-products* of nuclear power generation are more dangerous than those produced by burning oil or coal, because they are radioactive. Radioactivity is produced when some of the neutrons given out in the fission process miss uranium atoms, hit other substances and create new artificial radioactive substances. The main waste, however, arises from the two atoms into which the uranium atom is split. Both are radioactive. As the reactor goes on producing energy more and more of these radioactive fragments accumulate. For this reason the uranium fuel elements are removed after a time and the fuel material reconcentrated.

As more and more countries acquire nuclear power stations, the amount of radioactive waste material is growing. Many countries are unable or unwilling to make arrangements to reprocess this waste and it seems likely that only a few countries will build the necessary facilities. Britain has signed long-

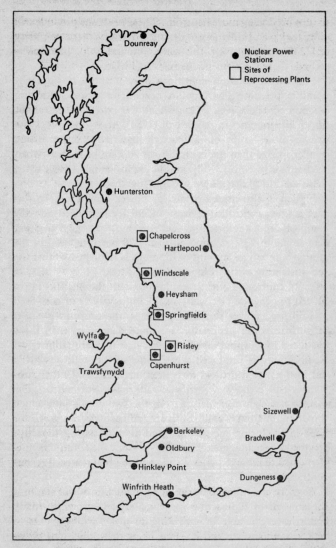

Nuclear power stations and reprocessing plants in Great Britain

term contracts with Japan and other countries to handle the latter's nuclear waste products. Even after reprocessing, some radioactive waste remains and the only solution at present is to seal this in suitable containers for 'disposal'.

Plutonium

Plutonium on the other hand is a potentially *useful* by-product of nuclear power generation and is made from the bombardment of the U238. It happens like this: when neutrons from the fission of uranium-235 hit atoms of U238, they are absorbed by the nucleus to produce another isotope – uranium-239 – which then undergoes its own radioactive decay process and eventually becomes plutonium (Pu239). For every gramme of uranium used in this type of nuclear power plant, up to a gramme of plutonium may be produced – and this plutonium is itself radioactive and can be used as fuel for further nuclear power generation. By choosing a suitable mixture of U235 and U238 and diluting the mixture with just the right amount of other non-absorbing atoms, the neutrons produced by the fission of U235 keep the reaction going to produce electricity *and*, simultaneously, plutonium from U238. By coincidence, naturally occurring uranium (99·3 per cent U238 and 0·7 per cent U235) *is* a suitable mixture and works just as described when it is diluted by pure graphite or heavy water (water composed of two deuterium atoms and one oxygen atom).

So nuclear reactors can be built to produce electricity *and* to 'breed' new fission material. Future nuclear reactions may then use this plutonium to produce further nuclear energy. But, unfortunately, plutonium can also be used to make atomic bombs, and its critical mass is only 5 kg. Indeed the first atomic reactors were intended to produce plutonium; they generated electricity only as a by-product. The very first nuclear reactor started production in 1942 and within a very short time other nuclear reactors supplied the plutonium used for the Alamogordo and Nagasaki explosions. The Hiroshima bomb was the only one of the first three to use uranium.

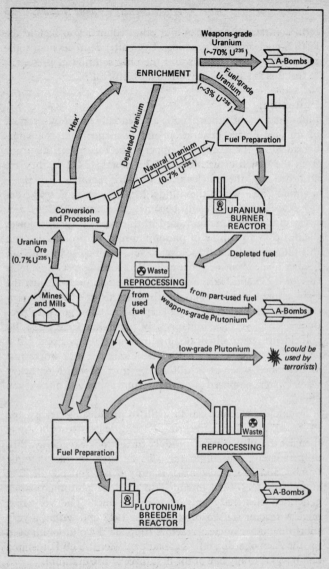

The uranium–plutonium fuel cycle

In theory any radioactive material can be used to make an atomic bomb. In practice, however, plutonium and uranium are the most suitable starting materials for bomb manufacture. 'Peaceful' nuclear power plants thus enable countries to obtain plutonium for a nuclear weapons programme. India exploded her first atomic bomb with plutonium developed from the peaceful application of nuclear energy in cooperation with Canada, a country strongly against the spread of nuclear weapons. There is no way to stop countries from acquiring stockpiles of plutonium once they make electricity from nuclear power.

The basic arithmetic of the problem is as follows: a reactor that produces one megawatt of electric power can produce about a quarter kilogramme of plutonium per year. (Future nuclear reactors will produce *more* plutonium than they consume.) Nowadays it takes about 1 kilowatt of electric power to satisfy the needs of one inhabitant of a country like Britain. So, if everyone were to reach the level of the current British standard of living and if their electric power were produced by 'plutonium-breeding' nuclear reactors, the actual production rate of plutonium would be over a million kilogrammes per year. As it needs only about ten kilogrammes of plutonium to produce a fairly simple nuclear bomb, the annual production of plutonium in future could be equivalent to over a hundred thousand Hiroshima-sized bombs.

Although this number of bombs will not be produced, it will be extremely difficult to prevent plutonium losses and, indeed, a loss of the order of 0·1 per cent of the envisaged annual plutonium production probably would not be noticed. Even this amount in the wrong hands could make enough bombs to destroy many of the world's major population centres.

Thermonuclear energy

To date, nuclear power plants have utilized nuclear fission as their source of energy. There are plants to develop *fusion* reactors to tap the energy released when two or more small atoms join together. However, commercial exploitation of this process

The Atomic Energy Commission [of the United States] 'loses' about 100 pounds of uranium and 60 pounds of plutonium (the basic ingredients of nuclear fission) each year, which is sufficient to make about ten atom bombs.

In most cases, when a loss is discovered, diligent clerical work usually corrects the error, but there have been instances where a loss has been attributed to espionage.

Nearly fifteen years ago, an American nuclear plant 'lost' 207 pounds, enough to make several bombs.

After a few months only 59 pounds had been recovered and, to this day, the AEC suspects that China or Israel may have acquired the remainder.

Nuclear specialists generally agree that a government-owned nuclear plant presents a near-impregnable target for the nuclear terrorist.

But as nuclear energy goes commercial, a number of privately owned energy plants will proliferate and will have only a fraction of the protective security of official plants.

Nuclear scientists further conclude that materials in transit present the weakest link in nuclear security.

This applies even to nationally owned plants in America, because once material has to be moved from one point to another, the national agent has to use private transport firms.

In the year ending 31 March 1974, the AEC recorded 455 shipments of special nuclear materials carried by civilian contractors under licence'.

(from the *Western Daily Press*, July 1974)

is a long way off, since the temperatures involved are so high that there is no known way at present to contain and control the reaction.

Unlike fission reactions, for which peaceful uses have been found, no one has succeeded so far in containing nuclear energy from fusion. All known materials melt and vaporize long before a million degrees centigrade is reached. Fusion actually takes place in the sun but is contained there by a blanket of thousands

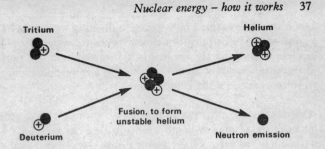

Tritium

Helium

Fusion, to form
unstable helium

Deuterium

Neutron emission

of miles of hot gas. With the technology available to us on earth the most promising idea is to keep the reaction within a 'magnetic bottle': in other words, to pass a very high temperature gas through a magnetic field and so tap the release of energy without any solid materials touching it. If this were successful, the world would have no need to fear an energy shortage in the future. Moreover this technique would not create undesirable waste products to the same extent as fission reactors.

But there *are* already fusion *bombs*. Thermonuclear bombs (H-bombs) are triggered by a vast amount of heat (the 'thermo' part) and work by the nuclear fusion of two or more small nuclei – for example, the joining together of two heavy hydrogen atoms to make helium. At temperatures of a million degrees centigrade or more, fusion reactions evolve vast amounts of energy. So a fusion bomb has big advantages over a fission bomb. Moreover, the size of a fission explosion is limited by the critical mass – if too much uranium or plutonium comes together the chain reaction will start too soon. There is no danger of this in a thermonuclear bomb; it can be as big and destructive as desired.

The way to obtain the heat to set off a fusion reaction is through a fission explosion. So an atomic bomb is needed to trigger a thermonuclear bomb! In effect a thermonuclear bomb is a fusion bomb encompassing a fission bomb. Whereas the power of atomic bombs is equivalent to thousands of tons of TNT (*kilotons*), the strength of a thermonuclear fission–fusion bomb may be measured in *megatons* (millions of tons of TNT equivalent). Most strategic nuclear weapons today are thermonuclear weapons in the range 0·1–10 megatons. (In addition, there are thousands of 'small', 'tactical' nuclear weapons, which are usually in the 5–100 kilotons range.)

The development of the H-bomb

Most of the leading A-bomb scientists were not keen on the H-bomb – not even Robert Oppenheimer, who had directed the A-bomb project. When US President Harry Truman authorized its development (on 30 January 1950), Dr Edward Teller – the 'father of the H-bomb' – failed to entice more than a handful to come back to Los Alamos. Bethe and Fermi helped although they had strong reservations. But the brunt of the work was carried out by scientists who were less well known than the brilliant 'stars' of the wartime project and who showed little public concern with the moral implications.

The first experimental detonation was conducted in the spring of 1951 at Eniwetok, an atoll in the Marshall Islands in the Pacific (America had become too small for unconfined nuclear tests). There was some thermonuclear reaction, but most of the energy still came from fission. The second Eniwetok test, on 1 November 1952, was more successful and released energy equivalent to about 10 million tons (10 megatons) of TNT. It was reported to have blown an island off the face of the sea.

This test revealed, however, that the concept of a simple fission–fusion bomb was impracticable for military purposes. The thermonuclear fuels used in the experiment needed massive, unwieldy refrigeration equipment and other complicated gear. Although the term 'H-bomb' is still used, the process of fusing hydrogen atoms (usually deuterium – 'heavy hydrogen') is merely a trigger for a secondary fission reaction.

The fission–fusion–fission bomb is an improved version of the thermonuclear bomb. First tested at Bikini Atoll on 1 March 1954 (see Plate VI), it comprises an ordinary fusion bomb, triggered by a fission bomb as described above, and encased in ordinary uranium. Although uranium-238 is unsuitable for a fission bomb, it can be induced to undergo fission by the very high temperatures of the fusion reaction. Because ordinary uranium is used, and there is no need to go through the expensive process of enriching it, the 'FFF bomb' has much more power for relatively little extra cost. From an analysis of the radioactivity released by the Bikini bomb, Professor Rotblat, by this time a vigorous opponent of the nuclear arms race, suggested that it comprised a plutonium core, a shell of lithium deuteride for the fusion reaction and an outer shell of U-238.

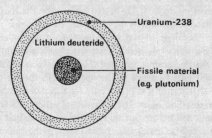

The voyage of the *Lucky Dragon*

Most of what is publicly known about thermonuclear bombs is due to an 'accident' to a Japanese fishing boat, the *Lucky Dragon*. Its crew of twenty-three were fishing for tuna some eighty-five miles east of Bikini Atoll when the first FFF bomb exploded.

At 3.42 in the morning the lines had been thrown, and the Fishing Master again checked the ship's position. It was rather warm and the wind was east-north-east at two miles per hour ... after ten minutes he signalled the engine room to stop the engine.

In the darkness before dawn, the *Lucky Dragon* drifted on the calm Pacific, rocking gradually in almost imperceptible swells. It was a scene of serene peacefulness ...

On the bridge the Fishing Master peered through the sextant. The North Star was obscured, but he took a fix on other stars well known to him from past sightings ... Glancing at his chart, Misaki noted that the nearest point of land was the tiny island of Naen, forty miles almost due south. The boatswain was on the bridge and observed that the sky was starting to cloud over.

Many of the crew, including the Captain, were asleep or were getting ready for breakfast. Shinzo Suzuki, however, could not sleep; he awakened almost instinctively when the engine stopped and wondered if all the lines had been thrown. It seemed early for the night was still dark and it usually took much longer to complete the job. He called to a passing seaman and asked if the lines were all set. Upon learning that they were, Suzuki remembered the lost lines and realized that this accounted for the early completion of the job. It was warm and somewhat sticky. Suzuki, unable to sleep any longer, climbed out of his bunk and went on deck ... He rested his arm on the roof of the after cabin and gazed absently into the somewhat overcast sky.

Suddenly the skies in the west lighted up and a great flare of whitish yellow light splashed against the clouds and illuminated the water. The startled seaman grasped the rough wood of the cabin with his hands and gazed in awe at the spectacle in the west. It seemed like minutes, though it was really only for seconds that he was transfixed by the dazzling light. It changed to a yellow red and then to a flaming orange red before Suzuki came to his senses and dashed back to his cabin to tell his mates what he had seen. As he entered the cabin, Takagi, a cabin mate, was humming a song. Suzuki blurted out, 'The sun rises in the West!' ...

The men on the deck were not speechless, but jabbered in excited tones, 'It's a pikadon!' While another said, 'I wonder if it is a pikadon?' ...

Everyone was shouting excitedly. 'What's the big red ball?' cried a shipmate. Another answered 'It must be the sun,' and was quickly doubted. 'No, it can't be the sun in the west!'

And again the word 'Pikadon!' was heard.

The glare in the west diminished in brightness as the colours seemed to spread out over the horizon and climb farther into the sky. No seaman had ever seen a sight like this before. Those who had crowded on deck after the first few minutes found it difficult to imagine what all the excitement was about, for by then the gaudy display of colours had faded or could be discerned with difficulty.

Captain Tsutsui was alerted by the burst of light flooding through the porthole near his bunk, but he was so drugged with sleep that he

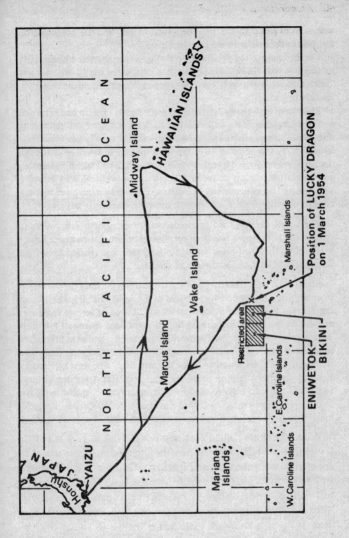

A map of the Lucky Dragon's *voyage, showing its position at the time of the explosion*

was slow to react. By the time he joined Misaki and the boatswain on the bridge the colour in the west had gone.

The darkness of the pre-dawn settled upon the shattered tranquillity of the tiny boat rocking in the limitless expanse of the Pacific. All was quiet. Gradually the crew's wonder turned to more mundane thoughts, namely breakfast ...

They went into the galley, fetched some bowls of soup and returned to the deck, where four or five other companions were still discussing the event. Scarcely five minutes had elapsed. The men began to eat their breakfast. A few minutes later the ship seemed to tremble as though shaken from below and a great sound-wave enveloped the ship, seeming to come at once from above and below. This was followed in a few seconds by two concussions like distant rifle shots. Crewmen instinctively threw themselves on the deck and covered their heads ...

The *Lucky Dragon* then proceeded on an east-north-east course to haul in the lines which had been set shortly before. Dawn broke before much of the line had been hauled up, and the crew relaxed somewhat as daylight helped to dispel some of their fears ...

About two hours after they had started hauling the lines the sky began to change in a rather odd way. It was as though a high fog were forming. Then a light rain or drizzle started to fall. Except for two engineers at work below decks and the Radio man and Steersman, all the crew were on the main deck hard at work. They were puzzled at first when tiny bits of sandy ash came swirling down on the decks. 'It looks like the beginning of a snowstorm,' one of them said. The men kept working, paying little attention to the unusual rain. But it became bothersome, and the men blinked as the irritating grains of whitish sand got into their eyes. Some ash drifted down and touched their lips, deposited on their ear lobes, and dusted the men's hats.*

When the ship reached port, some of the fish were sold before it was realized what had happened. Then radioactivity was discovered all over the ship and its cargo. Overnight the Japanese stopped eating fish. As for the fishermen, it was found that they had inhaled and swallowed radioactive fission products. All were sick and, despite intensive care, the Radio man Kuboyama died six months later (see Plate VII).

The disaster that struck the *Lucky Dragon*, eighty-five miles

* From *The Voyage of the* Lucky Dragon by Ralph Lapp, Penguin, 1958.

from the Bikini explosion, highlighted the fact that the new bombs were very 'dirty' – that is, they emitted large quantities of radioactive material. The third and outer shell of the fission–fusion–fission bomb allowed the thermonuclear bomb to be made small enough for military applications but also threatened life after a nuclear war. It is estimated now that the radioactive fallout from only a fraction of present-day nuclear bomb stockpiles would be sufficient to end all human life on earth today. The new situation was quickly appreciated by Winston Churchill:

> The atomic bomb, with all its terror, did not carry us outside the scope of human control or manageable events in thought or action in peace or war ... With the hydrogen bomb, the entire foundation of human affairs was revolutionized, and mankind placed in a situation both measureless and laden with doom.
>
> It is now the fact that a quantity of plutonium, probably less than would fill this box on the table – it is quite safe a thing to store* – would suffice to produce weapons which would give indisputable world domination to any great Power which was the only one to have it. There is no absolute defence against the hydrogen bomb, nor is any method in sight by which the nation, or any country, can be completely guaranteed against the devastating injury which even a score of them might inflict on wide regions ...
>
> I find it poignant to look at youth in all its activity and ardour and, most of all, to watch little children playing their merry games, and wonder what would lie before them if God wearied of mankind ...
>
> The problem is, therefore, to devise a balanced and phased system of disarmament which at no period enables any one of the participants to enjoy an advantage which might endanger the security of others ...
>
> The broad effect of the latest developments is to spread almost indefinitely and at least to a vast extent the area of mortal danger.†

Despite the risks of nuclear explosions, it is sometimes claimed that research should continue because it may have

* A debatable point this – JC.
† Prime Minister Winston Churchill, House of Commons, March 1955.

peaceful applications. The US 'Plowshare Program',* which attempted to find peacetime uses for nuclear explosions, showed this argument to be false. Conventional explosives proved more economical for long-trench digging, as for canals, and for relatively shallow excavations, as for harbours. Peaceful nuclear explosions were suggested also for oil-well drilling but, though this is technically feasible, the resulting oil flow is potentially radioactive. Similar objections exist for all other allegedly peaceful applications.

Yet although conventional explosives have been proved more practical, near-nuclear countries often pretend that they need nuclear-explosion technology for 'peaceful purposes'. In reality a country which develops nuclear-explosion technology is concerned above all with its destructive potential. In the twenty or more years since Churchill's warning, there have been *no* measures of disarmament which reduce the threat of the nuclear arms race. Shortly after America acquired her own H-bombs, Russia did the same and, in 1961, exploded the world's biggest thermonuclear device (57 megatons). Britain joined the H-bomb club by the end of the decade and France and China during the next (see the Table on pages 184–5).

Since 1961 tests of nuclear weapons have continued. With the development of lasers there is some prospect that a pure fusion bomb might be developed some time in the future. If this were to happen, there would be even less difficulty for additional countries to acquire nuclear weapons, since neither uranium nor plutonium would be needed. Perhaps these further developments are of no real consequence – world stockpiles of nuclear weapons are equivalent to many tons of TNT for every man, woman and child alive today.

* See the passage from Isaiah quoted at the head of this chapter. This is parodied in Joel 3:10 'Beat your plowshares into swords, and your pruning hooks into spears: let the weak say, I am strong.' So far Joel has it.

3. Nuclear war – what to expect

If we fight a war and win it with H-Bombs, what history will remember is not the ideals we were fighting for but the methods we used to accomplish them. These methods will be compared to the warfare of Genghis Khan who ruthlessly killed every last inhabitant of Persia.

Hans Bethe, H-bomb scientist

Nuclear explosions are not just very big bangs. They kill by heat, blast, radiation and by the subsequent radioactive fallout. An even greater number of deaths probably would be caused indirectly, by the social and economic disruption. As a starting point it is helpful to describe the effects of only one nuclear explosion – although, in a real war, many nuclear warheads might arrive together.

With a ten-megaton thermonuclear bomb the initial flash from the beginning of the fireball would be bright enough to blind temporarily and probably burn the eyes of people looking at it from 200 or 300 miles away. Within forty seconds a blindingly bright fireball would have grown about three miles across. This is where the thermonuclear reaction would be taking place and it would be as hot as the inside of the sun.

Then, depending on how high up it was when it exploded, the bomb would create havoc for many miles around. If it was exploded very high up, where the air is thin, most of the bomb's energy would go into heat and it would thus be an

Challenge to survival

Everything within a certain distance of a nuclear explosion will be totally destroyed. Even people living outside this area will be in danger from –

HEAT AND BLAST

FALL-OUT

Heat and Blast

The heat and blast are so severe that they can kill, and destroy buildings, for up to five miles from the explosion. Beyond that, there can be severe damage.

From Protect and Survive, *a government Civil Defence booklet,* HMSO, 1980

Fall-out

Fall-out is dust that is sucked up from the ground by the explosion. It can be deadly dangerous. It rises high in the air and can be carried by the winds for hundreds of miles before falling to the ground.

The radiation from this dust is dangerous. It cannot be seen or felt. It has no smell, and it can be detected only by special instruments. Exposure to it can cause sickness and death. If the dust fell on or around your home, the radiation from it would be a danger to you and your family for many days after an explosion. Radiation can penetrate any material, but its intensity is reduced as it passes through – so the thicker and denser the material is, the better.

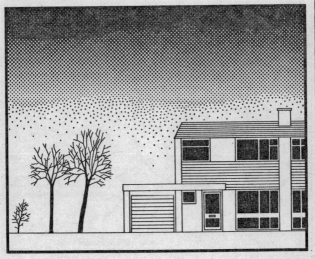

effective fire weapon. A ten-megaton bomb exploded thirty
miles up would send a searing wave of heat over an area of
5,000 square miles.

In a war most nuclear weapons are likely to explode near the
ground – so the flash might not be seen further than thirty
miles away. A ten-megaton bomb could produce a crater 240
feet deep (deeper than London's underground railway) and
perhaps half to one mile across, with a huge rim of piled-up
wreckage for up to twice that distance. The blast wave would
travel along the tunnels of any underground system and so kill
people sheltering in them ten or twenty miles away. People out
in the open up to twenty-two miles away would be burned
fatally; fires would be started up to twenty-eight miles away.

Everything within three and a half miles would be totally
smashed and there would be major damage to houses and streets
up to fifteen miles away. People sheltering in basements or
ground-floor rooms at this distance would be in danger from

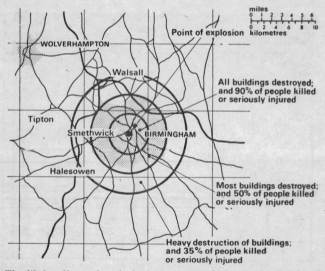

*The likely effects of a single 1-megaton explosion from a height of
3,000 yards above the centre of Birmingham. Source: UN data*

their homes collapsing. So the initial effects of blast and fire alone would be capable of killing over half the population of a city thus attacked.

Following this there would be further fire damage. The enormous number of fires that would be started over hundreds of square miles would not remain isolated. A 'firestorm' would be produced on a scale bigger than the big fire raids of the Second World War at Hamburg, Tokyo, Dresden and other cities, when the fires from thousands of incendiary bombs joined together to form huge pillars of fire which sucked in winds of up to 150 miles per hour (strong enough to uproot trees). People caught in the streets were burned to death and others in fire-proof shelters suffocated because the air that came in from the street was denuded of oxygen and scorchingly hot. Something similar, only worse, can be expected following a nuclear attack. The fire storm might well destroy everything within twenty miles.

People who survived the heat and blast would still have to face the third destroyer: radiation. There are three types from a nuclear explosion: alpha (α), beta (β) and gamma (γ) radiation. Alpha particles comprise 2 protons and 2 neutrons (in effect, the nucleus of the helium atom stripped of its electrons). A beta particle is a free electron given out during the decay of an unstable atomic nucleus. Gamma rays are high-energy electromagnetic radiation, similar to X-rays, which are given out by many radioactive nuclei during decay. The intense burst of nuclear radiation from the explosion would create in turn numerous radioactive substances which would then give off further radiation. At Hiroshima, people who survived within a mile of the explosion centre died later from radiation sickness. In addition many others who were some distance away from the explosion centre died from radiation carried with the dust and debris many miles away.

What happens is that the explosion sweeps up thousands of tons of earth and rubble and blows it up into the atmosphere forming the familiar mushroom cloud. The dust – fallout – settles back into the neighbourhood of the explosion during the

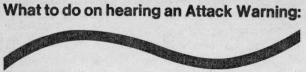

What to do on hearing an Attack Warning:

At home

If you are at home you should:

Send the children to the fall-out room.

Turn off the gas and electricity at the mains; turn off all pilot lights. Turn off oil supplies. Close stoves, damp down fires. Shut windows, draw curtains. Go to the fall-out room.

At work or elsewhere

If you can reach home in a couple of minutes try to do so.

If your are at work, or elsewhere, and cannot reach home within a couple of minutes, take cover where you are or in any nearby building.

In the open

If you are in the open and cannot get home within a couple of minutes, go immediately to the nearest building. If there is no building nearby and you cannot reach one within a couple of minutes, use any kind of cover, or lie flat (in a ditch) and cover the exposed skin of the head and hands.

Light and heat from an explosion will last for up to twenty seconds, but blast waves may take up to a minute to reach you. If after ten minutes there has been no blast wave, take cover in the nearest building.

From Protect and Survive, *a government Civil Defence booklet,* HMSO, 1980

What to do after the Attack:

After a nuclear attack, there will be a short period before fall-out starts to descend. Use this time to do essential tasks. This is what you should do.

Do not smoke.

Check that gas, electricity and other fuel supplies and all pilot lights *are* turned off.

Go round the house and put out any small fires using mains water if you can.

If anyone's clothing catches fire, lay them on the floor and roll them in a blanket, rug or thick coat.

If the mains water is still available also replenish water reserves. Then turn off at mains.

Do not flush lavatories, but store the clean water they contain by taping up the handles or removing the chains.

If the water supply is interrupted extinguish water heaters and boilers (including hearth fires with back boilers). Turn off all taps.

Check that you have got your survival kit at hand for the fall-out room. (See the list of survival items on pages 12-16.)

If there is structural damage from the attack you may have some time before a fall-out warning to do minor jobs to keep out the weather – using curtains or sheets to cover broken windows or holes.

If there is time, help neighbours in need, but listen for the fall-out warning and be ready to return to the fall-out room.

next twelve hours. Radioactive nuclei are mixed with the dust so that a very wide area is dangerously radioactive – about 2,000 square miles for a ten-megaton bomb. This radioactive dust is extremely poisonous if inhaled and this is why you are advised to stay indoors for several days after a nuclear attack.

Radioactive substances giving off alpha and beta particles are only really dangerous when they get inside your body. Alpha particles can travel only a few inches in air and cannot penetrate skin. Beta particles travel no more than twenty or thirty feet in air and about one mm. through human skin. Both can be stopped by a thin sheet of material so, although these particles comprise much of the energy of a nuclear explosion, they are not a major additional hazard in its immediate aftermath.

Gamma radiation is the biggest radiation hazard just after a nuclear explosion. Like X-rays gamma rays penetrate matter and, although they get weaker in the process, they never completely disappear. People can be affected by gamma radiation some distance away from a nuclear explosion.

Large doses of radiation cause radiation sickness. The first effects are usually noticed within hours – sickness and vomiting. Later there is more vomiting, diarrhoea, weakness and mental depression. The hair falls out. Bleeding starts from the mouth, nose and bowels. Very intensive treatment is needed for recovery and this is not likely to be available under the conditions following a nuclear attack.

Nuclear fallout is also a long-term hazard. The fine dust from the mushroom cloud can stay aloft for two or more years and return to earth thousands of miles from the point of the explosion. Radioactive nuclei break up because they are unstable, but they do not break up all at once. It is a matter of chance when they do. Some exist in an unstable form for a long time (years), others for only a short time (days). (The really short-lived substances last for only fractions of a second.) The nuclei obey the law of exponential decay – that is, in a given period of time a fixed fraction will decay. For example, for iodine-131, half will decay after eight days and then half of

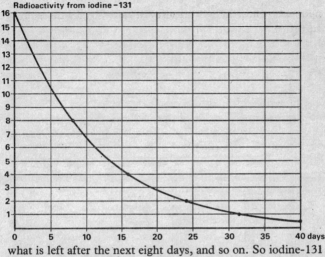

Radioactivity from iodine – 131

what is left after the next eight days, and so on. So iodine-131 is said to have a 'half-life' of eight days.

Some of the longer-lived radioactive substances in fallout dust can have even more serious effects than those previously described. The four most dangerous are strontium-90 (half-life: twenty-eight years), iodine-131 (eight days), caesium-137 (thirty years) and carbon-14 (5,670 years). These four are easily absorbed in our bodies, so that when they decay *all* their emitted radiation affects living matter. The effect is to change the chemical composition of living cells – a highly toxic form of internal poisoning.

The special danger of strontium-90 is that it is chemically similar to calcium and so is absorbed into our bones and blood. Growing children who drink milk from cows which have grazed on fallout-laden grass are especially vulnerable. So people born after 1955, when many atmospheric nuclear tests were conducted, have more strontium-90 in their bones than older people. By irradiation of bone marrow cells, or bone cells, strontium-90 may cause leukaemia or bone tumours.

The illustration overleaf shows how atmospheric nuclear explosions and strontium-90 pollution levels are related. Welsh

Reproduced from On the Warpath *by the author, Oxford University Press, 1976*

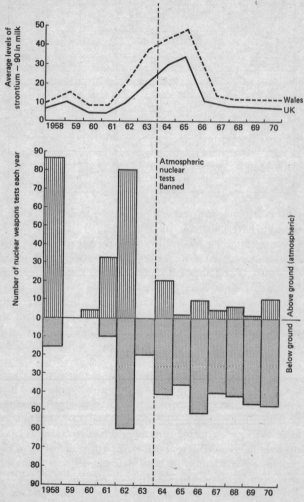

Average levels of strontium – 90 in milk

Number of nuclear weapons tests each year

Above ground (atmospheric)

Below ground

Atmospheric nuclear tests Banned

Wales

UK

Compiled from S I P R I data

hills are relatively calcium deficient so the milk from Welsh cows contains more strontium-90 than milk from elsewhere in the UK. It is ironic that the present generation of nuclear disarmament campaigners (born 1955–65) have more strontium-90 in their bones than the generation whose campaigns stopped the tests.

Iodine-131 is like ordinary iodine and about 20 per cent of ingested iodine-131 accumulates in the thyroid gland. This can lead, especially in young babies, to stunted physical and mental growth. However, as it decays quite quickly (with a half-life of eight days), iodine-131 is not as great a long-term hazard as strontium-90.

Caesium-137 behaves in the body like potassium and is distributed through the soft tissue. It has relatively penetrating gamma radiation which can reach reproductive organs and thus present a genetic hazard.

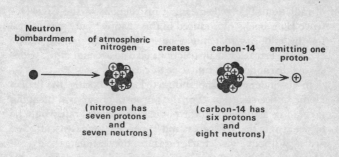

Neutron bombardment of atmospheric nitrogen creates carbon-14 emitting one proton

(nitrogen has seven protons and seven neutrons)

(carbon-14 has six protons and eight neutrons)

Carbon-14 can replace ordinary carbon anywhere in the body and decays to nitrogen-14. So carbon-14, like caesium-137, can cause abnormal children to be born. Even today children of Hiroshima and Nagasaki are more likely to be born dead or deformed than elsewhere – the effects of radiation are transmitted to the unborn generations.

At one time it was suggested that a 'clean' bomb might be developed, so that there would be less danger from fallout. But 'clean' bombs – in practice, pure fusion bombs – produce particularly large amounts of carbon-14 as a result of neutron bombardment of atmospheric nitrogen (the 7 protons and 7 neutrons of nitrogen become 6 protons and 8 neutrons, which is carbon-14). Since carbon-14 has a half-life of 5,670 years, it would be present over *thousands* of years, with the result that genetic mutations would be spread over hundreds of generations instead of only one or two.

Although scientists have failed to make the so-called 'clean' bomb, it now appears that truly 'dirty' bombs are practicable. The 'enhanced radiation weapon' (otherwise known as the 'neutron bomb') can kill people by radiation over a 1–2 kilometre range while leaving buildings and property reasonably intact after a few hundred metres.

Altogether, the chances of survival following a nuclear attack are not good. Only a few H-bombs would be needed to effectively destroy Britain's main population centres and it is doubtful whether many people would survive the after-effects of radiation. The well-meaning instructions of the Civil Defence Handbooks reproduced in this chapter* only make sense for the minority that might be left on the periphery of one explosion centre. The instructions take no account of the widespread disruption of a full-scale nuclear war.

In a confidential memorandum to local authorities the British Home Office suggests: 'For the purposes of survival planning it could be assumed that the population survival rate would be 60 per cent in the worst areas and 95 per cent in the least affected areas.' Without civil defence measures they estimate the overall casualties at 80 per cent nationwide; with civil defence this might be brought down to 40 per cent; and with a national shelter policy perhaps 20 per cent. But these figures are *not* estimates of survival rates after a *major* nuclear war – they are estimates based upon a nuclear war so 'small' that survival planning would be worth attempting.

This is why Civil Defence does make some sort of sense for neutral and non-nuclear countries like Sweden and Switzerland. They can expect to receive fallout with several hours

---

* *Protect and Survive*, HMSO, 1980.

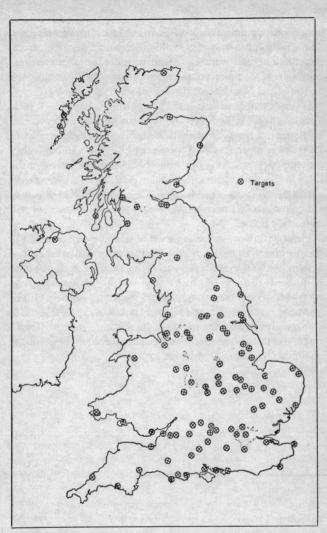

⊗ Targets

Possible British targets in a nuclear war. From Beneath the City Streets,
Peter Laurie

notice and are unlikely to suffer from the explosions directly. The situation for Britain is quite different, as we are a certain target in a nuclear war. The major pressure for fallout shelters comes from commercial interests attempting to exploit the public's fears of an oncoming nuclear war (see Plate VIII).

It seems that British Home Office planners have based their calculations on an assumed 200 megaton attack. However, this is less than 3 per cent of the known Soviet nuclear arsenal in 1980 and is much less than the Soviet Union would use if they contemplated attacking our military bases which threaten the USSR. So the Home Office plans either are inadequate or, alternatively, make sense because it is assumed that the Soviet Union already has been largely destroyed by an attack we will have made beforehand.

Plans have been made for an élite one in every hundred to shelter underground, if need be for months. But what sort of Britain would they emerge to after this time, even if the attack is 'limited' to only 200 megatons? Would any animals have survived? Would the water, gas and electricity supplies still be operating? Although military experts talk of 'acceptable levels of damage', for Britain the topic is hypothetical – no more than a fraction of the nuclear stockpiles in existence would be needed to annihilate the entire population.

4. Many ways of killing

International law limits the methods and weapons that belligerents may use against an enemy ... all arms, projectiles or material calculated to cause unnecessary suffering and unnecessary death are forbidden. Poison and poisoned weapons are prohibited. Most opinion also agrees on forbidding dum-dum bullets (designed to expand or flatten easily in the human body), suffocating and poisonous gases, bacteriological warfare, and radiological weapons.

Regarding nuclear weapons, the preponderance of legal opinion has condemned the effects of nuclear radiation from these weapons as being 'akin to those inflicted by the use of poison or poisoned weapons ... Thus, in principle, the use of such weapons is illegal' (*International Law Association, Report of the Fiftieth Conference held at Brussels, 1962*).

Most legal opinion does not regard the use of fire weapons such as flame throwers and napalm and incendiary bombs as illegal.

'The Laws of War', *Encyclopedia Britannica*, 1974 edition

Although nuclear weapons have not been used since 1945, their existence has profoundly influenced world events. The post-war period has been dominated by the nuclear arms race between the superpowers* with economic, social and military conse-

*The USA and USSR are so far ahead of the rest of the world in military strength that it has become commonplace to bracket them together as 'superpowers'. The term 'leading nuclear powers' includes the superpowers and, usually, Britain – in recognition of Britain's advanced knowledge of nuclear explosion technology. The term 'nuclear powers' also includes France and China, and perhaps India.

quences for all other nations. Whilst they and their respective allies have not risked direct confrontation, lesser powers have fought numerous 'small' non-nuclear wars. More people have been killed in these 'small' wars since 1945 than during any comparable period of 'peace'.

'It was going to be the ultimate weapon, but I can't lift it.'

The danger of nuclear war may be one reason for this increase. The risk of universal nuclear war has to some extent restrained military action by the more powerful countries and this has helped smaller countries and guerilla movements to continue fighting against vastly superior forces. Although US generals advocated the use of nuclear weapons in Korea (1949–53) and Vietnam (1962–72), the politicians dared not provoke Soviet intervention in support of her allies.

In practice nuclear weapons are unusable for virtually all present-day conflicts. For example, in Northern Ireland they would destroy the very people who need protecting. If used on a battlefield, the troops of both sides would be destroyed. So for all wars except those between nuclear powers, nuclear weapons are inappropriate. (Apart from one other possibility: that terrorists might obtain plutonium and blackmail a major nation. Although this danger is real, it is nowhere near as serious as the main nuclear arms race.)

This is why, ever since 1944, attempts have been made to make a really small nuclear bomb. These efforts became public in 1977, when US plans to develop the neutron bomb were announced. However, as a result of a worldwide outcry, production plans were postponed in 1978 (though the project is still 'live'). One crucial factor in the postponement decision was a realization that the use of any nuclear weapon, however small, would cross the threshold from conventional warfare and so make escalation into a full-scale nuclear war almost inevitable.

But nuclear weapons have influenced the *character* of modern warfare. In a nuclear war there would be no distinction between soldiers and civilians or between 'necessary suffering' and 'unnecessary suffering'. All the carefully worded legal definitions of humane warfare would be irrelevant, since friends, foes and neutrals would all die from radioactive fallout. By contrast, non-nuclear war can seem relatively humane (even when it violates previously accepted standards for conventional warfare). So under the shadow of nuclear warfare, conventional warfare has become far more terrible without evoking as much public attention.

Chemical and biological weapons

When a powerful nation fights a 'limited' war it cannot risk long-term effects like nuclear fallout. Moreover it is useful if buildings, factories and wealth are left untouched since there is no point in capturing a heap of useless rubble. Chemical and biological weapons (CBW) have been advocated as the best means of accomplishing this purpose.

Gas was used in the First World War, and the first extensive use of it then (in 1915) resulted in about 5,000 deaths. From then, until the end of the war in 1918, at least 125,000 tons of toxic chemicals were used, causing around 1,300,000 casualties of which about 100,000 were fatal. The gases used, mainly phosgene and mustard gas, were much less toxic than those available today and the means of delivery were very unsophisticated. 250 tons of VX (a modern nerve gas) could cause as many deaths as a 5 megaton thermonuclear bomb yet leave buildings, factories, roads, etc., undamaged.

Biological weapons (BW) would be delivered in the same way as chemical gases, but the extent and nature of their effects are less easy to predict. Because they affect living organisms, bacteriological agents (germs) can be carried by migratory birds,

Some lethal chemical weapons

Agents	Mechanism	Speed of action
Nerve agent G (e.g. Tabun, Sarin, Soman)	Interferes with nervous system	Seconds, by inhalation
Nerve agent V (e.g. VX)	Interferes with nervous system	Seconds, by inhalation, or minutes to hours through skin
Blister agent (e.g. sulphur mustard, nitrogen mustard)	Cell poison	Hours or days, but eyes affected more quickly
Choking (e.g. phosgene, cyanide)	Damages lungs	Immediate or up to three hours
Toxins (e.g. botulinus)	Neuromuscular paralysis	Hours or days depending on dosage

animals and travellers to localities far removed from the areas originally attacked. Biological weapons therefore share the disadvantage of nuclear weapons: they could kill people on the attacker's side.

This disadvantage was also demonstrated by the phosgene and mustard gas used in the First World War – it was sometimes carried back by the wind. Nerve gases, which can kill by touch, suffer from the same drawback. So chemical and biological weapons are extremely risky and this is one reason why BW have been outlawed.

The BW Convention of 1972 prohibits all biological weapons and provides for existing BW stockpiles to be destroyed. Unfortunately neither France nor China supports the treaty and we cannot be certain that even the signatory states have carried out its provisions. (Months after all BW were to have been destroyed, President Nixon learnt that US stockpiles were still intact – for 'technical reasons'.) Even if all BW were to be destroyed, they could be easily prepared once again. The difficulty of preventing secret unofficial production – they can be made in a hospital laboratory – makes BW especially repugnant to the major powers.

The production of poisonous chemicals is equally difficult to control but for a different reason. Many are widely used in peacetime – around 100,000 tons of phosgene are made in Britain every year for the manufacture of plastics, herbicides and pharmaceutical products. Ethylene oxide, 1 ton of which can be easily converted to 2 tons of mustard gas, is a major product of the petrochemical industry with a world-wide output of around 1,000,000 tons a year. Dimethylphosphite, which is needed to make the nerve gas Sarin, is used in the manufacture of pesticides. These examples show that it would be impracticable to prohibit the manufacture of chemicals that might be used for CW.

A more fruitful approach might be to prohibit the devices used to deliver BW and CW to their targets. A ban on rockets, bomber aircraft, bombs and shells would effectively prevent CBW being used. But it would also make atomic warfare impossible. So the effective prohibition of CBW is not likely until all ABC (atomic-biological-chemical) warfare is outlawed. Despite international law and the BW Convention, the threat of CBW remains.

Toxins appear to be the most effective and possibly the most efficient of the chemical weapons. A toxin is a chemical pro-

Grimbledon Down   Bill Tidy

Some lethal biological weapons		
Agents	*Diseases*	*Incubation period* (*days*)
Viruses	Tick-borne encephalitis	5–15
	Yellow fever	3–6
Rickettsiae	Rocky Mountain spotted fever	3–10
	Epidemic typhus	6–15
Bacteria	Anthrax	1–5
	Cholera	1–5
	Pneumonic plague	2–5
	Typhoid	7–21

duced by a living organism. Its advantage is that it is non-contagious: that is, it cannot multiply like bacteria. It therefore has many of the advantages of a biological weapon without the disadvantage of uncontrolled growth. The Botulinus Toxin is 1,000 times more toxic than the nerve gases and before evaporating could wipe out all life in a given area inside six hours.

CBW are weapons of genocide: they cannot discriminate between armed forces and civilians. As few governments ever admit that they are fighting an entire population, this presents a big *political* disadvantage: the use of CBW is an admission that the vast majority of the population are treated as enemies.

So conventional bombing is still used. With conventional bombing it can be said that the prime targets are military – even when most victims are civilians. Similarly mines and boobytraps are often stated to have military targets. Although such statements are usually misleading – because soldiers are better protected than civilians from such weapons – this is one reason why 'conventional' weapons raise less political protest.

Anti-personnel weapons

However, for certain types of warfare, the intention can be to kill or deliberately maim *civilians*. The weapons used are known as anti-personnel weapons (APW) and have two major military advantages. In the first place, badly wounded people need food and medicine and need to be tended. Secondly, the dead and buried disappear from sight, whereas the injured remain visible as a constant reminder of the horror of the war. So APW sap morale and tie up valuable resources.

Incendiary weapons

Incendiary weapons (fire bombs), such as napalm, were the earliest anti-personnel weapons. They're not much good at destroying buildings and most military targets, but they are very effective against people (see Plate IX). According to US military instructions the main object of fire bomb attacks is 'to kill, neutralize and demoralize'. (The manual does go on to mention that a secondary objective is to destroy 'or damage vehicles and equipment'.) Napalm, which is a jellified oily mixture, is the most well-known incendiary weapon and sticks to skin whilst continuing to burn. Magnesium and white phosphorus are newer types of fire bomb and have the additional property that they smoulder under the skin as the drops burn down to the bone.

Although napalm and similar devices have been used extensively for many years, there is some doubt concerning the legality of their use. A UK manual states 'their use against personnel is contrary to the law of war in so far as it is calculated to cause unnecessary suffering'. The US Army Manual, *The Law of Land Warfare*, states: 'The use of weapons which employ fire, flame throwers, or napalm, and other incendiary agents, against targets requiring their use is not violative of international law. They should not, however, be employed in such a way as to cause unnecessary suffering to individuals.'

In practice incendiary weapons are at least as useful as conventional explosives against people. So, despite the unnecessary suffering caused, napalm is normally employed against people. There may be some excuse for the production of napalm because it can be used against military targets. Other anti-personnel weapons do not have this justification. Fragmentation bombs, for example, cannot even puncture a truck tyre – although they cause people excruciating agony.

Fragmentation bombs

A fragmentation mine scatters hundreds of small pellets, or flechettes, which penetrate flesh and are not easily removed. Flechettes are irregular-shaped pellets which work their way through flesh like fishing hooks. So the surgeon who tries to remove a flechette cannot be sure whether it is still close to the point of entry. To make it even more difficult, some pellets are made in hard plastic which do not show up on X-rays and therefore cannot be found except by blind probing with a surgeon's knife. It is easy to see how such weapons use more medical resources than an equivalent attack with conventional explosives.

Gravel mines can be smaller than three inches square and are often covered with plastic or cloth. They explode when trodden on. These were used extensively in Vietnam. Whereas soldiers were protected by heavy boots, many a barefoot Vietnamese peasant lost a foot by these devices. The camouflage also meant that children were more commonly the victims – their inquisitive fingers sought out the scraps of cloth where adults walked past without interest.

Weapons which 'needlessly increase suffering' or which attack civilians rather than soldiers were outlawed as early as 1867 at the St Petersburg conference and this principle has been reaffirmed in every subsequent international agreement on the laws of warfare. Yet there was little outcry at their use in Vietnam.

Ecocide

The Vietnam War showed that even anti-personnel weapons and conventional bombing could not subdue people determined to resist. They learnt to live underground in the jungle and under extremely primitive conditions. So further measures were attempted.

Vast areas of land were sprayed with herbicide under operations code-named 'Food denial' and 'Cover denial'. 'Food denial' was meant to prevent local farmers supplying food to

the Vietnamese guerillas. 'Cover denial' meant stripping leaves, foliage and vegetation to remove the cover which gave protection from helicopter patrols. As a consequence vast tracts of land were destroyed for agriculture. Approximately one eighth of South Vietnam has been sprayed with herbicides and as a result much of this land will not supply food in the foreseeable future.

A vast expanse of woods [and] ... crop-producing land [was sprayed] and more than 1,000 inhabitants were affected. A large number of livestock were also poisoned and some of them died. The majority of the poisoned people did not take any food from these crops nor drink any of the water that had been covered or mixed with the sprinkled germ chemicals. They had only breathed in the polluted air, or the poison had touched their skin. At first they felt sick and some had diarrhoea; then they began to find it hard to breathe and they had low blood pressure; some serious cases had trouble with their optic nerves and went blind. Pregnant women gave birth to still-born or premature children. Most of the affected cattle died from serious diarrhoea, and river fish floated to the surface of the water, belly up, soon after the chemicals were spread.*

When defoliation failed to win the war, more systematic destruction was attempted. Land was levelled for perhaps a quarter of a mile on either side of highways and for half a mile round army camps and villages. Later, reploughing was encouraged to prevent the land recovering. As a consequence it

*From a South Vietnamese doctor's account of a chemical attack near Saigon, 3 October 1964.

has tended to harden by exposure to sunlight. In some areas the land solidified to rock and will never again be used for agriculture. This sort of attack upon the ecology of a country has become known as ecocide.

Conventional bombing also contributes to ecocide. Twenty-five million bomb craters have caused permanent damage to the landscape of South Vietnam, creating breeding ponds for disease-carrying mosquitoes. Few farmers risk walking between the craters for fear of unexploded bombs. The worst-affected areas are those that were subjected to 'carpet bombing'.

Carpet bombing was used by the Americans to maximize the damage on the ground and minimize the danger to their own pilots. Instead of attacking military targets one by one, formations of bombers flew together at a great height releasing their bombs at pre-set intervals. This laid a broad 'carpet' of bomb damage, equivalent in effect to ploughing a quarter-mile strip for miles and miles through the jungle. In addition to all the deleterious effects mentioned earlier with respect to bombing, ploughing and defoliation, the subdivision of the jungles prevents wild life and vegetation moving between the smaller areas left and makes recovery even more difficult.

The ultimate solution

With such weapons conventional warfare is not much different from a small nuclear war. Indeed the difference between conventional war and nuclear war becomes blurred when 1,500-lb. conventional explosive bombs are used. The real significance is political. Once nuclear weapons are used, an all-out global war is almost certain to follow. So anything short of nuclear weapons has become 'conventional' and, by implication, acceptable – because it is not as horrible as nuclear war.

Yet the 'conventional' Vietnam War was more terrible than any preceding war. In terms of tonnage more conventional explosives were dropped on Vietnam than were dropped during the Second World War – quite apart from the chemical weapons used, the defoliation and the anti-personnel weapons. And, since the war was essentially a political conflict, there was no

distinction made between soldiers and civilians or between 'necessary' and 'unnecessary' suffering.

Still the search goes on to find a technique, short of nuclear war, that would enable a powerful country to subdue a determined people. New ways are being developed to protect a sophisticated military force from retaliation.

The electronic battlefield is the ultimate solution. Instead of risking troops and manned helicopters and planes, pilotless aircraft will drop electronic gadgets all over the country from a great height. The gadgets will be equipped with listening and sensing devices, and perhaps roving television cameras which transmit signals back to command bases. Pilotless bombers will then be dispatched to attack targets selected by computers supplied with this field data. In this way no lives need be lost by the attacking power.

On the battlefield of the future, enemy forces will be located, trapped and targeted almost instantaneously through the use of data links, computer-assisted intelligence evaluation and automated fire control ... I am confident the American people will welcome and applaud the developments that will replace, wherever possible, the man with the machine.*

Some of these gadgets have already been tested and used. But they were somewhat primitive and the resourceful Vietnamese devised counter-measures. They moved the gadgets around, left motors running close to acoustic sensors and hung

* General William Westmorland (see Plate X), to an American Congressional committee, 1970.

bags of urine from trees to overload the sensors which detected smells. Although a lot was learnt, the techniques were not much use at that time.

Nor would these devices have been effective against a technologically advanced adversary. The methods depend upon a gross disparity in the relative strengths of the two forces. Neither America nor Russia would attempt to drop sensors over each other's territories for fear of provoking a nuclear war. So the genocide and ecocide of 'conventional' non-nuclear war is only feasible nowadays against guerilla movements and relatively weak military forces. The nuclear arms race remains top priority for the two leading military powers.

5. Weapons systems

With no advantage to be gained by striking first and no disadvantage to be suffered by striking second, there will be no motive for surprise or pre-emptive attack. Mutual invulnerability means mutual deterrence. It is the most stable position from the point of view of preventing all-out war.

Henry Kissinger

From about 1955 onwards the arms race has been concerned primarily with missiles and delivery systems. Although bombs can be made more powerful than 57 megatons, a scatter of smaller bombs can cause just as much destruction. With tons of TNT explosive equivalent for every man, woman and child alive in the world today, the USA and USSR do not need more nuclear explosives to kill people. For them it is far more important to ensure that bombs land on target – preferably targets which contain enemy nuclear bombs. Developments in technology, to make bombs smaller, enable delivery vehicles to become more effective in range and accuracy.

Alongside such developments in technology there have been changes in military strategy. Victory in a nuclear war must mean *total* destruction of the enemy – otherwise the other side can retaliate and the 'victor' may be as badly affected as the vanquished. So it is better to be the attacker in a nuclear war: the only way to 'win' is to launch a surprise attack so powerful that the enemy cannot retaliate.

This is one of the big differences between nuclear wars and all previous wars. There is no way a 'defender' in an impending nuclear war will be better off by letting the other side strike first. Once war seems unavoidable, it is best to attack quickly.

In the jargon of nuclear strategy, plans for a surprise attack are known as *first-strike strategy* and the ability to launch a successful first strike is known as *first-strike capability*. The response is to protect nuclear weapons so that there are always enough left (even after a nuclear attack) to hit back and inflict widespread destruction throughout the attacker's country. Provided this *second-strike capability* exists, and is known to exist, a sane military strategist will be deterred from starting a nuclear war. This is why they say that *mutually assured destruction* (MAD) has made the world safe!

Jargon

It is unfortunately necessary to learn terms like 'first strike', 'second strike' and 'mutually assured destruction' to follow the arguments of military strategists. However, they can be very misleading if accepted at face value. For example:

- a 'tactical nuclear weapon' can be bigger than the atomic bomb that destroyed Hiroshima;
- a 'limited nuclear war' could have more casualties than the First and Second World Wars combined;
- an 'acceptable level of damage' can mean more than 40 per cent of a population killed (e.g. 20 million dead in Britain);
- a 'counter-force' strategy involves attacks on military targets and is essentially a strategy to start a nuclear war;
- a 'counter-city' strategy involves attacks on civilians and is essentially a strategy to deter a nuclear war.

These last two examples are worth examining more fully as they illustrate how jargon makes policies seem more reasonable than they are. Mass murder ('counter-city') seems worse than destruction of weapons ('counter-force'). However, military targets are appropriate only if the intention is to launch a first strike. These targets have to be destroyed before the enemy

Nuclear jargon

Excerpts from the Press Conference of US Secretary of Defense James Schlesinger, 10 January 1974

Q. Could you amplify on the changing in targeting strategy?

A. I think that this has been discussed over the years, that to a large extent the American doctrinal position has been wrapped around something called 'assured destruction', which implies a tendency to target Soviet cities initially and massively and that this is the only option that the President of the United States or the national command authorities would have in the event of a possible recourse to strategic weapons. It is our intention that this not be the only option and possibly not the principal option open to the national command authorities.

Q. Can you just go a little further and tell me what you're talking about? What are you trying to do that is different? What is the change? What is the other option?

A. I'm not going to spell that out to you right now.

Q. Well, could you put it in English then, so that a layman can understand what you're driving at?

A. The main point that should be understood is that both sides now have, and will continue to have, invulnerable second-strike forces, and that with those invulnerable second-strike forces it is inevitable, or virtually inevitable, that the employment by one side of its forces against the cities of the other side in an all-out strike will immediately bring a counter-strike against its own cities. Consequently, the range of circumstances in which an all-out strike against an opponent's cities can be contemplated has narrowed considerably and one wishes to have alternatives for employment of strategic forces other than what would be, for the party initiating, a suicidal strike against the cities of the other side.

becomes aware that he is being attacked and retaliates. If, on the other hand, the point is to deter the opponent from attacking, it is ridiculous to aim at military targets – they will be empty at the time of retaliation, since the opponent will have used his weapons for his first strike.

So a counter-force strategy actually means a strategy for starting a nuclear war, whereas a counter-city strategy is one based on retaliation. The USSR has always lagged behind the USA in the nuclear arms race and boasts of the size of its nuclear warheads and of how many people it can kill (counter-city). By contrast the USA boasts of its missile accuracy and of how many military bases it can destroy (counter-force). Although it is certainly reprehensible to threaten mass annihilation (even in retaliation), a threat to start a nuclear war and initiate mass destruction is no better. In July 1975 US Defense Secretary James Schlesinger confirmed this point explicitly: 'Under no circumstances could we disavow the first use of nuclear weapons.'

Offensive and defensive weapons

The term 'defensive weapon' is another misleading piece of military jargon – it sounds rather soothing and almost nice. In reality, 'defensive weapons' are – if that is possible – even more of a threat than 'offensive weapons'.

'Offensive weapons' are intended for attack against military bases, towns, etc., while 'defensive weapons' are intended to repel such an attack (for example, by destroying attacking missiles). But the reason for developing 'defensive' weapons could be to ward off retaliation – to make a first strike feasible. (Conversely a second-strike strategy requires 'offensive' weapons to penetrate defences and so deter aggression.)

So 'defensive weapons' are not 'good'. An effective defensive system would enable an attack to be launched. Every weapon has a purpose *in the context of military strategy*: there are no peaceful nuclear weapons as such.

Missiles

The first atomic bombs were dropped from aircraft. But bombers have become increasingly vulnerable to anti-aircraft defences and they are, by modern standards, slow. (The fastest bombers would take several hours on the journey between Moscow and New York whereas missiles could arrive within the hour.) Since the late 1950s more and more reliance has been placed upon missiles – indeed the impetus for the space race began with military rockets rather than a desire for scientific exploration.

The first missiles were not very accurate over the USSR/ USA range and so could not be used against small targets – only against large cities. But nowadays missile accuracies are to within 200 yards (in 1980 perhaps thirty yards) and it is possible for an Intercontinental Ballistic Missile (ICBM) to destroy a hard military target.

Missiles are kept at instant readiness for firing. Formerly firing took several hours, thus giving the aggressor a big advantage: in theory the attacker could have destroyed all enemy missiles whilst they were still on their launch pads. (In response to this, missiles are now programmed to fire simultaneously and to leave their silos before the attacking missiles arrive.)

As well as ICBMs there are intermediate-range ballistic missiles (IRBMs) which, for example, could hit Moscow from missile sites in Europe; and submarine-launched ballistic missiles (SLBMs), the most modern version (Trident-2) having a range of 6,000 miles. Many of these missiles are able to deliver several nuclear warheads at once, spraying their targets as if with nuclear grapeshot.

Cruise missiles

All the missiles so far mentioned follow ballistic trajectories: that is, after the initial thrust, they proceed to their targets under free-fall conditions. By 1982 many intercontinental missiles may be powered for all or part of their flight, with navigation equipment on board to make automatic course corrections.

```
0 0 0 0 0 0 0 0 0 0 0 0 0 0 0 0 0 0 0 0 0 0 0 0  9 14 17 17 18 16 18 18
0 0 0 0 0 0 0 0 0 0 0 0 0 0 0 0 0 0 0 0 0 0 0 1 10 16 18 18 18 18 18 18
0 0 0 0 0 0 0 0 0 0 0 0 0 0 0 0 0 0 0 0 0 9 15 18 18 18 18 18 18 18
0 0 0 0 0 0 0 1 0 0 0 0 0 0 0 0 0 0 0 0 0 15 19 18 18 18 18 18 18 18
0 0 0 0 0 0 0 1 0 0 0 0 0 0 0 0 0 0 0 0 8 18 20 18 18 18 18 18 18 18
0 0 0 1 0 0 1 1 0 0 0 0 0 0 0 0 0 0 0 0 9 10 18 21 18 18 18 18 18 18
0 0 1 0 3 3 2 1 0 0 0 0 0 0 0 0 0 0 0 13 18 18 17 17 18 18 18 18 18
0 0 1 1 2 4 4 3 2 0 0 0 0 0 0 0 0 0 1 14 18 18 16 16 17 18 18 18 18
0 0 0 1 2 2 4 4 3 3 0 0 0 0 0 0 0 0 9 15 18 18 17 17 17 16 17 18 18
0 0 1 1 1 2 4 5 3 3 1 0 0 0 0 0 0 0 10 14 16 16 15 15 17 18 18 18 18
0 0 0 1 2 4 4 4 3 0 0 0 0 0 0 0 0 6 10 12 15 15 14 14 16 15 18 18 18
0 0 0 1 4 6 5 5 6 2 0 0 0 0 0 4 10 9 12 13 12 12 14 16 17 18 18
0 0 0 0 7 8 6 5 6 8 7 2 0 0 0 0 4 6 7 10 11 9 12 14 16 17 18 18
0 0 0 0 3 7 7 6 9 14 9 5 0 0 0 0 2 6 8 10 11 12 13 15 17 18 18
0 0 0 0 2 4 7 8 14 16 16 10 7 0 0 0 1 4 6 10 11 11 12 15 17 17 18
0 0 0 0 1 4 8 10 16 20 18 12 10 6 0 0 0 2 2 5 9 11 12 13 14 16 16
0 0 0 0 0 4 6 10 16 20 18 12 12 9 7 0 0 1 2 3 4 8 9 11 12 13 14 15
0 0 0 0 1 4 8 10 12 13 19 17 12 11 8 1 0 0 2 3 3 7 8 10 12 12 12 13
0 0 0 0 1 5 9 10 8 6 8 10 12 10 5 2 0 0 2 3 4 5 6 7 9 10 12 13
0 0 0 0 1 7 11 7 6 6 8 8 9 7 3 1 0 1 3 5 7 6 7 6 7 8 11 12
0 0 0 0 1 7 12 14 14 6 6 7 8 1 1 1 0 1 5 7 10 8 8 7 6 7 10
0 0 0 0 1 7 12 14 13 6 7 7 7 5 1 1 0 1 7 9 10 10 10 10 9 6 7
0 0 0 0 2 7 12 13 6 6 7 8 7 6 1 1 1 0 1 2 7 10 11 12 13 14 12 12 10
0 0 0 0 2 7 12 8 6 6 7 7 7 7 1 1 1 1 2 3 4 10 11 13 16 16 14 12
0 0 0 0 2 7 11 7 7 6 6 6 7 4 4 3 2 3 4 5 7 10 13 16 16 14
0 0 0 0 0 1 6 10 8 7 6 6 7 8 5 5 3 5 8 8 7 9 13 16 16 15
0 0 0 0 1 1 6 10 9 8 6 6 7 8 6 6 4 4 7 10 10 7 6 8 12 13 14 15
0 0 0 5 4 6 7 10 9 8 9 6 7 7 8 4 4 5 9 10 12 6 7 10 12 14 15
0 0 5 6 6 9 8 10 11 10 9 8 6 7 8 8 6 4 6 9 10 8 6 7 7 10 14 15
0 0 5 9 11 13 15 12 10 9 9 8 6 7 8 8 6 7 8 8 8 10 8 7 6 10 13 14
0 0 6 6 9 11 17 16 14 10 8 8 8 8 6 6 6 8 9 10 11 11 11 7 6 6 7 10 11
```

Long-range cruise missiles will find their way to the target by com-paring their 'memory' of a digital map of the terrain against observations whilst cruising

These 'cruise missiles' will be far more accurate than ballistic missiles. They carry their own guidance mechanism (which may be in communication with a Satellite Global Positioning System) and are controlled by an on-board mini-computer which corrects and changes the course during flight. In addition, they may be guided by reference to their own record of a digital map (see illustration). The accuracy claimed for cruise missiles suggests that they may parallel ballistic missiles for the purposes of a first strike.

Anti-ballistic missiles

Anti-ballistic missile (ABM) systems are intended for 'defence' against attacking missiles carrying nuclear warheads. It is not practicable to score direct hits on free-fall (ballistic) missiles coming at a speed of more than 2,000 miles per hour. But if *nuclear* warheads are used in 'defence', even a 'near miss' of, say, five miles can destroy an enemy missile. The burst of neutrons and gamma radiation from the 'defensive explosion' makes up for any inaccuracy.

Every military move has its counter-move. One reply to ABM has been to load several nuclear warheads on a single missile. When the ICBM nears its target, it separates into several fragments, each with a nuclear warhead. By then it may be too late to launch the extra anti-missile missiles and extremely difficult to decide where each should be aimed.

Missiles with many nuclear warheads are known as MRV missiles (Multiple Re-entry Vehicles). In their crudest form these allow the attacker to spread the destruction more economically over a wider area. Whereas the 1962 version of a Polaris missile carried a single 800-kiloton warhead with each of its missiles, the 1964 version was able to deliver three 200-kiloton MRV warheads. Although the total explosive power was less (600 kilotons), its capacity to cause death and destruction was considerably greater.

An ABM system

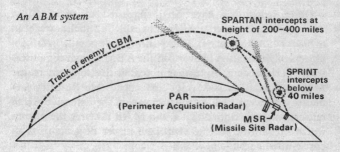

Track of enemy ICBM

SPARTAN intercepts at height of 200–400 miles

SPRINT intercepts below 40 miles

PAR
(Perimeter Acquisition Radar)

MSR
(Missile Site Radar)

MIRV

But MRV warheads are not very accurate. The next development has been MIRV (Multiple Independently targeted Re-entry Vehicles). In this instance each re-entry vehicle has its own guidance system aimed at a predetermined target. It is now possible to pack ten or more MIRVed nuclear warheads on a single missile.

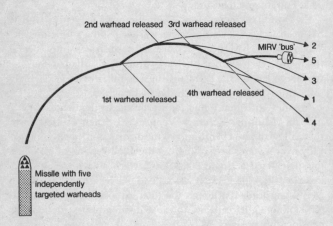

2nd warhead released   3rd warhead released

MIRV 'bus' → 2

→ 5

→ 3

→ 1

1st warhead released   4th warhead released   → 4

Missile with five
independently
targeted warheads

Other techniques have been suggested to avoid ABM defences. A forerunner missile might explode a nuclear warhead to black out ABM radars (an anti-anti-missile missile!). 'Decoy' objects might be used to overload the ABM system computers with spurious data. A further potential development of the MIRVed ICBMs is MARV (Manoeuvrable Re-entry Vehicles) which will change course to avoid the defensive ABM nuclear missiles. Both MIRV and MARV marry the proven worth of ballistic missiles with the newer developments in cruise-missile technology.

As a consequence of all these potential counter-measures it is now thought that ABM defences are probably impracticable and, in 1972, the Soviet Union and United States agreed not to waste too much more money on this aspect of the nuclear arms race. But, although MIRVs were said at the time to be necessary to counter ABMs, the ban on ABMs did not stop production of MIRVs – quite the contrary – and the implications of MIRVs became, in the mid 1970s, the most serious aspect of the arms race.

This can be illustrated by considering the nuclear balance that would exist if both sides had 1,000 ICBMs, with one ICBM at each missile site, and with no other nuclear weapons in existence. Neither could then risk a first-strike attack as this would need 100 per cent accuracy. At present there is no more than a 90 per cent probability that an ICBM will destroy a protected military target. So an attack of 1,000 ICBMs against the same number of missile sites would leave about 100 available for retaliation by the defender. Thus equality in ICBM numbers would allow *both* sides to have a second-strike capability, which is, as Henry Kissinger says, 'the most stable position from the point of view of preventing all-out war'.

The way to improve 'kill probability'* is to make more accurate missiles or to increase the explosive strength of the nuclear warheads. This can be countered by better protection for missile sites so that they can withstand bigger explosive pressures or, alternatively, by building *mobile* land-based missile launchers (such as the Soviet SS-20 or the US MX missile system described later). So far it has proved simpler and cheaper for the potential defender to improve his missile protection than for the attacker to achieve greater accuracy.

The simplest solution for the attacker is to build more missiles. With 2,000 missiles the probability of destroying the 1,000 missile silos would be raised to 99 per cent; with 3,000 missiles it would be 99·9 per cent. This illustrates that, for success, a

---

* 'Kill probability' is the k-value calculated on pages 94–5. A 5-kiloton bomb with an accuracy of 50 yards has a 96 per cent probability of destroying a missile silo hardened to withstand an overpressure of 300 pounds per square inch. In 1975 about half the US silos and all the Soviet silos were vulnerable to nuclear warheads of such strength and accuracy.

first strike needs at least three times as many warheads as there are targets. For the simple case of ICBMs only this would be extremely difficult to achieve – fortunately for world peace.

But with MIRVed warheads the chances of a successful first strike become more favourable, since 1,000 missiles could deliver ten times as many MIRVed nuclear warheads. Thus *both* sides could achieve a first-strike capability and *neither* side would have an effective second strike.

So the development of MIRV, though only one of many new weapons systems, was a major cause of the acceleration of the nuclear arms race during the 1970s.

Missile protection

ICBMs are built underground in deep silos for protection. Most of America's 1,064 ICBMs are stored in hardened silos so well protected that a 1-megaton nuclear bomb would need to fall within about a quarter of a mile to damage the missile (k > 16). Yet, with the improvements in missile accuracy

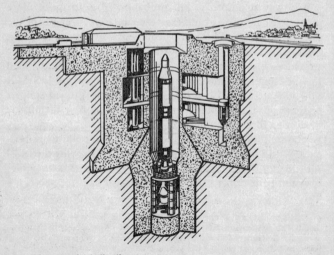

An underground missile silo

claimed for the 1980s, it is believed that even this degree of protection will prove inadequate.

'Mobile launchers' are not as accurate as ICBMs but they are better as *second-strike* weapons because of their relative invulnerability. They include ships, aircraft and submarines. Of these, ships have seemed the least important because they are slow moving and easily spotted. Their advantage is size: a single ship could carry hundreds of cruise missiles. Since warships can be easily destroyed, they are significant only in relation to a first-strike strategy.

Aircraft

Perhaps unexpectedly, bomber aircraft still have a future. This is due partly to the development of faster long-range aircraft but, more important still, to the introduction of short-range attack missiles (SRAMs) which replace conventional bombs. Using SRAMs, the aircraft need not get much closer than 100 miles to their targets and so they are almost invulnerable to anti-aircraft defences. (In 1980, in the run-up to the US Presidential election, President Carter revealed that the USA hoped to produce a 'stealth bomber', which would be undetectable by existing radar surveillance systems.)

B-52 and FB-111 strategic bombers carry twenty and six SRAMs respectively and thus, potentially, they more than double the number of nuclear warheads that America can deliver on Russia. At the time of writing, Russia has no comparable weapons. She would also need bases closer to America, in Canada and Mexico for example, to be able to threaten America with such short-range missiles.

MX

The MX (missile experimental) system is the most extraordinary scheme yet devised for protecting ICBMs. Over 50,000 million dollars is to be spent by the USA on 200 missiles, 4,600 missile shelters and 10,000 miles of roads, covering an area substantially greater than all of Wales.

	US SLBMs			Soviet SLBMs		
	Polaris A-3	Poseidon C-3	Poseidon C-4	SS-N-6	SS-N-8	SS-N-18
Date introduced	1964	1970	–	1968	1973	–
Number deployed (estimates for Sept 1980)	80	432	88	464	326	144
Number of MIRVs	3 (MRV)	10	8	1 (or 2 MRV)	1	3
Range (nautical miles)	2,500	2,500	4,000	1,300–1,600	4,300	4,050
Propellant	s	s	s	l-st	l-st	l-st
Throw-weight (kg)	500	1,000		700	700	
CEP (m)	900	500	500	1,000–2,500	1,000–1,500	550–1,000

Key: Propellant fuel: l = liquid, l-st = liquid-storable, s = solid, st = storable.

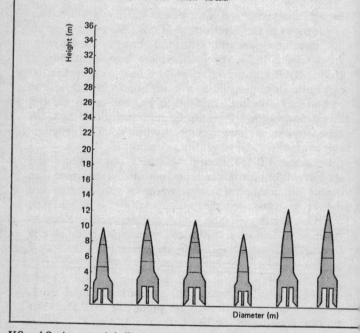

US and Soviet strategic ballistic missiles. From SIPRI *Yearbook 1980*

S ICBMs			Soviet ICBMs					
itan II	Minuteman II	Minuteman III	SS-9	SS-11	SS-13	SS-17	SS-18	SS-19
963	1966	1970	1966	1966	1969	1977	1976	1976
4	450	550	8	580	60	150	300	300
	1	3	1	1 (or 3 MRV)	1	4	1 or 8	6
3,300	7,000	7,000	6,500	5,700	4,400	5,000	5,500	5,000
	s	s	l	st	s	l-st	l-st	l-st
4,000	1,000	1,000	7,300	1,000	500	3,200	7,300	3,200
1,300	400	300	1,000–1,300	1,000–1,800	1,300	300–600	300–600	300–450

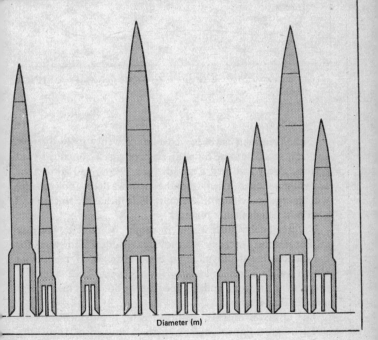

Diameter (m)

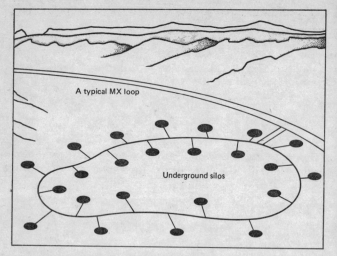

Loop road for one MX missile with twenty-three shelters. From SIPRI Yearbook 1980

Each MX missile can be moved to any of twenty-three different shelters, spaced at one mile intervals on a self-contained road system. Every so often, a missile (or a decoy) will go on tour and enter a shelter. Then, from the shelter, a decoy (or a missile) will emerge and continue the tour. This means the enemy will not know which shelter to attack.

Unfortunately, such a system might be used to increase missile numbers secretly – it provides the ideal framework for the clandestine deployment of extra missiles. If the Soviet Union builds a similar system it is likely that both sides will prepare for the worst and assume that the other has many more missiles than it admits.

The US MX missiles are planned for deployment in 1986 and are a great improvement over the Minuteman III missiles they will replace. Each will have ten MIRVed warheads instead of three and their accuracy will be improved by a factor of 3 (to below 100 metres – eventually to below 30 metres as measured by CEP).

The SS-20

This is a mobile Soviet ballistic missile, but only of intermediate range. It can carry three 150 kiloton MIRVed warheads (although some observers believe that most SS-20s prior to 1979 only had single warheads). Of the 120 deployed by 1979, about 50 were located along the Chinese border – the remainder are targeted on Western Europe.

Although the SS-20 is mobile, it is not as sophisticated as the MX system. It is launched directly from the transporter and does not use a shelter system. Until 1979 the SS-20s had been replacing the older SS-4 and SS-5 IRBMs. By mid 1979 about 140 of these older weapons had been dismantled.

The SS-20 greatly increases the strength of the Soviet nuclear forces in Europe and their ability to avoid destruction from a NATO attack. For a short period, until 1983, the Soviet Union will have more advanced IRBMs in Europe than NATO (see table on page 93). After 1983, the proposed introduction of 464 ground-launched cruise missiles (GLCMs) and 108 new Pershing II missiles will restore the advantage NATO has enjoyed in Eurostrategic weapons ever since 1962.

Air-launched cruise missiles (ALCMs)

From 1982, the USA plans to equip all its 151 operational B-52G bombers with twenty ALCMs each. These can be pre-programmed to follow a zig-zag path to avoid air defences and, with a warhead of up to 200 kiloton yield and an accuracy of perhaps thirty metres, will have a nearly 100 per cent ability to destroy any missile silo. When all 3,000 ALCMs are deployed, the USA should have the ability to destroy all ICBM and IRBM silos presently known to exist in the Soviet Union.

ALCMs, as such, are not covered by the SALT-2 agreement but the bombers that carry them are counted as if they were MIRVed missiles. Nonetheless, by 1985 these weapons may account for a quarter of the strategic nuclear warheads possessed by the USA.

The multirole Tornado

Not to be completely outdone, Britain, Italy and West Germany were, in 1976, cooperating to produce hundreds of Multi-Role Combat Aircraft (MRCA) which could be used to carry thermonuclear bombs. At the prices then prevailing the 385 MRCA for Britain would cost £4,000 million.

When the MRCA (in 1977 renamed the Tornado) is deployed in the early 1980s, about 220 of Britain's 385 Tornados will replace forty-eight 1960-vintage Vulcan bombers and sixty Buccaneer nuclear strike bombers. It is clear that these will be able to deliver at least as many nuclear warheads as the proposed fleet of four or five Trident submarines. Many people within the military establishment believe that the Tornados will be more than sufficient to provide Britain with a nuclear deterrent and that the Trident submarines are not needed for this purpose.

Submarines

Nuclear submarines have been highly effective second-strike weapons for the past two decades. They are nuclear in two senses: they fire nuclear warheads and they are powered by nuclear reactors. They can stay underwater for three months at a time and, except when in shallow water or close to islands, are undetectable (although this situation looks like changing within a decade). Their role is to continue on patrol underwater for long periods – even after a nuclear war in which their home country may have been destroyed. This invulnerability makes them ideal for retaliatory action later on.

The earliest of the nuclear submarines, Polaris, carried more explosive power in their sixteen SLBMs than was used in all bombing throughout the Second World War. The SLBM range of 1,500 miles, fired from under the surface, gave them the ability to destroy all the major cities of the Soviet Union. They were relatively inaccurate (one or two miles perhaps) but this was unimportant as they were intended primarily for retaliation against people (second strike), not for attack against military bases.

If that was all they could do, they would be a perfect second-strike weapon. Unfortunately to some extent they could also be used in a first strike. They could sneak close to military targets, such as harbours, well within their 1,500-mile range, and then score direct hits. It seemed possible that Polaris might take part in a first-strike attack. Although this was denied by America and Britain, the Russians saw Polaris as a first-strike threat and seven or eight years afterwards developed a similar nuclear submarine fleet – which America and Britain then saw as a Russian threat.

Poseidon is an improvement on Polaris, with far more accurate and longer-range SLBMs. It is not clear why these improvements were necessary if Poseidon is intended merely for a second-strike strategy: Soviet cities were vulnerable already. So suspicions were intensified as Poseidon replaced Polaris.

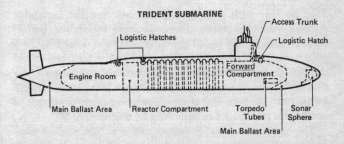

TRIDENT SUBMARINE

Moreover yet another generation of nuclear submarines is being produced. This new American underwater long-range missile system (ULMS), using Trident submarines, has a range of 6,000 miles, an accuracy equivalent to the best of the present generation of ICBMs and will carry ten MIRVed warheads on each of its twenty-four SLBMs. A fleet of more than thirty Trident submarines is envisaged. The additional targets that will be reached by the Trident SLBMs (compared with those that can already be reached by Poseidon) are the Soviet missile sites in Kazakhstan. If the object of nuclear submarines is mere deterrence, there is no reason for adding extra *military* targets to the list. The new submarines may well be part of a planned development of a first-strike capability.

In 1980, the British government announced agreement with the US government to build in Britain four Trident submarines, each to be armed with British warheads. These submarines will have only sixteen missiles (as for Polaris) but it is expected that each missile will carry from six to ten MIRVed nuclear warheads (compared with three MRV missiles for the 1964 version of Polaris). In this respect, the new purchase will more than triple the destructive capability of Britain's sea-based 'deterrent'.

The Trident decision has met strong opposition and it is possible that it will be overturned in favour of a cheaper way of maintaining Britain's nuclear status.

Anti-submarine warfare

Side by side with these developments come the inevitable counter-measures. Early proposals were for 'hunter-killer' nuclear submarines to tail the Polaris-type submarines. At a predetermined moment all the 'hunter-killer' submarines would destroy their Polaris quarries. Fortunately this proved impracticable – *very* fortunately, because the prospect of nuclear submarines chasing and dodging each other throughout the oceans was recognized as hazardous by all concerned.

The more 'promising' developments in anti-submarine warfare (ASW) are similar to those described earlier in relation to the electronic battlefield. The oceans will be sown with electronic devices to detect changes in temperature, noise, vibration and anything else that may indicate the presence of nuclear submarines. These gadgets will be stationed permanently on the ocean bed or will float at pre-set depths, sending back signals for evaluation. The central control station would eventually have sufficient information to keep a continuous record of the movements of all submarines. It would then be relatively simple to destroy all the enemy submarines by explosions underwater. Assuming a maximum of forty enemy nuclear submarines on patrol at any time, no more than forty nuclear warheads would be needed. (During 1979 the maximum number of Soviet submarines normally on patrol did not exceed fifteen.)

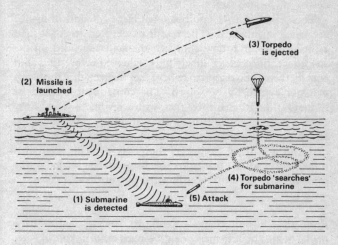

(2) Missile is launched

(3) Torpedo is ejected

(4) Torpedo 'searches' for submarine

(1) Submarine is detected

(5) Attack

The US has a large underwater surveillance centre at Brawdy in south-west Wales. From Brawdy, submarine cables run to a point 200–300 miles west of southern Ireland, picking up signals from an array of hydrophones. This system helps to track the movement of Soviet submarines which might threaten the USA (they would not need to pass this way to threaten Britain or Europe).

This makes Brawdy an absolutely certain target in a war between the USA and the USSR: the Soviet Union would have to destroy Brawdy very quickly to protect her second-strike forces. Although this fact is crucial to Britain's security, the existence of this US facility has not been officially admitted.

(It is recorded, however, in the 1977 Defense Procurement Report of the US House of Representatives.)

At this stage in the arms race, a technological breakthrough in ASW would be far more serious than, for example, further improvements to missile systems. The ability to locate the Soviet nuclear submarine fleet reliably would make a first-strike feasible – the US already has enough accurate missiles to destroy all located targets.

This programme is ambitious, but large amounts of money are being spent on it. The resources devoted to ASW and associated research now approach the sum expended on the space race. Success is unlikely to be achieved before 1985, but equally there is no reason to believe that the technical problems will not eventually be solved. The consequences could be serious. If the Russians feel that, with a few more years work, the USA could obtain a first-strike capability, they may panic and precipitate conflict to pre-empt that eventuality. Alternatively, and more probably, they may escalate their own military expenditure to counter the threat to their second-strike capability. So the arms race shows no sign of slowing down.

Death rays

From time to time claims appear that Soviet scientists have made, or are about to make, new weapons quite unknown here. In practice this has not happened: the USA has been first in every major weapons development since 1945.

These stories have a simple purpose: to scare people into agreeing to more military spending. In 1977, advocates of cruise missiles 'discovered' a new Soviet weapon – a proton beam said to be able to destroy all conventional US ballistic missiles and aircraft but not the low-flying cruise missiles.

Although the USA is itself spending about 200 million dollars each year on research into lasers and particle beam weapons, these are not expected to have wide applications (except perhaps for anti-satellite activities in space). Although the speculations about Soviet death rays do not stand up to scientific examination, this has not stopped widespread publicity for the idea. Even the weapons of science fiction play a part in the arms race.

Tactical Nuclear Weapons (TNW)

Most of this chapter has been concerned with 'strategic nuclear weapons', a misleading term which, in current usage, refers to those weapons which could be delivered by the USA and the USSR directly upon each other.

At the other end of the scale there are 'battlefield' nuclear weapons, which are supposed to be usable only in a 'limited nuclear war'. These 'mini-nukes' are intended for a limited war over battlefields of only a few hundred square miles.

In between there are weapons with yields of 0·01 to 1 megaton

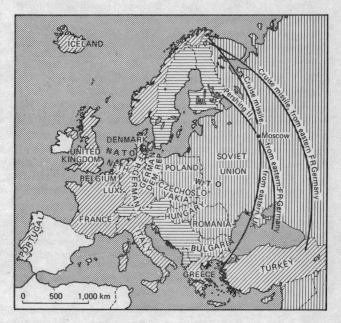

Target coverage of proposed NATO theatre nuclear weapons. From SIPRI Yearbook 1980

delivered by missiles with ranges of over 1,000 miles (tabulated opposite). Depending on how they may be used, they are known as 'tactical', 'theatre' or 'Eurostrategic' weapons.

The term 'tactical', as opposed to 'strategic', is applied when the nuclear war is 'controlled' in its ferocity. The term 'theatre', as opposed to 'global', is applied when the nuclear war is 'confined' to a geographical area.

If these weapons were to be used in a 'limited' war in Europe, the continent would be devastated. Although Europe may be a 'theatre' when viewed from the USA and its devastation a 'tactic' to ward off the destruction of America, the effect on Europe would be equivalent to an all-out war with strategic weapons. It should be appreciated, moreover, that the Soviet Union is part of Europe and feels as threatened by the Eurostrategic weapons as by the US strategic forces.

British nuclear weapons

Britain's present 'contribution to NATO's strategic deterrent' comprises four Polaris submarines equipped with sixteen Polaris SLBMs. In addition, Britain contributes to NATO's TNW forces. These include bombs which can be delivered by RAF strike aircraft and depth bombs delivered by RN helicopters. Nimrod maritime patrol aircraft can deliver US nuclear depth bombs. The British Army of the Rhine has British-owned Lance missiles and artillery which can deliver US nuclear warheads.

In addition to these weapons systems, Britain plays host to over one hundred US military establishments in the UK, most of which contain facilities for US nuclear forces. It has been estimated that Russia will have earmarked for attack more military targets in Britain than anywhere else in the world.

Major Eurostrategic weapons

State	Weapon designation	Year first deployed	Max. range (km)	No. of RVs	Yield	CEP (m)	No. deployed in 1979
Missiles							
USSR	SS-4	1959	2,000	1	1 Mt	2,400	390
	SS-5	1961	3,700	1	1 Mt	1,250	80
	SS-12	1969	~800	1	1 Mt	..	72
	SS-20	1977	~4,000	3	150 kt	400	~120[b]
	SS-N-5	1964[a]	~1,200	1	1–2 Mt	..	18
USA	Pershing IA	1962	~750	1	60–400 kt	450	180[c]
	Pershing IA	1962	~750	1	60–400 kt	450	72[d]
	Pershing II	(1983)	~1,600	1	10–20 kt	45	0*
	GLCM	(1983)	2,500	1	200 kt	90	0†
UK	Polaris A-3	1967	4,600	1	3 × 200 kt	800	64
France	S-2	1971	3,000	1	150 kt	..	18
	M-20	1977	5,000	1	1 Mt	..	64

State	Weapon designation	Year first deployed	Range[e] (km)	Weapon load (t)	Nuclear weapons per aircraft	Speed (Mach)	No. deployed in 1979
Aircraft							
USSR	Tu-16 Badger	1955	6,500	9.1	2	0.8	318
	Tu-22M Backfire	1974	9,000	8.0	4	2.5	50
USA	FB-111A	1969	10,000	17.0	6	2.5	66
	F-111E/F	1967	4,900	12.7	2	2.2/2.5	156
UK	Vulcan B2	1960	6,500	9.6	2	0.95	48
France	Mirage IVA	1964	3,000	7.3	1	2.2	33

[a] On board Golf-2 submarines in the Baltic.
[b] The figure is for launchers. Probably only 80 of these are targeted on Western Europe.
[c] Deployed in Western Europe.
[d] Deployed in FR Germany under joint US-FRG command.
[e] The maximum combat radius, which allows a mission to be fulfilled and the return of the aircraft, is less than half this maximum range.
RV = Re-entry vehicle. .. = Number unknown.
* 108 will be deployed in 1983.
† 464 will be deployed in 1983.

(from *SIPRI Yearbook 1980*)

Soviet and American strategic weapons

The effectiveness of a nuclear warhead depends upon its explosive power and the accuracy of its delivery system. More formally the lethality (k) of a nuclear warhead depends on its strength or 'yield' (y) and the accuracy of delivery (CEP). Accuracy is measured by 'circular error probability' (CEP) – the radius of a circle about the target in which 50 per cent of the bombs may be expected to fall (in nautical miles). So lethality is increased with powerful bombs (i.e. large y) and high accuracy (i.e. small CEP), the exact mathematical formula being:

$$k = y^{\frac{1}{2}}/(CEP)^2.$$

The relative effectiveness of the Soviet and American armoury is therefore measured from the total lethality of all the deliver-

	Missile numbers (*n*)	Warheads per missile	Warhead numbers (*N*)
USA			
Minuteman III	550	3	1,650
Minuteman II	450	1	450
Titan	54	1	54
(Total ICBMs)	(1,054)		(2,154)
Poseidon	496	10	4,960
Polaris A-3	160	1	160
(Total SLBMs)	(656)		(5,120)
Total (all missiles)	1,710		7,274
USSR			
SS-9	288	1	288
SS-11	1,010	1	1,010
SS-13	60	1	60
SS-8	109	1	109
SS-7	100	1	100
(Total ICBMs)	(1,567)		(1,567)
SS-N-6	528	1	528
SS-N-8	180	1	180
(Total SLBMs)	(708)		(708)
Total (all missiles)	2,275		2,275

able nuclear warheads of the two countries – the sum of the products of k times N. The results *for missiles only* are set out below.

In order to have a better than 90 per cent chance of destroying a US missile silo, Soviet warhead lethality (k) would need to exceed 16. By contrast, because Soviet silos are much less protected, US ICBM warheads only need half the k-value to achieve the same result.

Information from Congressman Robert L. Leggatt, *US Armed Forces Journal International*, February 1975.

SIPRI estimates for US and Soviet missile effectiveness are lower because different assumptions are made for accuracy (CEP) and yields (y), but the relative strengths are about the same.

Yield (megatons) (y)	Total megatons (N.y)	Accuracy (CEP)	Warhead lethality (k)	Total lethality (k.N)
0·17	280	0·2	7·7	12,659
1·0	450	0·3	11·1	5,000
5·0	270	0·5	11·7	632
	(1,000)			(18,291)
0·04	198	0·3	1·3	6,446
0·6	96	0·7	1·5	232
	(294)			(6,678)
	1,294			24,969
25·0	7,200	0·7	17·4	5,025
1·0	1,010	1·0	1·0	1,010
1·0	60	0·7	2·0	122
5·0	545	1·5	1·3	142
5·0	500	2·0	0·7	73
	(9,315)			(6,372)
1·0	528	1·5	0·4	235
1·0	180	0·8	1·6	281
	(708)			(516)
	10,023			6,888

The Dynamics of the Arms Race

Robert S. McNamara

The United States must not and will not permit itself ever to get into a position in which another nation, or combination of nations, would possess a first-strike capability against it. Such a position not only would constitute an intolerable threat to our security, but it obviously would remove our ability to deter nuclear aggression.

We are not in that position today, and there is no foreseeable danger of our ever getting into that position ... Our alert forces alone carry more than 2,200 weapons, each averaging more than the explosive equivalent of 1 megaton of TNT. Four hundred of these delivered on the Soviet Union would be sufficient to destroy over one third of her population and one half of her industry. All these flexible and highly reliable forces are equipped with devices that ensure their penetration of Soviet defenses ...

The most frequent question that arises is whether or not the United States possesses nuclear superiority over the Soviet Union. The answer is that we do ... the most meaningful and realistic measurement of nuclear capability is the number of separate warheads that can be delivered accurately on individual high-priority targets with sufficient power to destroy them ...

One point should be made quite clear, however: our current numerical superiority over the Soviet Union in reliable, accurate and effective warheads is both greater than we had originally planned and more than we require ...

How this came about is a significant illustration of the intrinsic dynamics of the nuclear arms race.

In 1961 when I became Secretary of Defense, the Soviet Union had a very small operational arsenal of intercontinental missiles.

However, it did possess the technological and industrial capacity to enlarge that arsenal very substantially over the succeeding several years. We had no evidence that the Soviets did plan, in fact, fully to use that capability. But, as I have pointed out, a strategic planner must be conservative in his calculations; that is, he must prepare for the worst plausible case and not be content to hope and prepare merely for the most probable.

Since we could not be certain of Soviet intentions, since we could not be sure that they would not undertake a massive buildup, we had to insure against such an eventuality by undertaking a major buildup of our own Minuteman and Polaris forces. Thus, in the course of hedging against what was then only a theoretically possible Soviet buildup, we took decisions which have resulted in our current superiority in numbers of warheads and deliverable megatons. But the blunt fact remains that, if we had had more accurate information about planned Soviet strategic forces, we simply would not have needed to build as large a nuclear arsenal as we have today . . .

In recent years the Soviets have substantially increased their offensive forces. We have been watching and evaluating this very carefully, of course; clearly the Soviet buildup is in part a reaction to our own buildup since the beginning of the 1960s. Soviet strategic planners undoubtedly reasoned that, if our buildup were to continue at its accelerated pace, we might conceivably reach in time a credible first-strike capability against the Soviet Union.

(from *The Essence of Security*, 1968)

6. The arms race

I remember President Kennedy once stated ... that the United States had the nuclear missile capacity to wipe out the Soviet Union two times over, while the Soviet Union had enough atomic weapons to wipe out the United States only once ... When journalists asked me to comment ... I said jokingly, 'Yes, I know what Kennedy claims, and he's quite right. But I'm not complaining ... We're satisfied to be able to finish off the United States first time round. Once is quite enough. What good does it do to annihilate a country twice? We're not a bloodthirsty people.'

Nikita Khrushchev

'Minimum deterrence', according to former US Defense Secretary Robert McNamara, needs about 400 thermonuclear warheads. With only moderate accuracy these could destroy about two thirds of Soviet industry and kill about sixty million people (excluding subsequent deaths from fallout, social disruption and starvation). Few countries would risk starting a nuclear war if this were the expected scale of retaliation.

With twice as many thermonuclear warheads (that is, 800) McNamara estimated that the industrial destruction would be around three quarters and the immediate death toll about eighty million. (This relatively small increase is because a lot of Soviet industry and population is widely dispersed in the countryside.) So, assuming that American policy stopped at minimum deterrence, about 400 thermonuclear bombs would be adequate whilst any more than 400 would be hardly worth the extra cost. Similar arguments apply to the Soviet Union.

Yet, by 1972, the Soviet Union and the USA each possessed far more SLBMs, ICBMs, aircraft and other missiles than either needed for minimum deterrence. Indeed, submarine-launched missiles alone provided sufficient warheads for 'minimum deterrence'. In addition both had over 1,000 ICBMs and the USA had several hundred bombers within striking range of the Soviet Union. 'I can go into my office and pick up the telephone and in twenty-five minutes seventy million people will be dead,' declared President Nixon at the height of his Watergate troubles.

Moreover missile numbers *underestimate* the degree of 'overkill' since most ICBMs now carry multi-warheads. At the time of the SALT-1 agreements (May 1972) the number of deliverable nuclear *warheads* held by the USA and the USSR was

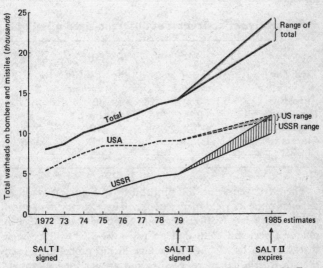

Strategic nuclear warhead inventories, USA and USSR, 1972–85. From SIPRI Yearbook 1980

about 5,700 and 2,100 respectively – both well above the MAD minimum of 400 – that is, the minimum needed for both to inflict unacceptable damage on each other. By January 1979, the US Department of Defense estimated that these numbers had reached 9,200 and 5,000 respectively (excluding the European theatre forces which, always remember, threaten Britain and the USSR but not the USA).

From time to time it is claimed that a nuclear war won't be so bad because the yield (megaton power) of the average nuclear warhead has been reduced over the years. In reality a scatter of small bombs spreads destruction more effectively than a single blockbuster. Moreover smaller nuclear warheads may be guided more accurately to their targets. This explains why the Polaris A3 missile, which originally had a single 1-megaton warhead, was 'improved' to carry ten 50-kiloton MIRV warheads. Although this drops the yield per missile from 1 to 0·5 megatons, the destructive capability is increased for all but very large cities.

Comparative effectiveness of different-sized missiles

	Number of targets destroyed	
Type of target	*One 10-megaton warhead*	*Ten 50-kiloton warheads*
Airfields	1·0	10
Hard-missile silos	1·0	1·2–1·7
Cities of 100,000	1·0	3·5
Cities of 500,000	1·0	0·7
Cities of 2,000,000	0·6	0·5

The effectiveness or 'kill probability' of a nuclear warhead depends upon its yield in megatons and its accuracy in nautical miles. The relative effectiveness of the Soviet and American missile forces are compared on pages 94–5; it will be seen that America has a huge advantage in kill probability, even though Russia has more missiles and greater total megatonnage. On the 1979 figures America had more than twenty and

Russia more than ten times the MAD minimum. The introduction of cruise missiles will increase America's 'strategic superiority' even more – but to what purpose?

In 1979 the USA may have had a 95-per-cent chance of destroying all Soviet missile silos, airfields and submarine bases in a first strike. But, assuming she had done so and had also destroyed the Soviet nuclear submarines in their bases, this still would have left about 400 Soviet SLBMs available for minimum deterrence. So the United States, despite its enormous technological lead, even in 1979 had little immediate prospect of acquiring a first-strike capability and cannot use its power in any effective manner. Henry Kissinger expressed this frustration as 'the great paradox of the nuclear age. Power has never been greater; it has also never been less useful.'

So why continue?

Each additional round of American military spending has been justified on the grounds that the Soviet Union has been catching up with some new weapon or other. In 1977, when *Overkill* was first published, the complaint was that the Soviet Union had tested MIRVed missiles – a stage reached by the United States seven years earlier. Previously the Americans claimed to need MIRVs because of the (unsuccessful) Soviet ABM construction around Moscow in 1961 (though the American MIRV development actually started in 1958). In neither instance was there a real danger that the Soviet Union threatened the nuclear stalemate: none the less American counter-measures were taken and so the stalemate *was* threatened by the acceleration of the nuclear arms race.

By the time of this edition of *Overkill*, scares about Soviet MIRVs have died down and Soviet SS-20s have become the new frightener. The SS-20s are indeed very formidable weapons but their deployment, at least until 1979, has been as a one-for-one replacement of other intermediate-range missiles. By no stretch of the imagination are they a *new* threat to Western Europe comparable with that posed to the USSR by *extra* deployment of cruise missiles.

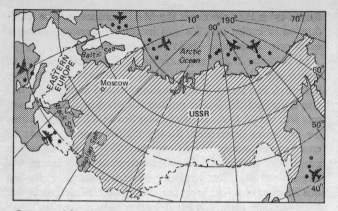

Coverage of Soviet targets by cruise missiles carried in aircraft which stay 300 km outside WTO territory, for a range of 2,500 km. From SIPRI Yearbook 1978

Here is the nub. Every development by one side is interpreted, rightly or wrongly, as a threat by the other. Logically neither side need worry if they have enough to deter a nuclear attack. In this nuclear stalemate, a halt to all so-called improvements would not harm either side. In practice the arms race has a momentum of its own and has never slackened.

Whatever views are held about the politics and intentions of the Soviet Union, and the supposed level of her conventional armed forces, it must be admitted that the United States has led the nuclear arms race. Whether you consider the first nuclear bombs, ICBMs, MIRVs, nuclear submarines, SRAMs or ASW, the United States has been the pacemaker, usually with a lead of several years.

Yet this lead has not been decisive. The United States has never held a first-strike capability. At the same time American forces were too sophisticated and heavily armed for the fighting in Vietnam, which partly explains why small (that is, Hiroshima-strength) 'tactical' nuclear weapons have been developed for 'limited nuclear war'. Some thousands of tactical nuclear weapons have been provided for the conventional forces deployed in Europe. The United States – in collaboration with her allies – has built up an impressive nuclear armoury, many times more powerful than that possessed by the Soviet Union and her allies.

Who is winning?

But is anyone really ahead? If both sides can destroy each other, neither has an advantage in real terms. There are three kinds of nuclear balance.

There is the *destructive balance*, which stopped being meaningful once each side became able to wipe out the other a few times. (This was reached before 1960 when both had obtained more than 400 nuclear bombs.)

Then there is the *second-strike balance* (minimum deterrence or mutually assured destruction). Once each side has reached the MAD stage (that is, the ability to deliver 400 or more nuclear bombs even after being attacked), this balance also stops being meaningful.

Lastly there is the *first-strike balance* in which the USA has a huge lead which, fortunately, still falls short of the ability to achieve a successful first strike. If this ever were achieved, the second-strike capability of the Soviet Union will have been eroded and nuclear war could result.

Unfortunately there are always some people ready to urge that we need more arms to catch up with a mythical Soviet lead, and the publicity given to their views means that most people still think that new nuclear weapons are needed. A typical example, from *The Times* of 10 September 1973, is reproduced overleaf and, although the writer took part in the decision to MIRV Polaris, Poseidon and Minuteman missiles, thus *decreasing* megatonnage, he complains of the fact that Russian missiles have more megatonnage than America's!

America's MIRVed ICBMs of the 1975 vintage were able on average to deliver three times as many warheads as the Russian ICBMs. As Henry Kissinger has succinctly commented: 'You are hit by warheads not missiles.' So the Soviet missile lead is worthless by comparison with the American warhead lead: the greater Soviet megatonnage merely showed that they were in fact ten years *behind* the Americans. In effect the Russians were still, in 1973, developing a massive second-strike capability for retaliation against big cities whilst the Americans were developing a first-strike capability.

The newest Soviet warhead, the SS-9, is 500 times more powerful than the United States' newest warhead, the Poseidon MIRV. If the Soviets choose to run a MIRV race, they could outpower the United States twenty times over. When the US MIRV their 4-megaton Poseidon, they split it into 50-kiloton warheads making a total of half a megaton for the missile. The Soviets could MIRV their 25-megaton SS-9 (of which they have 300) into ten 1-megaton warheads, making a total of 10 megatons per SS-9. To equate these two missiles would be dishonestly to conceal a Soviet advantage of 24,950,000 tons of explosive power.

The obvious riposte to the above would be to say that United States submarines prowl the seas carrying nuclear missiles which can hit any target with zero warning. But the true state of the game happens to be that the new Soviet ballistic missile submarine, which will carry 4,000-mile-range missiles, a much greater range than the best United States submarine-launched missiles, can be stationed in a stand-off posture opposite both United States coasts with atomic warheads targeted at every major city in the country . . .

Soviet nuclear superiority is clearly established by the SALT Agreements which President Nixon signed in Moscow with fanfare and formality in May 1972. These agreements proclaim to all the world that the Soviets are number one in military power and that the United States is now a poor second.

> Walter Walker
> Former Commander-in-Chief,
> Allied Forces Northern Europe
> (from *The Times*, September 1973)

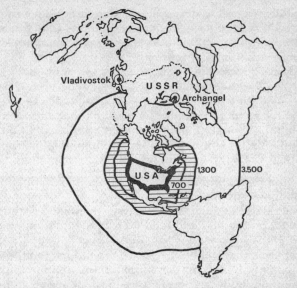

Sea areas from which Soviet SLBMs could hit American targets within 200 miles of the American border. Their older missiles have a range of 700 nautical miles; their current missiles, 1,300 nautical miles; and a proposed missile, 3,500 nautical miles

Geography

A straight comparison of nuclear-submarine numbers is equally misleading. A realistic comparison has to allow for the number on patrol and where they are in relation to their targets. Here the Americans have a big advantage because they are based at Holy Loch in Scotland and at Guam in the Pacific. These bases enable the American submarine fleet to be constantly within firing range of the Soviet Union. By contrast, Soviet submarines have to travel to their patrol area and this takes time. Moreover, in practice the USA succeeds in keeping 20–25 nuclear submarines on patrol at all times, compared with only

12–14 Soviet nuclear submarines, of which only 3–4 normally are in the Atlantic and so threatening the USA. Thus, despite having a bigger fleet, the Soviets have *fewer* submarines on useful patrol than the Americans.

Geopolitics are also important in comparing missiles and aircraft. Whereas America has IRBM silos within range of the Soviet Union and can fly aircraft along Soviet borders, the USSR does not have such well-situated allies. So, quite apart from the advantage of greater accuracy, and their possession of SRAMs, the US superiority is even greater than indicated and appears likely to continue so for the foreseeable future.

Quality versus quantity

General Walker's claim that new Soviet submarines 'will carry 4,000-mile-range missiles' was not confirmed even seven years later when the first 4,000-mile-range American Trident SLBM was commissioned (in 1980). It should be noted, moreover, that in the early 1970s most Soviet submarines were, in reality, merely submersible ships and needed to surface in order to fire their missiles. So the 25:14 advantage the West enjoys with respect to the numbers of nuclear submarines actively on patrol is even more valuable than it appears: the Soviet submarines are far more vulnerable than the Western fleet.

These factors show that missile range on its own does not indicate the relative effectiveness of American and Soviet submarines. The military balance is complex, involving as it does missile numbers, accuracies, megatonnage, base locations and qualitative factors such as reliability and performance. Scare stories of a Soviet lead constantly appear to justify more improvements to Western weaponry but all independent assessments confirm Kennedy's boast of American superiority.

The naval balance

In the last twenty years the Soviet navy has extended its operations and now appears regularly at ports in the Mediterranean, Pacific, Caribbean and Indian Ocean. It is this wider

Naval general purpose forces: active strengths, 1977

	USSR	Other WP	WP total	USA	Other NATO	NATO total
Aircraft carriers				13	3	16
ASW cruisers + 30,000 tons[a][b]	1		1			
ASW cruisers − 30,000 tons					2	2
Cruisers	35		35	25	7	32
Destroyers	112	1	113	91	92	183
Frigates	108	4	112	166	64	230
Corvettes	106	6	112		35	35
Attack submarines diesel[c]	156	6	162	10	129	139
Attack submarines nuclear[c]	80		80	65	9	74
Amphibious warfare vessels + 4,000 tons	14		14	65	29	94
Replenishment, support and transport vessels[d]	85		85	40	98	138
Coastal and ocean-going mine warfare vessels	289	86	375	25	248	273

[a] ASW: anti-submarine warfare.
[b] There would be some dispute as to whether Soviet ships now being launched in this category should properly be called ASW cruisers or aircraft carriers.
[c] Includes submarines armed with cruise missiles.
[d] Excludes small tugs, tenders, etc., and all merchant shipping which might be requisitioned in war.

(from *The Defence of the Realm in the 1980s*, Dan Smith, Croom Helm)

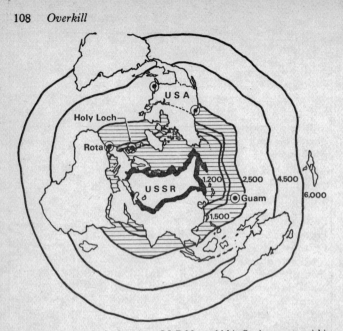

Sea areas from which American SLBMs could hit Soviet targets within 200 miles of the Soviet border. The range of the older Polaris missiles is 1,200 and 1,500 nautical miles; of the newer Polaris and Poseidon missiles, 2,500 nautical miles; and of the proposed Trident, 4,500 and 6,000 nautical miles

deployment, rather than an increase in numbers, that forms the basis for concern in NATO countries. Such expansion challenges Western domination of the seas in the Third World.

The table shows that the active strengths of NATO and the Warsaw Pact in 1977 gave NATO an overall advantage in aircraft carriers, destroyers, frigates and amphibious warfare vessels, whereas the Warsaw Pact was well ahead only in corvettes, mine-warfare vessels and diesel attack submarines. The big advantages often claimed for the Warsaw Pact navies are derived by the simple device of restricting the comparison to selected areas, notably the eastern Atlantic.

Military spending

According to the Stockholm International Peace Research Institute (SIPRI), the Warsaw Pact spends about 30 per cent less on armaments than NATO. Nevertheless, it is widely believed that the Warsaw Pact spends more. Why is this so?

The most common trick has been to measure military spending in comparison with the wealths of the countries concerned (using their Gross National Product, or GNP). The Warsaw Pact countries are not as wealthy as NATO countries and so, *as a proportion of GNP*, they spend more on arms. This GNP comparison is of interest because it shows that Warsaw Pact countries suffer proportionately more from the waste of their resources on armaments and so are less able than NATO countries to keep going in the arms race. However, the comparison is used by NATO propagandists to confuse people into

THE BALANCE OF READY FORCES IN THE EASTERN ATLANTIC

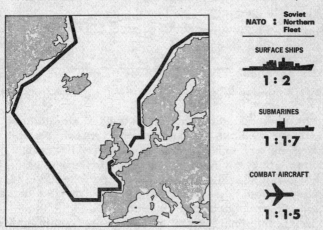

This illustration, reproduced from the 1976 British Defence White Paper, makes the Soviet military forces seem superior by confining the comparisons to limited geographical areas

believing that Warsaw Pact countries spend more *in total* than NATO countries, which is simply not true.

In recent years NATO's accountants have tried a more complicated way of misleading public opinion. They have calculated what it would cost to buy Soviet military weapons and armed forces in US dollars! This makes Soviet military spending seem very high indeed because relatively 'cheap' items (such as the Soviet conscript army) would cost very much more in the US (where army recruits are relatively well paid).

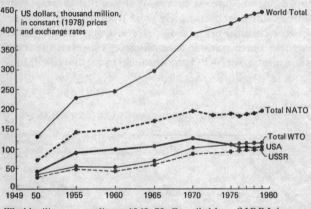

World military expenditure, 1949–79. Compiled from SIPRI data

As it happens, a Soviet accountant could do the same trick in reverse and inflate US military expenditure. This is because prices are very different in the two countries. For example, to buy US cruise missiles in roubles is, firstly, impossible or, secondly, if allowed would cost the Soviet Union far more, relatively speaking, than the actual dollar cost in the USA. This is therefore not a good way to compare costs.

It is best to admit, however, that there is no really satisfactory way to compare military expenditure, especially with exchange rates being so artificial. The SIPRI figures are probably the best available and are sufficiently accurate to show, if proof is needed after comparing military capabilities, that NATO is far from lagging behind the Warsaw Pact in expenditure. Moreover, Soviet military budgeting has to allow for many potential enemies (and unreliable allies) along her borders, so only a proportion of the cost of her forces can be compared with NATO's military spending.

Conventional forces

Nuclear forces are not the only factor in the military balance. The nuclear superiority of the West is said to be matched by the superior conventional forces of the Warsaw Pact (the alliance between Russia and the East European countries). As Europe would be the theatre of operations, the argument with respect to front-line bases is reversed. The bulk of the Warsaw Pact forces are close to their presumed military objectives in Western Europe whereas most American forces are an ocean away. So the Soviet Union and her allies have stronger front-line bases for conventional warfare.

These arguments have validity but omit other aspects. One factor is the antagonism between the Soviet Union and China. A large proportion of the Soviet Union's forces is stationed along the Chinese border and only a small proportion could be used effectively in Europe. Although newspapers often quote figures which show Soviet military superiority, US Pentagon studies in 1962, 1968 and 1973 reached the conclusion that NATO conventional forces have been at least as strong as the Warsaw Pact in Europe throughout this period, even on a strict numerical basis.

According to James Meacham, Defence Correspondent of the *Economist*, writing in the October 1975 issue of *NATO Review*:

NATO today could probably fight the Warsaw Pact to a standstill in a conventional war in Central Europe. Its forces are large enough, although not as large as they should be; its equipment is better, although not as good as it should be for the money that is spent on it; and its disposition is at least adequate, if not ideal ... Although the Warsaw Pact's numerical superiority is clear, it is by no means overwhelming.

THE MILITARY BALANCE ON NATO'S CENTRAL FRONT
(READY FORCES)

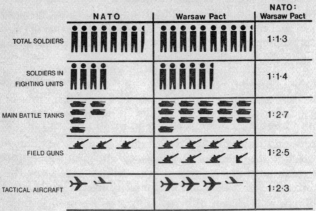

	NATO	Warsaw Pact	NATO : Warsaw Pact
TOTAL SOLDIERS			1 : 1·3
SOLDIERS IN FIGHTING UNITS			1 : 1·4
MAIN BATTLE TANKS			1 : 2·7
FIELD GUNS			1 : 2·5
TACTICAL AIRCRAFT			1 : 2·3

This illustration, reproduced from the 1976 British Defence White Paper, makes the Soviet military forces seem superior by omitting tactical nuclear weapons, anti-tank weapons, etc. (where NATO has an overwhelming lead).

If it should succeed in concentrating a superior force, say 3 or 4 to 1, in a small area, it could very likely achieve breakthrough. But presumably NATO commanders would be doing something to redress the balance. NATO's equipment is, by and large, a lot better than the Warsaw Pact's.

The fact that the Warsaw Pact has almost twice the number of *divisions* as NATO does not in itself mean that they are stronger. Each Warsaw Pact division has only about *half the soldiers* of a NATO division and is less well equipped. NATO divisions are manned overwhelmingly by regular troops and possess at least 6,000 tactical nuclear weapons; by contrast most Warsaw Pact soldiers are conscripts and they have not usually been entrusted with such weapons.

Tanks

NATO superiority in conventional weaponry was confirmed by former Head of Defence Intelligence, General Daniel Graham, when talking about the standard Russian battle tank, the T-62:

> The T-62 is really a T-54 tank (first manufactured in 1948) that has been modified a little here and a little there. It has the same engine in it that the Soviets had in their tanks in World War II. There are some drawbacks to that. It isn't a powerful enough engine. Our tank does outrange their tank. I have been in a T-62 and it has a very cramped turret, and you have to be a left-handed midget because you have to load the darn thing from the wrong side of the breech. And you have to be about my size. If they run out of left-handed midgets in the Soviet Union, they are going to be in big trouble with the T-62.

One interesting aspect of the 'tank gap' is that it has widened because of NATO's policy of tank replacement. Unlike the Warsaw Pact countries, NATO has scrapped its older models and concentrated instead on anti-tank weapons. NATO now has about 200,000 extremely accurate anti-tank guided missiles to repel no more than 25,000 Warsaw Pact tanks (of which 80 per cent are obsolete by NATO criteria). By comparison, NATO has about 12,000 modern tanks with faster rates of fire, more ammunition and greater accuracy on the move than the 5,000 or so 'modern' Soviet tanks.

The explanation of the Warsaw Pact's numerical superiority appears to lie in their use for internal security by Eastern European governments. These governments possess more than half the total and virtually all of these are thirty-year-old models. It is ludicrous to include all such tanks in the East–West military balance.

Morale

The internal politics of countries have another direct bearing on the military balance. Although Warsaw Pact countries probably would remain united in the face of a NATO attack, this seems much less likely if the Soviet Union contemplated an attack across Germany. It doesn't seem credible, therefore, that the Warsaw Pact forces could be used for aggression, whatever their innermost intentions may be.

(These political considerations may not matter so much to a government contemplating a *nuclear* first strike – in theory this could be launched at the press of a button. With regard to conventional weapons, however, both sides seem to be strong enough to counter an attack but neither has the military strength or the political will to try to start hostilities.)

Military balance

The foregoing has not been intended as an apologia for the level of Soviet conventional forces. The purpose has been to show that claims of massive Soviet superiority are quite un-founded and to show that neither side has a clear military advantage in nuclear or conventional forces. Neither side dare risk a conventional war; if they did, this could very easily escalate into a nuclear war which would destroy both. None the less the arms race has been fuelled by claims that the other side had an overwhelming military lead – particularly evident in the case of the United States, where arguments are conducted in public. For example, before 1960 Senator J. F. Kennedy gained much support in his election campaign by blaming the Republicans for allowing the Soviet Union an enormous lead in missiles. After he became President, and after a big increase in US missile expenditure, it was 'discovered' that the 'missile gap' did not exist.

Similarly MIRV was developed because of a mythical threat

of a Soviet ABM and, in 1969, the US Congress sanctioned expenditure on the Trident submarines and the B-1 bomber in response to an alleged Soviet MIRV development. Two years later the photographic evidence for Soviet MIRVs was admitted officially to be worthless. Unfortunately many of the predictions of Soviet intentions are self-fulfilling since the decision to step up US arms expenditure naturally stimulates the Soviet Union to do the same.

The Soviet Union has had valid reasons for believing that America might be ahead and perhaps cannot be blamed for staying in the race. Nonetheless in certain respects they too have undertaken unjustified military developments. For example, the abortive attempt in 1961 to build ABM defences around Moscow provided a useful post-justification for the US MIRV developments. But this is the only instance of a past Soviet initiative that could have been honestly misinterpreted as an attempt to obtain first-strike capability.

A more serious and recent development began in 1976 when the Soviet Union joined the 'MIRV club'. As argued earlier, these are unambiguous first-strike weapons and the American initiative to develop MIRV must be deplored. In this case Soviet military strategists appear to have successfully argued for parity – they want the same opportunity to start a nuclear war. It would have been more acceptable had they decided to make the Soviet nuclear submarine fleet more invulnerable or provided greater missile protection: this would discourage an American-inspired nuclear war for less cost and risk.

Why so many?
There can be only two reasons why a country wants more nuclear weapons than the MAD minimum. Either it is worried that its nuclear forces might be destroyed to below this level if the other side launches a first strike, or it wants more nuclear warheads *in order to make possible its own first strike*.

A US Congress study in 1978 looked into the vulnerability of the USA to a Soviet attack. They concluded that, even without mobile basing of MX missiles, the USA would still have about 4,900 thermonuclear warheads left over for retaliation and, moreover, if they had a bit of warning beforehand, about 7,500 would survive the Soviet attack. These warheads would be able to destroy about 90 per cent of military targets in the USSR, about 80 per cent of industrial targets and all Soviet government centres and kill about 90 million people. Even then the USA would have about 1,000 nuclear warheads left over for contingencies.

It doesn't seem, then, that the USA needs MX and cruise missiles and Trident submarines as an insurance against a Soviet first strike.

By contrast, an American first strike in 1980 against the Soviet Union could have destroyed virtually all ICBM silos, long-range bombers (on the ground) and the in-port nuclear submarines. This would have left the Soviet Union with about 400 nuclear warheads (mainly SLBMs) for retaliation. If the theories of deterrence have validity, the Soviet Union may well feel the need for more nuclear weapons, especially when MX, cruise and Trident are deployed.

The Soviet government must have been even more worried in 1980 by the revelation of the contents of 'Presidential Directive 59'. This says that US nuclear forces now are to be aimed 'primarily at military targets'. *It confirmed that the US government was seriously studying the possibility of starting, waging and winning a nuclear war.*

One of the great ironies of the 1970s was this acceleration of the nuclear arms race in a period of detente between the superpowers. There is a much greater appreciation of the dangers of nuclear war and of the spread of nuclear weapons, but this has not been matched by moves to halt, let alone reverse, the construction of new weapons. All previous arms races in history have ended in war. If the nuclear arms race continues, sooner or later, by accident or design, there will be a nuclear war.

7. How war might start

The danger of outbreak of war by accident ... grows as modern weapons become more complex, command and control difficulties increase, and the premium is on ever-faster reaction.

Dean Rusk
US Secretary of State, 1962

Accident? ...

Many people think that a nuclear war is quite likely to start by accident. Preparations for quick retaliation are so extensive that a mistake could set off a train of events that could end with a nuclear holocaust.

It is not easy to obtain information on nuclear accidents. The US and Soviet authorities only admit to having had accidents when they become public knowledge anyway.

SIPRI estimated in 1977 that there had been 'somewhat over 100 nuclear weapon accidents and incidents over the past 25 years' and provided 'data on some 113 such events'. It seems probable that the true figure is much higher: the USA alone probably has about 30,000 nuclear weapons at home or abroad.

Faulty electronics

NATO has radar and scanning systems to detect missile launches, aircraft flights, submarine movements and any other unusual events which might herald a surprise attack. The Soviet Union probably has something similar. Each of these 'early-warning' systems depends upon complex and sophisticated electronic equipment which constantly scans areas of many thousands of square miles. Just as television sets and computers break down from time to time, so do these. On average each instrument gives a false signal about once every three months.

In 1961 a mistaken interpretation by America's early-warning system led the US strategic air force to fly off to bomb Russia. After two hours flying the aircraft were recalled as, by then, it had been discovered that the original signal was merely a moon echo. If the same mistake happened today, ICBMs could land in Moscow within an hour, long before the recall signal could be sent.

'*How was I to know our formation flying would show up on their early-warning system?*'

On another occasion atmospheric disturbances completely disrupted the NATO early-warning system and it was thought that the Russians might have exploded a nuclear bomb to deliberately black it out. A flight of geese in a formation akin to that of a fighter bomber has been another source of confusion. Any one of these or similar errors could have led to a nuclear war.

In 1980, on two occasions at least, the main US computer system detected a Soviet attack without even the excuse of a faulty input signal. Now that computer systems have become so sophisticated, and apparently dependable, there is a greater risk that human operators will rely on computer outputs rather than their own commonsense.

Early-warning systems use a variety of techniques, and a vast amount of information is collected. Ground-radar systems, similar to those used in the Second World War, detect oncoming aeroplanes and missiles; over-the-horizon (OTH) stations monitor radio signals bounced off the ionosphere to give advance indication of missile launches (the ionosphere is disturbed by rocket exhausts); and satellites keep a constant watch over the world's surface for unusual events of any kind. With so much data available, the process of deciding whether an event is unusual or dangerous has to be assigned to special electronic equipment – people would take too long over this task.

As early-warning systems become more sophisticated and swifter counter-attacks are envisaged, there will be less opportunity for second thoughts if an attack is started in error. In the near future it will be possible to launch a counter-attack by electronic signals rather than human intervention. Early-warning systems could be coupled directly to missile-firing systems, and so missiles launched automatically on receipt of a warning signal. Then, in the event of an error, there would be no possibility of recall.

People are a good safeguard against faulty equipment. At present the early-warning systems are able to *instruct* people to fire missiles, but human beings are still responsible for the ultimate decision. And, to safeguard against a single person taking a rash step, missile-firing systems usually require two or more keys to be turned simultaneously at separate locations.

Another common safeguard at the moment is an '*electronic*

key' which has to be received by radio before a human operator
can launch the missiles. However, if the missiles are being used
in retaliation, radio messages might be drowned by the interference from nuclear explosions. So it is likely that ways have
been devised to get round these remote-control electronic
keys.

Remote-control electronic safeguards have their own dangers. On one occasion an H-bomb plane had its electronic key
activated by a tune from a Spanish 'pop' station and was thus
primed for action. Despite all precautions, there is no certainty
that an accidental missile firing will not occur one day.

Collisions

There have been at least thirteen accidents involving planes
carrying nuclear bombs and, on one occasion, a B52 bomber
crashed over South Carolina with a 10-megaton bomb on board.
The bomb was equipped with five interlocking safety devices
to prevent an accidental explosion but, on recovery, four of the
five safety devices were found to have been triggered by the
fall. Had the bomb exploded, it could have been interpreted
as a surprise Russian attack and America might have 'counter-
attacked'.

Britain's nuclear submarines have been involved in several
minor collisions. One surfaced under a fishing boat in the
middle of the Irish Sea. On another occasion, two of the submarines contrived to hit each other! In 1976 the US House
of Representatives Intelligence Committee learnt that US
nuclear submarines on patrols in Soviet waters had collided
with 'hostile vessels' nine times in the previous sixteen years.
The consequences of a major collision would not be funny. An
accident to any bomb carrier or store could lead to a misunderstanding that might precipitate nuclear war.

Collisions on land may seem unlikely but they do occur.
Bombs are carried by road and rail and run the same risks as
other cargoes. There have been many accidents to bombs even
when stationary in missile silos. In 1980 a workman dropped
a spanner onto a fuel tank in a Titan missile silo, causing an

explosion which threw an 8-megaton bomb a few hundred yards away.

People

There is also a risk that the people in charge of nuclear weapons may make a mistake or go berserk. The type of person who is put in charge of a missile silo or goes to sea in a Polaris submarine is carefully chosen to be cool in emergencies and convinced of the rightness in some circumstances of mass destruction.

In an interview with Jonathan Steele of the *Guardian* (reported on 9 October 1975), one young officer of the US base at Omaha, Nebraska, put it this way: 'We have two tasks. The first is not to let people go off their rockers. That's the negative side. The positive one is to ensure that people act without moral compunction.'

Imagine being cooped up in a submarine for three months on end, never seeing daylight and sleeping next to weapons of mass destruction. Such conditions are not normal and they can create special psychiatric problems. Similarly those who man missile silos go down into the bowels of the earth each day to check missiles whose purpose is to kill thousands of people at the press of a button. These men undergo regular psychiatric checks and often become disturbed mentally.*

To overcome the danger of men going berserk, crews have been supplied with pistols and have been given instructions to shoot anyone who appears likely to fire missiles without proper authorization. This is a rational precaution against the possibility of madness but it cannot help but contribute to the abnormal atmosphere. In addition to everything else that might cause worry, each man knows that his companion has a loaded

---

*A New York psychiatrist, Dr Jonathan Serxner, has investigated the mental state of Polaris submarine crews. Despite lectures, classes, cinema shows and other entertainments, religious services and a library, he found feuds and various minor psychiatric disturbances (about one in twenty of the men needed treatment). There was a chief petty officer who, after five weeks at sea, had delusions of persecution and heard voices. He was given heavy sedation and later transferred from submarine service.

pistol which he has a right and duty to use, should he believe (or say that he believes) his colleague has gone mad.

Nor is it only the people in charge of the missiles and submarines that could cause an inadvertent nuclear explosion. Thousands of tactical nuclear weapons are scattered around Europe under the control of field commanders. Although their working conditions are not as claustrophobic as those of the submarine and missile silo crews, they also can suffer mental disorders. In 1972 a homesick US pilot climbed into a bomber aircraft at a US H-bomb base in East Anglia, flew off and crashed in the English Channel whilst being 'pursued' by other American airforce planes.

One possibility that is often overlooked is that the generals might not wait for authorization to use the weapons under their control. Lord (formerly General) Montgomery wrote in the *Royal United Services Institute Journal*, November 1956:

> . . . if we are attacked, we use nuclear weapons in our defence. That is agreed; the only proviso is that the politicians have to be asked first. That might be a bit awkward, of course, and personally I would use the weapon first and ask afterwards.

Then there are statesmen who go berserk. In 1949, two months after his retirement, former US Secretary of Defense James V. Forrestall committed suicide by jumping from a sixteenth-storey balcony. He had become so convinced of the Communist 'threat' that when a fire engine disturbed his sleep he ran out in his pyjamas screaming that the Russians were coming. The most serious aspect of his mental illness was that many Defense Department officials and journalists accepted his anti-Soviet hallucinations whilst he was still in office.

Confidence-building

The danger of war by accident, miscalculation, insanity or simply human error is sufficiently serious for America and Russia to have agreed on exceptional measures to try to prevent these eventualities. The Hotline Agreement signed in 1963, with supplements in 1971, means that the leaders of the two nations can now quickly confer. These bomb-proof telex lines are supposed to prevent war by misunderstanding. In the event of an accident or an international crisis it enables the leaders of the two superpowers to talk to each other. If it is all a misunderstanding they quickly reassure each other and unintended full-scale war can be avoided.

But the Hotline cannot inspire complete confidence. Suppose the plane that crashed in South Carolina had caused a nuclear explosion. The American President might not know exactly what had happened and might suspect that this had been an attack from the Soviet Union. He would use the Hotline to ask whether this was the case and the Soviet leader would say that his country was not responsible. But the American President would have expected that reply anyway since a country planning a surprise attack would not use the Hotline to say 'yes, but it's a secret'! So, even with the Hotline, suspicions could lead to a superpower chief to presume that an attack was in progress.

Thus the Hotline Agreement is no guarantee against war by accident. There needs to be mutual trust and confidence between the leaders. So constant contacts outside times of crisis are very important. If the leaders know each other personally, they may be less likely to believe that the other is capable of duplicity.

On non-vital matters there is now considerable exchange of information. At the Helsinki conference in 1975 it was agreed that each side would warn the other of all military manoeuvres. Now, when there are to be large troop movements in Eastern Europe, the West knows in advance that this is to happen as a routine manoeuvre and does not fear that it is a prelude to a Soviet attack. In the same way tests of missile firings are announced beforehand to avoid being mistaken for the beginning of a nuclear first strike. These exchanges of information help to build confidence in each other's intentions.

In addition to measures which depend upon the voluntary supply of information, activities can be checked unilaterally. Atmospheric nuclear explosions can be detected by satellites which circle the earth testing for radioactivity. Military stations monitor signals from the ionosphere indicating when missiles have been launched. So the American President, at the time of the South Carolina crash, could have been told immediately that there was no indication of a recent Soviet launch.

The straightforward way to prevent an accidental nuclear war is to abolish all nuclear weapons. But, failing actual disarmament, weapons have been developed which are less likely to lead to accidents. For example, the old liquid-fuelled rockets were more likely to blow up on their launch pads than the modern solid-fuelled rockets. No one wants to see a nuclear accident lead on to the holocaust, and very deliberate measures are taken to avoid this eventuality. Nevertheless, with perhaps forty or fifty thousand nuclear devices in various sites around the world, the possibility of accidental nuclear explosions cannot be ignored.

Escalation? ...

During my six years on the NATO Military Committee I never missed an opportunity of saying, loud and clear, that the actual use of tactical nuclear weapons could only end in escalation to total global nuclear destruction, and for that reason no one in their senses would contemplate their use. (*Lord Louis Mountbatten*)

The borderline between rational and irrational behaviour is never more blurred than when the topic of 'limited nuclear war' is discussed. This idea supposes that countries will fight with 'small' nuclear weapons over 'small battlefields' (that is, drop Hiroshima-strength bombs all over Europe) but will stop short of all-out nuclear war. It has been suggested as a humane alternative to the inflexible massive nuclear retaliation advocated, for example, in the 1958 British Defence White Paper:

It must be well understood that if Russia were to launch a major attack, even with conventional weapons only, the West would have to hit back with strategic weapons.

It is dangerous to believe, however, that *any* nuclear war will not lead to universal destruction, for the first use of nuclear weapons then becomes more acceptable. This theory of 'limited nuclear war' forms the basis for official NATO strategy in the event of a European war and largely owes its adoption to former British Defence Minister, Denis Healey. In the event of our appearing to be losing a conventional European war, NATO will drop 'nukes' (big nuclear bombs) on cities such as Prague and Warsaw and use 'mini-nukes' (small nuclear bombs) on the battlefields. The obliteration of 'less important' targets will convince the Russians that we are serious so – the theory goes – they will stop fighting.

The difficulty is that the Russians may then decide to destroy 'less important' cities like London, Manchester and Glasgow to stop us fighting. What do we do then? In the words of Morton Halperin, formerly US Deputy Assistant Secretary of Defense, 'The NATO doctrine is that we will fight with conventional forces until we are losing, then we will fight with tactical nuclear weapons until we are losing, and then we will blow up the world.'

'Well, I'm sure the Prime Minister and all those Generals must know more about it than we do . . .'

If the horror of nuclear war is not sufficient to prevent hostilities breaking out in the first place, is it likely that statesmen and generals will suddenly become cool and rational during a war? At the start of the 1980 Iraq–Iran war, all the 'experts' predicted a short confrontation in which neither side would attack the other's oil installations for fear of retaliation. How wrong they were! If one accepts Lord Mountbatten's prediction of inevitable escalation, it means that either the NATO strategy is a sham and the so-called tactical nuclear weapons are a gigantic bluff or, alternatively, that the NATO strategy is serious and those in charge are not 'in their senses'. Either way it is clear that conventional hostilities in Europe might easily be a prelude to an all-out nuclear war.

The 'flexible' response strategy is worse in some ways than the 1958 policy of massive retaliation for, by making nuclear war apparently more acceptable, it may bring forward the day on which nuclear weapons are first used. It also allows NATO to 'increase its options and to be able to counter aggression at any level by an appropriate choice of responses, leaving the enemy in doubt as to which response would be selected'.* The 1958 strategy of massive retaliation, by contrast, at least had the virtue that it deterred *all* hostilities. The new strategy justifies the development of all kinds of conventional armaments whilst at the same time doing nothing to remove the risk of an ultimate nuclear conflict.

Moreover one man's limited nuclear war is another man's holocaust. The use of even 10 per cent of the 7,000 tactical nuclear weapons in Europe would destroy the entire region where the nuclear exchanges occurred. Nor is Europe the only possible flash-point for a nuclear war. In October 1973 President Nixon put all US forces, including those based in Britain, on a world-wide nuclear alert, the occasion being another round in the Arab–Israeli conflict. So a nuclear war need not necessarily arise only from a direct Soviet–American misunderstanding: a dispute elsewhere in the world could trigger the sequence of events.

*NATO Handbook, 1975.

Whilst neither of the superpowers has a first-strike capability, no one *in their senses* will risk an all-out nuclear war. Unfortunately this is no guarantee against the possibility of war by accident, misunderstanding or uncontrolled escalation. For true security the world needs nuclear disarmament.

8. Arms control

Eminent authorities declare that both the US and the Soviet Union now possess nuclear stockpiles large enough to exterminate mankind three or four – some say ten – times over. What is the point of limiting arsenals like that? The only practical effect would be to give an air of legitimacy to the continued possession of an armoury of death which, on every ground of morality and common sense, ought to be destroyed.

Philip Noel-Baker, Nobel Peace Prizewinner

With the sole exception of the Biological Weapons Convention, there have been *no* disarmament agreements since 1945, nor are any in sight. The agreements that have been reached merely limit areas in which arms may be used or the numbers of weapons that may be produced. Ironically, they often have the effect of accelerating the arms race in areas not covered by the agreements.

The 1972 SALT-1 agreement shows the weakness of a partial measure. It was agreed to limit the number of missiles in under-

I *Alamogordo: the first atomic explosion, 16 July 1945*

II *General Leslie R. Groves and Dr J. R. Oppenheimer looking over the remains of a tower from which the test bomb was exploded*

III *Hiroshima: the first A-bomb target, 6 August 1945*

IV *Nagasaki: the second A-bomb target, 9 August 1945. Scene near the explosion centre (picture first released December 1975)*

pallito
STOCKINGS

News Chronicle

LATE LONDON EDITION

TUESday FIELD DAY

No. 30,958   TUESDAY, AUGUST 7, 1945   ONE PENNY

On this Bank Holiday the course of world history may have been altered

FORCE OF NATURE HARNESSED:
ATOM BOMB ON JAPAN

Power equal to 20,000 tons of T.N.T.

Next step is to control the force
— Sir John Anderson

ALLIES BEAT GERMANS IN BATTLE OF SCIENCE

From ROBERT WAITHMAN, News Chronicle Correspondent

WASHINGTON, Monday.

IT MAY BE THAT THIS BANK HOLIDAY WEEK-END THE COURSE OF WORLD HISTORY WAS CHANGED. FOR AT 11 A.M. IN THE WHITE HOUSE TODAY PRESIDENT TRUMAN ANNOUNCED THAT BRITISH AND AMERICAN SCIENTISTS, WORKING TOGETHER, HAD "HARNESSED THE BASIC POWER OF THE UNIVERSE," AND THAT A FEW HOURS EARLIER THE FIRST ATOMIC BOMB HAD FALLEN ON A JAPANESE CITY.

This is something far more bigger than any of the stories of war-time scientific discoveries that have yet appeared; its implications, for both good and bad, are still hidden.

President Truman says that "further examination" is necessary of "the possible methods of protecting us and the rest of the world from the danger of sudden destruction." More reassuringly, Secretary of War Stimson says that the means has been found of releasing the atomic energy "and explosively but in regulated amounts."

Equal to 2,000 of Britain's "Grand Slams"

But both Mr. Truman's and Mr. Stimson's statements make it clear that much more has still to be learned about the use of information that has been produced by the greatest scientific gamble in history.

Meanwhile its use in the form of the atomic bomb against the Japanese has been revealed with a great sense of drama. At about 7 p.m. yesterday an American plane flew over Hiroshima, a Japanese army base, and released the first bomb.

It was a bomb equal in power to 20,000 tons of T.N.T., or 2,000 times as powerful as Britain's "Grand Slam"—until now the world's biggest bomb, weighing 22,000—and so powerful that it obliterated an entire island in the English Channel when it was first tried out.

Mr. Stimson said today that after the atomic bomb had exploded on Hiroshima reconnaissance planes were sent to the spot, but they found the target area covered with such an impenetrable cloud of dust and smoke that they had to fly back until the atmosphere cleared sufficiently for photographs to reveal what happened to the army base at Hiroshima, and perhaps to the nearby city and its 350,000 inhabitants.

Even more powerful forms are on the way

The Secretary of War went on to say that with an improved form it would be possible that will increase "by several fold" the effectiveness of the present atomic bomb.

But "possession of this weapon by the United States may in its present form prove a tremendous aid in shortening the war against Japan."

At the moment we cannot know just how details of the bomb or its working. A working fact does not come from the Office of Censorship saying—"In the interest of the highest national security it is requested that editors and broadcasters continue to withhold information without appropriate authority concerning the scientific processes, formulas and mechanism of the operation of the atomic bomb : the location, procurement and consumption of uranium ores ; the quantity and quantity of production of these bombs; their physics, characteristics and future military employment."

Work on the atomic bomb was carried out at two big plants and several here where in the United States, and at a 56,000-acre plant in Canada. A total of 1540 millions has been spent on the work.

first atom bomb vaporised tower

WASHINGTON, Monday.

first experimental atomic bomb explosion in history took place on top of a steel tower in the desert of New Mexico, in thunder, lightning and rain, and scientists and Army experts crouched in timber and earth shelters abrasion.

a burst was 5.30 a.m. on of the air than all agents, New Mexico.

What is meant by atomic energy

By a Scientific Correspondent

ATOMS in the central part of the atom are composed of electrons, protons and neutrons.

A hundred million of tiny solar systems laid side by side on a pin's head would occupy a distance of only a quarter of an inch. Yet if the energy of the atom could be released, it would be practicable for the operation of, for example, a power plant.

The Germans made efforts

Gen. Groves, in a statement here today said: "We knew there were definite and serious chances throughout the entire programme. While we did not know where success would come, we knew it was worth doing, particularly after our intelligence learned that the Germans were making efforts to solve the problem—how otherwise we were unable to do.

"Of the bomb itself about all that can now be said—on the authority of President Truman and Secretary Stimson—is that it is now being manufactured, that the enemy cannot find it at a temperature effective for the destruction;

"IT CAN BE DONE," HE SAID IN 1941

SIR GEORGE THOMSON
In August 1941, his committee told the Government that an atomic bomb could be developed before the end of the war.

TARGET, AND RESULT

HIROSHIMA, on South-West Honshu, port and army production base, is roughly four by three miles.

Many hours after being hit by Atom Bomb No. 1 the whole area was still covered by an impenetrable dust-cloud.

From one point to another the same damage expected to be found or would result from five 1,000-plane R.A.F. raids on Berlin, or an attack by 2,000 Super-Fortresses, or nearly three times the total tonnage dropped on London in the 1940-41 blitz.

British and U.S. scientists pooled skill

THIS revelation of the secrets of nature, long mercifully withheld from man, should arouse the most solemn reflections in the minds and consciences of every human being capable of comprehension.

These solemn words are contained in a statement as the new bomb which had been prepared by Mr. Churchill. The statement was issued by the Prime Minister Mr. Attlee, from 10 Downing Street, last night.

"We must indeed," says Mr. Churchill, "pray that there useful agencies will be made to conduce to peace among the nations, and that, instead of wreaking measures we have leave upon the entire globe, they may become a perennial fountain of world prosperity."

Mr. Attlee's statement said:

Everybody will have seen the important statements which have been made by President Truman and by Mr. Stimson, the United States Secretary for War, about the atomic bomb.

The members of the release of energy by atomic forces have been closed, and the science here been dropped on Japan by the United States Army Air Force.

President Truman and Mr. Stimson have mentioned in their statements the names and the contributions of the men who in this country...

Some account is now required of the part which this country has played in these memorable events. This account has been prepared to be issued to the Press.

Before the change of Government Mr. Churchill had prepared a statement which I am now quoting it in the form in which he wrote it.

Churchill's statement

And here is what Mr. Churchill said in his statement:

By the year 1939 it had become widely recognised among scientists of many nations that the release of energy by atomic disintegration was a possibility.

The possibility which promised to be realised before the British Isles could be brought to a gunfire.

Before the outbreak of war, research into the problem was proceeding in Germany as well as in Great Britain, the United States and France.

Nevertheless, no material either of the quality or in quantity that would be of real value...

Hidden cities housed the workers

EVEN the children of the people who built the atomic bomb did not know what they were doing. They lived in three little secret "atomic cities," the largest of which, under the shadow of the Great Smokies, sprang up in two years to a population of 75,000.

All of them could keep their secret because, even inside the cities, few knew what was going on. Men worked on sections of the whole, and few indeed could put the pieces together and see the whole. The work was split into so many compartments that not even...

Self-contained

A Scientific correspondent of Reuter writes: These hidden cities were self-contained and isolated from the rest of the world. They were complete with shops and places of amusement, libraries and churches.

The men and women who were building the bomb lived in these cities and stayed there—they were "on the inside."

It is extremely doubtful whether they knew what it was they were building. Only a handful of men at the top knew the full story.

Progress in 1941

IN the largest accidental attack on a single objective yet made the R.A.F. hurled 400 of Gen. MacArthur's Far East Air Force bombers and fighters against Tarumizu, an important factory centre on the east shore of Kagoshima Bay on South Kyushu.

Munitions of the Strategic Air Forces struck at Tokyo for an hour in daylight yesterday and a Guam communique disclosed that the Jap industrial town of Tarumizu, on Kyushu, was completely destroyed in Sunday's raid by 500 Super-Fortresses.

Maximum priority

THE bomb communiques thereby to point into the effect of...

LET the BELLS RING but . . .

Let the bells ring for the half is done! But after the bells a task remains. The roof is safe, the fireside smiles, but sons are away

While they still fight shall we forget— with a world to mend and wounds to heal?
The bells that ring to bid us rejoice

News Chronicle 8 & 13

v

VIII *A nuclear shelter being installed in Barnet (1980)*

VI (*top left*) *A test explosion on the island of Bikini*
VII (*bottom*) *Two of the fishermen from the* Lucky Dragon

IX (*left*) *On the Golan Heights. A destroyed Syrian armoured vehicle with a victim of a napalm attack*

X (*bottom left*) *General William C. Westmorland, Commander of US forces, in South Vietnam in 1965*

XI (*right*) *A nuclear-powered submarine during sea trials*

XII (*right*) *A ground-launched cruise missile*

XIII *Palomares: the dangers of nuclear accidents were well illustrated when a B-52 bomber collided with a tanker aircraft during a mid-air refuelling operation over the Spanish village of Palomares on 17 January 1966. Following the collision three 10-megaton H-bombs fell on the land and a fourth into the sea. Those that fell on land were recovered quickly though one had been damaged, causing radioactive contamination nearby. Fifteen U S warships and two submarines searched for many weeks before the fourth bomb was recovered. The photographs show (top left) a typical refuelling operation; (middle) debris from this accident; (bottom left) checks against radioactive contamination of farm livestock; (top right) U S soldiers hosing down soil in case of radioactivity; and (bottom right) on 19 March thousands of barrels of contaminated soil about to be loaded for transportation to South Carolina, U S A, for disposal*

XIV *Soviet missile*

XV *A subsidence crater caused by an underground, intermediate-yield atomic explosion. It left a crater 125 feet deep and 425 feet in width, and a chimney which reached the surface and caused this visible depression*

XVI *An aerial photograph of central London. Many important features could be picked out with careful study*

XVII *US President Eisenhower with British Prime Minister Macmillan (1*

XVIII *CND President Bertrand Russell and Chairman Canon L. John Collins (1959)*

XIX *Aldermaston march (1960): foreground – Jacquetta Hawkes,*
Canon Collins and Ritchie Calder; behind – Michael Foot and John Horner

XX *Committee of 100 sit-down (1961)*

XXI (*top left*) *Easter 1969: Mme Thi Binh speaks for Vietnam NLF at Trafalgar Square*

XXII (*bottom left*) *Easter 1970: trade union banners lead march from Crawley*

XXIII (*right*) *Mgr Bruce Kent attempting to exorcize the evil at the Faslane Polaris base (1973)*

XXIV (*below*) *One of many demonstrations in 1980 against the proposed stationing of cruise missiles*

XXV, XXVI *26 October 1980: march and rally*

ground silos and nuclear submarines but not to halt 'qualitative improvements' to the missiles. But, before the 1972 agreement, America was MIRVing these missiles (having concluded that this was a cheaper and more effective way of adding to her nuclear armoury). She did not intend (or have the immediate ability) to build new missiles anyway. Secretary of State Henry Kissinger, in his briefing to the US Congress, explained:

For various reasons during the 1960s the United States had, as you know, made the strategic decision to terminate its building programs in major offensive systems and to rely instead on qualitative improvements.

By 1969, therefore, we had no active or planned programs for deploying additional ICBMs, submarine-launched ballistic missiles or bombers. The Soviet Union, on the other hand, had dynamic and accelerated deployment programs in both land-based and sea-based missiles.

The purpose of an arms control agreement, therefore, may well be to secure a temporary military advantage under the guise of halting the nuclear arms race. In this sense arms control does not necessarily indicate a step towards disarmament. President Nixon made this clear at his Press Conference on the SALT-1 agreement:

... the offensive limitation is one that is particularly in our interest because it covers arms where the Soviet Union has ongoing programs, which will be limited in this five-year period, and in which we have no ongoing programs.

A further problem with arms control treaties is that they often accelerate the arms race during the negotiating period: more arms are made beforehand as 'bargaining chips'. At the same press conference President Nixon justified the previous expenditure on ABM:

I can say to the members of the Press here that had we not had an ABM program in being there would be no SALT agreement today because there would be no incentive for the Soviet Union to stop us from doing something that we were doing; and, thereby, agree to stop something they were doing.

Accordingly, there are usually two results of partial arms control measures: frenzied competition in the shortly-to-be-controlled weapons just before the agreement; and even more frenzied competition in the uncontrolled weapons afterwards.

Historically arms control measures have never halted an arms race. This is because, by their very nature, they are 'deals' between competitors to resolve temporary problems: they do not tackle the root causes of the conflict. In the case of the PTBT it was agreed to halt radioactive pollution of the atmosphere – not the nuclear arms race. In the case of the SALT-1 agreements military and economic needs coincided with limitations on the numbers of ICBMs and SLBMs.

Moreover arms control agreements can help countries secure an advantage over their potential rivals. When the PTBT was signed by the USA, USSR and UK, these countries had already conducted a large number of nuclear tests in the atmosphere. By contrast France and China were not as advanced

The frequency of nuclear tests between 1951 and 1973. Note the extra large number just before the Partial Test Ban Treaty (PTBT) was agreed in 1963

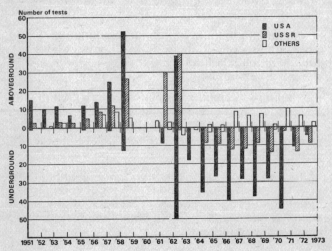

and were not ready or able to carry out all their tests below ground. The PTBT seemed to France and China to be a device to keep the three leading nuclear powers permanently ahead.

So France and China refused to sign the PTBT and have suffered world-wide unpopularity by conducting atmospheric nuclear tests, whereas the leading nuclear powers received little protest when they continued their nuclear tests underground, at a far higher rate than France and China, and with the American testing rate 40 per cent *above* the pre-PTBT level. (Ironically, there have been more nuclear test explosions since 1963 than in the years that preceded the PTBT 'limitations' on testing.)

The same issues are involved in the 1974 USA/USSR 'threshold limitation' of nuclear tests to a ceiling of 150 kilotons.

An M.P. called Frank in Tahiti
Said he felt that he just wasn't free:
"If the French want to test,
Then surely it's best
If they blow up their bombs in Paree?"

Mayor Francis Sanford, French Polynesia's Representative to the French National Assembly, was reported in the Fiji Times (November 1972) as saying: 'They tell us the tests are clean. If it is true, why don't they let off the explosions in France?' The same paper had earlier (September 1971) reported the French Ambassador to Fiji, Count Christian de Nicolay, as claiming that the risk was lessened by having the tests in the Pacific: 'Below you in France you have 50 million people; here there is nothing.'

The leading nuclear powers have conducted many tests above 150 kilotons and no longer need big tests. All foreseeable developments are in miniaturization. France, China and India are hardly likely to accede to such a threshold agreement before they too have reached this stage.

International arms control treaties

1925	Geneva Protocol	Poisonous gases and chemical and biological weapons banned. Signed by eighty-four countries – but *not* USA.
1959	Antarctic Treaty	All military activities (including manoeuvres, testing, etc.) prohibited in Antarctica. Ratified by twenty countries.
1963	Hotline Agreement	Establishment of a direct communications link between the national command centres of the USA and USSR. (Two supplements added in 1971 and a separate UK/USSR agreement made in 1977.)
1963	Partial Test Ban Treaty (PTBT)	All nuclear tests prohibited except those conducted underground. Signed by USA, USSR and UK and over 100 other countries – but *not* France and China.
1967	Outer Space Treaty	Outer space, including the moon, not to be 'appropriated' by any country; and no nuclear weapons to be put on the moon or in orbit around the earth.
1967 and 1968	Treaty for the Prohibition of Nuclear Weapons in Latin America (Treaty of Tlatelolco)	Part 1: Latin American countries agree to being a nuclear-free zone. *Not* ratified by Argentina. Part 2: Nuclear powers recognize and agree to be bound by the Treaty.

If all nuclear tests had been banned in 1963, this would have meant that the three leading nuclear powers were *genuinely* foregoing the development of improved nuclear arms. There is a distinct possibility that the Comprehensive Test Ban Treaty (CTBT), if it is eventually agreed, will be too late to halt all

1968	Non-Proliferation Treaty (NPT)	Nations without nuclear weapons to take no steps to procure them; and nations with nuclear weapons not to help any non-nuclear nation to obtain them. Signed by USA, USSR, UK and over 100 other countries – but *not* France, China, Cuba, Israel, India, Pakistan, Brazil, Argentina or South Africa.
1971	Sea-bed Arms Control Treaty	The placing of weapons of mass destruction on the sea-bed prohibited. *Not* signed by France or China.
1972	Biological Warfare Convention	All biological weapons that exist to be destroyed; and no more such weapons to be manufactured. *Not* signed by France or China.
1972	Strategic Arms Limitation Talks. Interim Agreement (SALT-1)	Specific limitations on the numbers of ABMs, intercontinental land-based missiles and missiles launched from US and Soviet submarines.
1974	Threshold Agreement	USA and USSR agree not to test nuclear weapons with a yield of more than 150 kilotons (supposed to come into force in 1976).
1978	ENMOD Convention	Prohibits military or other hostile use of environmental modification techniques.
1979	SALT-2	Limits numbers of strategic delivery vehicles of USA and USSR (not ratified by USA in 1980).

possible developments of all possible nuclear bombs for the USA and USSR. In that event it is likely that the other nuclear powers will again refuse to participate, on the grounds that the CTBT will discriminate in favour of the leading nuclear powers.

The failing of the treaties so far mentioned is that they are not all-embracing. The same applies to the 'geographic treaties' (Latin America, Antarctica, Outer Space and the Sea-bed). These are almost irrelevant. Nobel Peace Prizewinner, Philip Noel-Baker, commented that 'while disarming Antarctica, we put 7,000 nuclear weapons in Europe; we should have disarmed Europe and put those weapons in Antarctica.'

Admirable as it is to have any region nuclear-free, the effect of these limitations has been to divert public attention from the intensified competition elsewhere. Disarmament will not be accomplished through more and more arms control measures of this nature, useful as they may appear.

Paradoxically, comprehensive disarmament may be easier to implement than arms control, for it involves the total destruction of familiar weapons rather than partial limitations over unfamiliar objects. Moreover suspicions that continue with arms control are allayed as complete disarmament proceeds. All sides to a disarmament agreement will take good care to verify that the others honour the treaty: with arms control the incentive is to break the treaty on the assumption that other countries are doing the same.

Verification

Even though the SALT-1 agreements and the Biological Weapons Convention were agreed without special provisions for verification, it is often claimed that other treaties are impracticable because of the risk of cheating.

The popular form of the argument claims that arms control and disarmament are impracticable because the Soviet Union will not accept inspection in her territory. The Soviet Union is indeed extraordinarily sensitive on this matter, especially when you consider that most of her 'secrets' are known to the

West through the use of satellite and other spy techniques. However, on-site inspection has not been considered necessary for *any* of the arms control agreements so far mentioned and there is reason to believe that this issue will not be relevant for any future possible treaties either.

Take the problem of detecting underground nuclear tests. The PTBT banned atmospheric nuclear tests only, because underground nuclear explosions were said to be undetectable. Have a look at the photograph (Plate XV) of the effect of an underground nuclear test. It would have been easily seen from a satellite. Moreover, before the actual explosion, earth-moving and other activity would have been noticeable as preparations went ahead. If the explosion had been conducted farther underground, to avoid the cave-in and collapse, then, correspond-

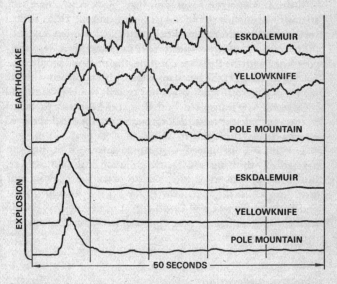

Seismic records of underground nuclear explosions are readily distinguished from earthquakes by their shorter duration. The three upper traces were produced by a Libyan earthquake, the bottom three by a French nuclear test in Algeria

ingly, a truly massive excavation would need to have taken place beforehand. So clandestine underground nuclear tests *can* be seen by satellite observation.

Nor is that all. Underground nuclear tests can be detected by the same seismic observation stations that are used to monitor earthquakes. In 1963 negotiations for a comprehensive test ban treaty ended with America and Britain insisting on seven annual on-site inspections to check against Russia cheating whilst the Russians would only agree to three. The Russian view that seismic detection was sufficiently sensitive to detect underground explosions above 10 kilotons without on-site inspection is now generally agreed. If a threshold agreement at, say, 20 kilotons had been signed in 1963, the world would have been spared much of the succeeding arms race.

There was also the suggestion that 'black box' monitoring stations be installed in the Soviet Union and the USA so that seismographic records could be investigated without any need for permanent on-site inspectors. If the Americans were truly concerned with the Russians cheating, this proposal should have been acceptable. If the Russians were truly concerned with the danger of American spies, black box records would have allayed these fears. As it transpired, both Russia and America preferred to continue nuclear tests underground once they had achieved all they needed through atmospheric nuclear tests.

The PTBT is indeed a great advance, for it has cut dramatically the major radioactive pollution of the atmosphere. But it has not halted or even slowed down the nuclear arms race. And whilst the signatories to the PTBT continue to test underground, France and China repeat what America, Britain and Russia were doing at the equivalent stage in their nuclear developments.

Satellite observation

So the main stumbling block in the way of disarmament is simply a lack of willingness to disarm. Nevertheless, for public consumption, it is still claimed that the technical difficulties of verification are more significant. It is worth-while examining this issue in more detail.

Although military expenditure is mostly for weapons and fighting forces, much is devoted to spying. Aerial photography has proved most useful and the major military powers now have very accurate knowledge of the disposition of each other's forces and weapons, missile accuracy and numbers and many other matters of considerable military importance. These spying techniques could equally well be used to verify disarmament measures.

Spy photography is not confined to the visible-light spectrum and hence to the hours of sunlight. It is possible to use the infra-red band and also certain radar wavelengths. Whereas the visible-light wavelengths can only be used during daytime hours, infra-red photography allows observation at night and, to some extent, penetration of camouflage. Radar wavelengths have not proved as useful as visible-light and infra-red photography.

The accuracy of spy photography can be gauged from the photographs brought back from the moon. On the Apollo missions a typical camera had a focal length of two feet and, from an altitude of approximately sixty miles above the lunar surface, obtained three-foot ground resolutions (that is, it picked up objects as small as about three feet). Cameras for satellite photography have a focal length of more than eight feet and so, from an altitude of say 100 miles, the ground resolution would be just over a foot. The clarity of the pictures from photoreconnaissance satellites is now limited more by atmospheric effects than anything else.

Artificial satellites are better than aircraft for photographic reconnaissance because they have no engines and so do not vibrate. This means that the clarity of photographs from artificial satellites can be as good as from aircraft, despite the greater height from which they are taken. They are also preferable because, apart from the technical advantages, aircraft are vulnerable to anti-aircraft fire from below – as US pilot Gary Powers found out in 1960 when his U-2 flight was abruptly terminated.

In general it is easier to find an object on a photograph than to decide what it is. All the same an extended object such as a railway can be distinguished even when its width is less than the minimum ground resolution: it is even possible to pick out telegraph wires. In practice, analysis is limited primarily by the huge amount of data collected.

If all the Soviet Union were constantly photographed in minute detail, every existing US computer would be involved on this task alone. To overcome this difficulty, *two* sets of photographs are taken: the first to identify interesting targets (*surveillance*) and the second to rephotograph the more interesting areas in greater detail (*close-look*).

Early surveillance satellites stayed aloft for three to four weeks and carried a wide-angled, low-resolution camera. When near to an appropriate ground station, the exposed film (already developed aboard the space craft) was scanned by on-board electronic devices and the resulting signals were transmitted to earth by radio. This provided the information needed for a subsequent close-look expedition. As high resolution (that is, detailed accuracy) was not needed for surveillance, the photographs were rarely recovered.

The earliest US reconnaissance satellite (SAMOS) was first used in 1960, shortly after Gary Powers's flight over the USSR. SAMOS was placed in a polar orbit varying in altitude from 300 to 350 miles. Later satellites had an orbital life of three to four weeks with a perigee (lowest orbital point) about 100 miles above the earth's surface. Since 1966 these have provided constant and virtually full coverage of the USSR and complete coverage of China.

Close-look cameras have a very high resolution and a relatively narrow field of view. Early close-look satellites were larger than those used for surveillance and remained in near-polar orbit for about five days before film recovery – which was usually accomplished by the ejection of a capsule containing the film and its collection from the sea. (More often nowadays the capsule is recovered in mid-air. When the capsule falls to about ten miles from earth, a parachute opens and is caught by a trapeze-like cable attached to a transport aircraft.)

The Discovery recoverable-capsule satellites are heavier than surveillance satellites and have a lower orbit (perigree typically eighty miles) to take detailed (close-look) photographs. From about 1971 onwards a new generation of observation satellites was introduced, known unofficially as the Big Bird. It is launched by the powerful Titan 3D booster rocket, weighs about 10 tons and combines area surveillance with close-look, the latter taking place on the orbit immediately after the surveillance orbit over the same spot.

A Soviet espionage programme similar to that of the US appears to be taking place with their Cosmos satellite launches. This programme incorporates a long and consistent series of eight-day and thirteen-day flights, presumably for reconnaissance. They probably look at the same things as the Americans but they use different techniques. For example, there are no Soviet satellites in high orbits as are used as part of the US Vela nuclear detection system (to record fallout radioactivity and explosion X-rays). Nor does the Cosmos programme include satellites with orbits that might be expected to provide early warning of a nuclear attack.

The 'amateur' analysis of Cosmos satellite launches carried out by the Kettering Grammar School (Northants) tracking group suggests that there may be several different types of flight within the eight-day and thirteen-day groups. The thirteen-day satellites sometimes make small manoeuvres, about half are recoverable and, for more than a decade, at least one such satellite has been in orbit for two thirds of the time. Although details of the Soviet programme are still a matter of conjecture, there can be little doubt that this scrutiny of the USA and her NATO allies is as thorough as the American and NATO scrutiny of the Soviet Union.

Certainly since 1962, and probably earlier, the United States has had detailed information on the number and location of Soviet strategic missiles. In 1967 President Johnson claimed that satellite reconnaissance was worth 'ten times' as much as the US space programme because 'I know how many missiles the enemy has'. Intelligence analysts are continuously watching silo construction and transport to and from launch sites and, although photography does not penetrate buildings, infra-red and multi-spectral techniques also indicate what goes on inside – particularly when new activities involve changes in standard operating procedures. Multi-spectral analysis is achieved by taking photographs of the same area through different colour filters, thus obtaining highly accurate prints of the colour spectrum of the objects photographed – rather like a three-dimensional view from above.

It has proved impossible to hide large objects by camouflage. If the surrounding ground has temperatures or emission characteristics which differ from the nearby terrain, this will show on an infra-red picture. Moreover the installation of camouflaged objects takes time and can be observed by satellites. Few, if any, items of major military significance are small: missile sites and similar military installations cannot escape detection. In the same way the development and testing of new weapons involves activities which can be observed by spy satellites – which is why we can compare strategic nuclear forces (as in Chapter 6).

The photographs help to identify missile systems, to detect changes in operating procedures and to monitor testing programmes. The satellites are used to watch industrial facilities, including shipyards, for the construction of submarines and plants and for the assembly of missiles. Virtually all the problems of verification of arms control and disarmament agreements have therefore been *solved* by technical advances in satellite photography and analysis.

Other types of observation

Even the *performance* of military equipment can be deduced. Since as early as 1955 U S radar in Samson, Turkey, has tracked missile tests from the Soviet launch site at Kasutin Yar, north-west of the Caspian Sea. Several fixed land-based radars are also available: they watch where Soviet re-entry vehicles fall. From their trajectory it is possible to decide if the missiles have

one or more warheads and whether these are guided to targets
(MIRVs) or are simply fragments scattering on burn up.

Over-the-horizon (OTH) radar is used to monitor missile
tests. Stations at Okinawa (an island south of Japan), Cyprus
and Orford Ness (now abandoned) can detect disturbances in
the ionosphere caused by the gas exhaust of a rocket. Since
each type of missile disturbs the ionosphere somewhat differently, it can be identified by its characteristic OTH signa-
ture. All Soviet long-range missiles can be discovered this way.

Apart from photography, other verification techniques are
available. Electronic eavesdropping is one of the most useful,
since conversations over radio and telephone links are easily
'tapped'. Indoor conversations can be bugged. Electronic eavesdropping satellites can listen in to short-range radio trans-
missions. As no government can arrange all its business
outdoors, it follows that the *intentions* of the military are often
known even before construction of new weapons begins.

All these observational techniques were developed for military reasons and were originally intended to provide early
warning of new military developments or even of an attack.
But they also provide the means by which arms control and
disarmament agreements can be monitored.

SALT-2

This chapter opened with an exposé of SALT-1 and concludes
with a condemnation of SALT-2. The new treaty, like its
predecessor, claims to limit strategic weapons and to lay the
basis for disarmament. In reality, it allows each of the superpowers to add another 4,000 nuclear warheads to their arm-
ouries by 1985 – at which time it is estimated the USA and
the USSR will have 14,000 and 9,000 respectively – excluding,
as always, the Eurostrategic weapons, which remain totally
uncontrolled.

By comparison with SALT-1, the number of 'acceptable
strategic delivery vehicles' has been raised by 50 per cent,
because cruise missiles were not mentioned previously. This

shows how SALT-1 only limited the known missiles, not the ones that were on their way.

The SALT negotiators thought about this problem and discussed whether to prevent new weapons being developed. In the end they decided on an amazing clause which allows each side to deploy no more than one completely new ICBM system in the lifetime of the treaty, which is five years. As the normal development period of the weapons system exceeds ten years, this clause effectively sanctions all future ICBM improvements.

While any agreement may be better than none (and the vehement opposition in the USA suggests that the treaty could restrict the arms race to some extent), no one should be duped into believing that SALT negotiations are leading to disarmament.

SALT-2
Limits on strategic delivery vehicles

2,250 total for all ICBMs, SLBMs and heavy bombers

with **1,320** maximum for MIRVed ICBMs and SLBMs and heavy bombers with LRCMs

with **1,200** maximum for MIRVed ICBMs and SLBMs

with **820** maximum for MIRVed ICBMs

9. Disarmament

Over the years they have worked their way over the whole canvas of the subject and could now well produce watertight treaties at the drop of a hat, if only the political decisions were taken.

The Times
on the 508th meeting of the
UN Disarmament Committee

Satellite observation and other unilateral inspection methods have proved more than adequate for arms control treaties such as SALT-1. The same techniques have even greater potential for disarmament since, whilst it might be possible for a country to disguise the type of weapons it holds, it would be extremely difficult to disguise the fact that it holds weapons of some sort.

For example, an agreement to limit MIRVed missiles but not all missiles might be difficult to monitor without on-site inspection and suspicions would continue. Similarly, an agreement not to allow cruise missiles to carry nuclear warheads would be easier to circumvent than a treaty to ban all cruise missiles, whatever they carried. Better still, an agreement to disarm by destroying *all* missiles could be checked by satellite photography and there would be little opportunity for cheating.

But cheating, or the fear of cheating, is not the only obstacle to disarmament. Whilst arms were being destroyed, it might be feared that one side had a *temporary* military lead and would be tempted to exploit this advantage. For example, if one side originally had more missiles than the other, then the destruction of missiles would be of greater help to the side previously having fewer missiles. So the process of disarmament has to maintain *relative* military strengths as it proceeds. Otherwise, if a political dispute arose during this period, war, or at least rearmament, could be started once more.

Although General and Complete Disarmament (GCD) would leave all sides equal – with nothing – the road to GCD is complicated by this need to maintain at least a rough balance for all parties. This is why the plans for GCD almost agreed by America and Russia in the early 1960s all envisaged a short period (five to ten years) to dismantle the entire war machines of the superpowers.

One proposal put forward from the Pugwash Movement appears to overcome most difficulties. It would be for each country *itself* to divide its territory into areas which are to be completely disarmed. Then it would be for the other side to decide the *order* in which the areas disarm. (This would be rather like sharing an orange between two squabbling children: one child divides the orange and the other chooses. This procedure makes sure that the divider takes good care that the orange is exactly equally divided.)

Each country would divide its own territory into, say, twenty geographical areas which it considers of equal military significance. The other side then would choose which one of these twenty areas should be completely disarmed. If this processs took about six months, at the end of that period all parties would have reduced their armaments by 5 per cent and thus would be in the same relative position with respect to each other. Then, by choosing the second areas for disarmament, in the following six months a further 5 per cent of the armaments would be eliminated and again all would remain at the same relative strength. This technique could make General and Complete Disarmament a manageable process and gradually extend the areas over the world in which there would be total disarmament.

Although this proposal has not been adopted (or discussed), arms control by systematically extending nuclear-free zones is a realistic prospect. At one time the British and American governments were in favour of first Central Europe, and later the rest of Europe, becoming nuclear-free. For over twenty years, however, the Soviet Union and her East European allies have remained formally committed to a nuclear-free Europe. Rather than test these claims by detailed negotiations, NATO spokesmen merely assert that the Warsaw Pact countries are insincere. Although the Warsaw Pact conditions for a nuclear-free Europe might prove severe, there would be little diplomatic risk in entering into negotiations on this topic.

In other parts of the world there are nuclear-free zones already: in Latin America and Antarctica, with good prospects for Africa and parts of Asia. This may help disarmament, since negotiations between the superpowers would be simplified if all other powers were non-nuclear.

The Comprehensive Test Ban Treaty (CTBT)
In 1973 Kurt Waldheim, Secretary General of the United Nations, pressed for an agreement to ban all nuclear weapons tests as 'the most important single measure to halt the nuclear arms race'. But although the USA and USSR then seemed to be moving towards agreement on a CTBT, progress was sufficiently slow to allow military planners to continue with all the nuclear tests they 'needed'. So France and China, and the 'near-nuclear' countries, are able to claim that the superpowers intend to keep their lead and are making no concessions to the rest of the world. It now seems unlikely that a CTBT (if it is ever agreed) would make much difference to the USA/USSR arms race or that it would influence others.

The problem has not been technical for, as described earlier, nuclear explosions can be detected whether above or below ground. The objections have come from the military and political pressure groups, not the scientists. Soviet scientists, however, have come up with one complication. They argue that 'peaceful nuclear explosions' (PNEs) should be excluded from a CTBT on the grounds that nuclear explosions might be useful for earth-moving, oil recovery, etc. Since there is no certain way of distinguishing between a peaceful and a warlike explosion, this would make the treaty meaningless – another example of the maxim that 'the only reliable ban is a complete ban'!

The Non-Proliferation Treaty (NPT)

This treaty is probably the most serious attempt so far made to halt the nuclear arms race and it had been ratified by 111 countries by 1980. In effect it is a 'deal' between nuclear and non-nuclear powers in which *non-nuclear powers* agree 'not to receive . . . manufacture or otherwise acquire nuclear weapons or other nuclear explosive devices . . .' (Article II) provided that *the nuclear powers* 'pursue negotiations in good faith on effective measures relating to cessation of the nuclear arms race at an early date and to nuclear disarmament and on a treaty on general and complete disarmament, under strict and effective international control' (Article VI).

As with so many other partial measures, the NPT was signed for a variety of reasons and so is built on fragile foundations. The nuclear powers appreciate the danger of nuclear proliferation but they are not as concerned about their own nuclear weapons. The non-nuclear powers fear a world-wide nuclear war and see the commitment to nuclear disarmament in Article VI as a major feature of the treaty.

Countries such as India, South Africa, Israel and Brazil did not sign the NPT on the grounds that it contained no guarantee of nuclear disarmament and so seemed more like a device to prevent near-nuclear countries like themselves from acquiring nuclear status. Another weakness of the treaty is that it does not stop the transfer of nuclear-power technology to non-nuclear countries. But such a transfer enables a non-nuclear country to make plutonium, and thus to construct an atomic bomb. In exactly this way India (a non-signatory) developed her first nuclear explosive device by using plutonium manufactured in a nuclear-power plant supplied to her by Canada (a signatory of the NPT).

Whether or not the NPT succeeds depends above all else upon the progress made by the nuclear powers towards nuclear disarmament. If good progress is made, the non-nuclear countries will not have the same urge to join the nuclear arms race. The Strategic Arms Limitation Talks (SALT) have been presented as the response of the nuclear powers to this commitment under Article VI of the NPT. The patience of the non-nuclear powers wore thin at the second review conference for this treaty, held in 1980. It was not possible to agree on a statement which explained the failure of the SALT negotiations, and many non-nuclear countries now feel free to reconsider their attitude to acquiring nuclear weapons.

If the SALT negotiations lead to nuclear disarmament, there will be good prospects that no more countries will 'go nuclear'. Unfortunately, at the time of writing, the so-called spirit of détente has not even curbed the nuclear arms race. As shown in Chapter 6, the limitations on missile numbers following SALT-1 have prevented neither increased numbers of nuclear warheads nor improvements in accuracy to make the warheads much more lethal. Moreover, the SALT-2 agreement remains unratified by the USA and new weapons systems have been devised to circumvent even the meagre limitations of the 1972 SALT-1 agreement.

The Long-Range Cruise Missile (LRCM)

Chief amongst these is a Long-Range Cruise Missile (LRCM) which can be launched from a variety of vehicles (submarines, ships and even a passenger-carrying 747 jet). As this modern-day 'buzz-bomb' is not a free-fall ballistic missile, the US government argued that it was not covered by the SALT-1 limitations.

The LRCM has great accuracy (CEP = approximately 100 feet) which gives it a very high lethality at a relatively low cost.

At 1975 prices the 'cost per unit kill probability' of the Minuteman III ICBM was around $700,000. By comparison the LRCM unit lethality will cost no more than $3,000.

Another serious aspect of LRCMs is that, unlike all the ICBMs, SLBMs and the other strategic-weapons delivery systems described earlier, they have some immunity from satellite inspection. The high accuracy of the LRCMs depends upon the light, miniature and relatively inexpensive electronic devices which are mounted on a missile that is typically under one yard in diameter and less than six yards long. These missiles can be loaded with nuclear *or* conventional explosives. It will be extremely difficult for satellite observations to monitor how many possess nuclear warheads and impossible to assess how many are programmed for intercontinental targets.

LRCMs will make nuclear proliferation far easier than hitherto. Because they can be used to carry conventional explosives, they may be sold to any country that shows a commercial interest. Countries that could not consider ICBMs and SLBMs because of their cost, and hence have not acquired nuclear weapons, might change their attitude if LRCMs became available.

The LRCM is a good example of the way in which technological advances can outstrip political and military needs. Partial Arms Control agreements such as SALT-1 do no more than impair the advances in new weaponry whilst the momentum of these developments renders the previous arms control measures worthless. The limitations on ICBMs and SLBMs will contribute no more to peace in 1980 than would the banning of bows and arrows in 1939. A *total* halt in all arms developments is an essential prerequisite for any disarmament. Without this there can be no guarantee that any partial measures, however well considered, will not be superseded by ever more dangerous new weapons.

Weapons for their own sake?
The cruise missile has been described as 'a solution in search of a problem'. Although the idea has been discussed for many

years its purpose still is not clear. Consider the following:

1. if the cruise missile is intended as a second-strike weapon (against people), why does it need high accuracy and a hardened nose-cone?
2. if it is intended as a first-strike weapon (to destroy military targets), why is it so slow? (it would take a couple of hours to reach the Warsaw Pact countries from Britain, long enough for Soviet missiles to be launched);
3. their slow speed and high accuracy make cruise missiles suitable for 'battlefield' use, so why are they to be located in Britain?

Perhaps there *is no logic* to the arms race. Maybe the weapons come first and the attempted justification second. Lord Zuckerman goes one step further:

> The decisions which we make today in the fields of science and technology determine the tactics, then the strategy, and finally the politics of tomorrow.

The United Nations

The United Nations is the world's most important forum for discussing disarmament, but it does no more than its member states are prepared to accept. In 1978 the United Nations devoted a complete session to the problems of disarmament (the UN Special Session on Disarmament – UNSSD – held from 23 May to 1 July). The final document of the UNSSD, adopted by consensus, provides a realistic blue print for an end to the arms race.

However, although adopted by consensus, there is little sign that governments feel any obligation to carry out these proposals. The British government's comments were succinct:

> The Declaration suffers from a lack of balance through insufficient emphasis on measures to limit conventional weapons and on the need to prevent the spread of nuclear weapons.

Translated this means, 'we have an advantage in nuclear weapons and we mean to keep them'.

From the UNSSD Final Document

Removing the threat of a world war – a nuclear war – is the most acute and urgent task of the present day. Mankind is confronted with a choice: we must halt the arms race and proceed to disarmament or face annihilation . . .

The ultimate objectives of the States in the disarmament process is general and complete disarmament under effective international control.

Nuclear weapons pose the greatest danger to mankind and to the survival of civilization. It is essential to halt and reverse the nuclear arms race in all its aspects in order to avert the danger of war involving nuclear weapons. The ultimate goal in this context is the complete elimination of nuclear weapons . . .

The achievement of nuclear disarmament will require urgent negotiation of agreements at appropriate stages and with adequate measures of verification satisfactory to the States concerned for:
- cessation of the qualitative improvement and development of nuclear-weapons systems;
- cessation of the production of all types of nuclear weapons and their means of delivery, and the production of fissionable material for weapons purposes.

(July 1978)

Unfortunately, the UN is used by governments primarily as a means to restrict the weapons of other countries, not their own. It may open the door to disarmament but the peoples of the world will need to push their governments through.

Would disarmament measures be circumvented?
The way that countries have circumvented arms control measures leads many people to believe that this would happen also with disarmament. In addition, even if complete disarmament were to be achieved, there seems nothing to prevent countries

rearming once more should they so desire. If these views are correct, genuine disarmament must be a hopeless dream.

There are three good reasons for discounting these fears, two of which have been mentioned already. In the first place, disarmament is much easier to control than is arms limitation in the midst of a continuing arms race. All methods of delivering nuclear weapons, such as LRCMs, would be automatically prohibited in the context of disarmament and so would their use for conventional explosives. So new technological advances are unlikely to supersede the terms of a disarmament measure as has so often occurred with arms control.

Secondly, the process of disarmament is far more likely to lead to an increase in mutual trust and understanding and lowering of tension than is arms control. Whereas disarmament strikes at one of the main causes of the arms race – mutual fear – arms control can actually increase suspicion since the balance of terror is maintained exactly as before and every action is scrutinized to detect potential new developments.

The third reason is more complex. As is well known, many powerful industrial and commercial interests rely upon the arms race for their prosperity and have good reason to fear disarmament. They put pressure on governments and make disarmament more difficult. In 1961 President Eisenhower warned:

We have been compelled to create a permanent armaments industry of vast proportions ... We must not fail to comprehend its grave implications ... In the councils of governments we must guard against the acquisition of unwarranted influence, whether sought or unsought, by the military–industrial complex.

Once disarmament got under way the power of the military–industrial complex would be reduced. This would be so whether the industries switched to peaceful production or suffered a decline at the expense of other industry. In either event there would be more people with a vested interest in maintaining the momentum of disarmament and less with an interest in additional production of armaments. Thus, provided disarmament proceeded at a reasonable pace, once under way there would be less and less internal opposition to the policy.

In summary, disarmament is not only more desirable than arms control, it may be easier to implement also. Once effected it would be hard to return to the conditions of the arms race because the major reasons for that race, both external (mutual fear) and internal (vested interests), will have been removed.

10. War as a way of life

War is horrible. There is no question about it. But so is peace. And it is proper ... to compare the horror of war and the horror of peace and see how much worse it is.

Herman Kahn

War in our time has become an anachronism. Whatever the case in the past, wars in the future can serve no useful purpose.

Dwight Eisenhower

Mankind is accustomed to war. For thousands of years there have been wars between tribes, kingdoms and nations. Historians can show that much of this bloodshed has actually benefited human progress. Warlike behaviour is now thoroughly ingrained in our make-up with the result that many people believe disarmament is not practicable.

There is moreover some evidence that human beings have an innate aggressive instinct which may have been necessary for survival in the past. So the argument that 'You can't change human nature' is used as an explanation and excuse for past wars and for the continuing arms race. It is often claimed that the popularity of war games and war stories indicates that warfare satisfies a basic biological need.

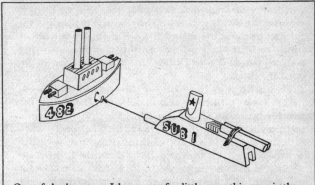

One of the best toys I have seen for little ones this year is the Ship and Submarine. A wooden destroyer, of sorts, is rapidly assembled from a collection of pieces and a spring-loaded core is laid in the heart of the ship. From the ship's side protrudes a small end of a dowel. You then take the submarine and push in its longer dowel of a torpedo until it engages with a click. Hold the sub firmly, aiming the torpedo at the destroyer and press the firing lever. The entire destroyer blows up, all the pieces flying about and falling on the floor, but not close enough to the submarine's 'captain' so as to hurt him. Then you start rebuilding the ship for more destruction.

Solid and likely to last for ages, and to give pleasure for that long.

(from *The Times*, 9 November 1973)

Yet war has not *always* been a feature of human society: at one time it was unknown. It became significant at a particular stage in history and, by the same token, could disappear in the future. An understanding of the history and evolution of warfare is beyond the scope of this book, but the following brief review may help explain how war may be eradicated.

War is only an invention

Margaret Mead

Warfare, by which I mean recognized conflict between two groups *as groups*, in which each group puts an army (even if the army is only fifteen pygmies) into the field to fight and kill ... is an invention like any other of the inventions in terms of which we order our lives, such as writing, marriage, cooking our food instead of eating it raw, trial by jury or burial of the dead, and so on ...

There are peoples even today who have no warfare. Of these the Eskimo are perhaps the most conspicuous examples, but the Lepchas of Sikkim ... are as good. Neither of these peoples understands war, not even defensive warfare. The idea of warfare is lacking and this idea is as essential to really carrying on war as an alphabet ... is to writing. But whereas the Lepchas are a gentle, unquarrelsome people ... the Eskimo are not a mild and meek people; many of them are turbulent and troublesome ... The personality necessary for war, the circumstances necessary to goad men to desperation are present, but there is no war ...

[In contrast are] the pygmy peoples of the Andaman Islands in the Bay of Bengal. The Andamans also represent an exceedingly low level of society; they are a hunting and food-gathering people; they live in tiny hordes without any class stratification; their houses are simpler than the snow houses of the Eskimo. But they knew about warfare ... Tiny army met tiny army in open battle, blows were exchanged, casualties suffered, and the state of warfare could only be concluded by a peacemaking ceremony ...

So simple peoples and civilized peoples, mild peoples and violent, assertive peoples, will all go to war if they have the invention, just as those peoples who have the custom of duelling will have duels and peoples who have the pattern of vendetta will indulge in vendetta. And, conversely, peoples who do not know of duelling will not fight duels, even though their wives are seduced and their daughters ravished; they may on occasion commit murder but they will not fight duels.

(from *Warfare Is Only an Invention –
Not A Biological Necessity*, 1940)

What is 'war'?
War is not simply a large-scale domestic squabble. It is an *organized* activity requiring active and continual *preparation*. For this reason it must not be confused with the spontaneous arguments and occasional fisticuffs that often enliven family life. Domestic disputes took place, no doubt, in early primitive communities but there were neither special weapons available for killing people nor trained professional fighters. The weapons of early communities were used for hunting and farming, not against fellow human beings (except presumably in the heat of the moment).

There were good reasons for this. Early communities lived at subsistence level and there was neither wealth nor better living standards to be obtained from murder. On the contrary the widely dispersed population of early societies needed many hands for the collective work of hunting and food gathering so that all might prosper. Inter-community fighting would have been suicidal, because numbers were essential for survival as a community. Just as farming is a relatively recent human activity (about ten thousand years) so is war (about five thousand years) – and even today some communities exist without knowing armed conflict.

But, granted that warfare is an invention, why was it adopted by, for example, the North American Indians, and not by their near-neighbours the Eskimos? One might have expected martial behaviour to become dominant in all communities, but this has not happened in every case. Societies do not automatically adopt warfare once it has been invented: other conditions also have to be satisfied. War has first to be worthwhile for the community, *as a community* – a condition never satisfied for the Eskimo peoples who live in widely dispersed settlements and have little scope for territorial disputes. The degree of sophistication of a society and its technology has little relevance since primitive communities, given the conditions of economic conflict, do make war.

Communal warfare

War has been a consequence of man's success as a species. As mankind became more populous, tribes began to fight over each other's territory. Thus began economic conflict between human beings – the first essential prerequisite for war.

However, the character of this early fighting was very different from what followed. An entire community fought to defend or occupy a pasture or hunting ground, but the outcome of the battle did not alter the way of life of the victor or the vanquished – all remained hunters or farmers. Indeed it often happened that the surviving members of the defeated tribe became full members of the victorious tribe. This early fighting may be termed *communal warfare* and has more in common with civil wars or guerrilla wars than most major wars of history.

As economies developed beyond subsistence level, communities grew larger and more sophisticated. People began to specialize in certain tasks: for instance, some became tool-makers, some craftsmen and others remained unskilled workers. As a result disagreements began to arise about how the society's wealth should be shared. Some people claimed to deserve more than others because of their special skills. Eventually the old communal societies collapsed.

The new social structures that then arose were divided into a hierarchy of specialists; depending upon status and property ownership, people belonged to particular classes. Egyptian, Greek and Roman societies were extreme examples of 'class-divided societies' with ten or twenty times as many slaves as freemen.

Professional warfare

For our purpose, the important point is that a divided society needs power to regulate and maintain these divisions. The task of coercion was entrusted to the warrior, whose job was to keep 'law and order' for the slave owners (often the warriors were themselves slave owners) and to obtain a ready supply of new slaves. In short, warriors fought on behalf of the community (or, more accurately perhaps, on behalf of the rulers of the community).

This is the second feature of most modern warfare: it involves societies with *professional* fighters. These police the community internally and defend the community against external foes, and are maintained by the rest of the community through taxes of various kinds.

As antagonisms within a community grew, and were formalized and contained by laws and traditions, so antagonisms between communities also developed. Eventually 'empires' were established, in which widely separated communities were controlled by allegiance to a dominant tribe (for example, the Tartars under Genghis Khan) or a city (for example, Rome or Alexandria). The central authority then exacted tribute in the form of slaves, goods and taxes and so became even more powerful. At its zenith the Roman Empire controlled most of present-day Europe as well as parts of Africa and Asia Minor.

Antagonisms between empires made their boundaries a constant battleground and it became necessary to make continual preparations for warfare. From this time onwards, war has been a *permanent* feature of developed society. As a result, war between communities became a major preoccupation of the rulers, and many rulers were chosen for their fighting ability. From being an occasional collective activity on the part of the entire community, war became a continuous specialized activity on behalf of the rulers.

It would be wrong to suggest, however, that such wars only benefited rulers. The Roman Empire brought order and a more developed society to its colonies and probably raised living standards in the process. Trade routes were made secure by warfare: over 1,000 years after the fall of the Roman Empire the exchange of English wool for Indian spices benefited communities along the entire length of the trade route. But generally, as trade and shipping developed and new countries were discovered, trading relationships changed in character. They became unequal and the cause of continual friction.

Spanish and Portuguese adventurers stripped the largely pacific civilizations of the Americas of gold and silver and the English plundered their homeward-bound ships. The Anglo–Spanish wars of the sixteenth century resulted from this rivalry for plunder. This kind of war was simply state-aided piracy.

It is clear then that, until the nationalist wars of the nineteenth century, war was primarily a contest between monarchies for territory or money, and the aristocratic élite were the only people with an interest in victory. Most people had to be persuaded to fight to support wars: they were therefore often fought for ostensibly idealistic reasons – religious wars are a good example. The Crusades aimed to secure access to the Holy City for pilgrims, but in addition they helped to secure trade routes to India and the East.

Nationalist wars

Nowadays nearly everyone is concerned to avoid the tragedies that war brings. This change was well under way long before the advent of modern weapons. People cared about the outcome of the Napoleonic wars: the whole French nation was mobilized, not just the ruling élite. The genius of Napoleon was not only military but political: he was able to enthuse masses to rally behind the national flag. Chauvinistic propaganda had become an essential instrument of warfare.

The failure of the Americans in Vietnam illustrates how difficult it is to win a war today without the complete support of the people. Although the US forces suffered many military setbacks they were at all times vastly stronger than the Vietnamese: even now they have the military strength to annihilate Vietnam. The American government failed because they lost the political will to continue the fight – in other words they were unable to convince enough Americans that they were in the right. By contrast the people they were fighting were convinced of the rightness of their cause and, despite their far greater losses, continued their struggle.

Although the chivalrous professionals-only war has long disappeared, the concept lingers on. As late as 1920 the

President of the International Committee of the Red Cross wrote:

The Committee considers it very desirable that war should resume its former character, that is to say, that it should be a struggle between armies and not between populations. The civilian population must, as far as possible, remain outside the struggle and its consequences.

The 'civilized warfare' embodied in the 'rules' of the St Petersburg, Hague and Geneva Conventions owes much to this philosophy. Although medieval knights might act cruelly against rebellions from their own serfs, they would not use the medieval equivalent of APW against non-combatants. Warfare

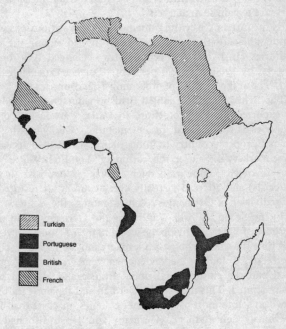

The conquest of Africa, 1880

was strictly a matter for the leaders of society. Fortunately people are no longer prepared to remain 'outside the struggle' and this offers hope that wars may eventually be abolished altogether.

World wars

The eighteenth and nineteenth centuries saw vast industrial, social and economic changes in the richer countries, especially Britain. Many more goods were produced than the people could buy (or needed). Whereas the early empires guaranteed *supplies* of raw materials (wool, slaves etc.), empires now also could guarantee *markets* for manufactured goods. The expansion of empires in the nineteenth century resulted from the economic pressure to gain such markets.

By the turn of the century unequal trading relationships were commonplace with the whole world divided among the rich countries. (In 1876 11 per cent of Africa belonged to European powers; by 1900 it was 90 per cent.) Further expansion then had to be at the expense of other industrial countries.

The British Empire enabled British manufactured goods to be exported, under protection, to India, Canada and other countries as well as securing raw materials. Germany, the last major European country to industrialize, was denied access to these markets and suffered accordingly. The First World War thus involved competition over *exports* (as opposed to raw materials) and affected virtually every country. It resulted in the redivision of Germany's colonies amongst the victors.

In the Second World War Japan and Germany again tried unsuccessfully to re-divide the world in their favour. However, this time the war did help the Germans and the Japanese, albeit indirectly. Colonial independence movements were strengthened and the empires of Britain, France and Holland soon disintegrated. This means that German and Japanese industry now can sell to most of the former colonies, markets that were previously denied them. (Germany and Japan also had the incidental advantage that, after the war, they were not allowed to waste too much on arms: this enabled them to invest more money in industrial plant and machinery than did their competitors.)

Competition between British and German industrialists continues today but without bloodshed. The main reason is that the really powerful industrialists are *multinational* nowadays and no longer desire the old type of wars. When the British part of a multinational company does badly, investment is switched elsewhere, for example to Germany. So war between the rich industrial nations is now less likely.

Minor wars

These trends do not mean that all wars are over; on the contrary

The conquest of Africa, 1914

they have intensified other types of conflict and are partly responsible for the *increased* frequency of wars since 1945.

The 'sport of kings' is over because people are no longer prepared to remain 'outside the struggle' when the struggle is simply to make their rulers richer. But this greater political awareness has been responsible for warfare in which people try to change their governments – civil wars, wars of independence, etc.

Most wars since 1945 have been for national independence and, in general, these have succeeded in ending the unequal trading relationships of former empires. Very often the newly independent countries have placed severe restrictions on the activities of foreign investors and used their newly acquired strength to raise prices of raw materials (like oil) substantially. The potential for conflict with former colonial powers thus continues after independence. Wars of independence, and post-independence power struggles (often exacerbated by foreign powers), have greatly increased the incidence of bloodshed in the world since 1945. Moreover many local conflicts now have world-wide implications because they threaten multinational corporations. So these organizations tend to meddle in political affairs to a greater extent than hitherto.

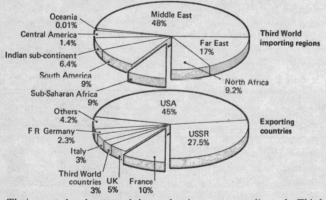

The importers' and exporters' shares of major weapon supplies to the Third World, 1970–79. From SIPRI *Yearbook 1980*

So the economic and political interests of rich industrial nations and multinational corporations are often involved in the minor wars. And, although governments and industrialists may no longer wish to see their own people fighting, they are not averse to maintaining it elsewhere. In the Nigerian civil war (1968) French arms were supplied to the Biafran 'rebels' and British and Russian arms to the Nigerian government. In a certain sense the old-style wars continue – but with other people's lives.

The arms trade

The arms race between the superpowers has its own direct influence on the frequency of minor wars. Most of the arms employed are supplied by only a few nations (over 85 per cent from the USA, USSR, UK and France). The motives for the supply of arms may be political (to make friends) or commercial (to make money).

The reasons for the special profitability of arms sales deserve study. Consider what happens when motor cars are sold to, say, India. It may follow that Pakistan will buy more cars but, after a while, fewer cars will be needed and demand will level off in both countries. In contrast, when military equipment is sold to India, Pakistan will require more arms which, in turn, will stimulate further sales to India. In common with drugs, arms have the big commercial advantage that sales stimulate demand. British arms sales have steadily increased over the years despite the economic crises at home. Britain is in danger of becoming 'no longer a nation of shopkeepers but a nation of gun makers'.*

In contrast to the 'inter-war period' (1918–39), when the build-up of armaments was often attributed to the greed of private arms manufacturers, today the export of weapons is controlled by governments. Less than 5 per cent of the arms trade is in the hands of private dealers and only a minute proportion of these dealers operate without government approval. (Over half of British arms manufacture is government-owned.)

*Mary Kaldor, *The Times*, October 1975.

So an understanding of the arms trade is crucial, because it is one means by which the competition between rich countries is extended throughout the world and absorbs local disputes and wars.

It is not always appreciated that the arms trade subsidizes the main arms race. Weapons development costs have become so enormous that, for the manufacturers to stay in business, the weapons have to be sold to many customers ('To arm ourselves, we must arm the world.')* Conversely, a halt to the arms trade would do much to reduce the pace of new weapons development.

Scientific progress

It is sometimes argued, notably by Lord Zuckerman, that scientists bear the main blame for the arms race. They are so interested in the gadgets and devices that, or so it is claimed, they go on developing new weapons without thinking of the consequences. Once a new device has been invented, the military then work out how it might be used.

> The men in the nuclear laboratories of both sides have succeeded in creating a world with an irrational foundation, on which a new set of political realities has in turn had to be built. They have become the alchemists of our times, working in secret ways which cannot be divulged, casting spells which embrace us all. (*Lord Zuckerman*)

It certainly is true that some weapons seem to have been developed for no clear purpose. The contradictory characteristics of the cruise missiles (those described in the chapter on disarmament) might be explained by this theory ('a solution in search of a problem'). But even if many scientists do ignore the possible implications of their work, it is wrong to blame the arms race on any one group. If society pays for over one third of its qualified scientists to work on weapons, society as a whole has to share the blame for the consequences.

* Anthony Sampson, *The Arms Bazaar*.

The military–industrial complex

War then is a human activity related to social, economic and political factors. Victory brings economic advantages, sometimes to everybody and usually to rulers and those who influence the rulers of society. This is why President Eisenhower warned against the power and influence of 'the military–industrial complex'. Because arms sales are very profitable, armaments manufacturers are very rich and powerful. They can have a good deal of influence on government policies. If a disarmament proposal looks like succeeding, they can influence public opinion and governments, so that the negotiations fail.

Compare the relative indifference of political and military 'experts' when a railway line or coal pit is closed with the furore if 'defence cuts' are suggested. In the former instance we are told that economic progress necessitates that the workers concerned become unemployed. By contrast armaments factories are kept open, allegedly to preserve the workers' livelihoods. An example of this thinking came from Roy Mason, UK Defence Secretary, speaking in Parliament in May 1976: 'If the MRCA contract is cancelled ... 24,000 jobs would go immediately ... There would be hardly an aircraft industry left.'

Most armaments factories can be switched to peaceful production. Lucas Aerospace workers have prepared a plan for alternative peaceful employment for their factory which, given the political will, could be quickly implemented. Their advanced electronics knowledge has already come up with a kidney machine, a device to help spina bifida children and retarda braking systems for road transport vehicles. After a particularly bad coach disaster in Yorkshire, in May 1975, the *Sunday Times* commented:

last week's crash might have been avoided if the coach had been equipped with an extra braking device such as an electro-magnetic retarda which is being fitted to an increasing number of coaches in this country.

But the Lucas factory, which makes these retardas, has had to restrict production because of the demands of the more profitable armaments departments of their factory.

Soviet pressure groups

US President Eisenhower used the term 'military–industrial complex' to describe the pressure groups who were opposed to his attempts to improve relations with the Soviet Union. The groups included military people, private industrialists, workers in the arms industry and politicians who had made their mark by advocacy of more defence spending. The term describes those people in a capitalist society who, for a variety of reasons, have a vested interest in the continuation of the arms race.

Within the Soviet Union there is no privately owned industry and hence there are no private industrialists to make a commercial profit from weapons manufacture (or fallout shelters). But all the other components of the military–industrial complex exist and there can be no doubt that they influence Soviet government policy. The military will tend to exaggerate the US threat to help ensure they obtain the weapons they believe they need. The workers in weapons factories will fear for their jobs. Bureaucrats may fear a more open society if international tension is relaxed. While they will operate in different ways from their American counterparts, and the Soviet government may be less responsive to outside pressures, it would be foolish to ignore the influence of such groups in the formulation of Soviet policies.

Wars will cease ...

The slogan 'Wars will cease when men refuse to fight' has attracted thousands to the pacifist philosophy of life. This is little more than a pious hope. Throughout history wars have been conducted by a very tiny minority. Today, even if less than one in a thousand were prepared to fight, mankind still could be annihilated by a nuclear war. Peace is not simply a matter for individual action: it requires a concerted effort by everyone who desires peace to enforce disarmament upon those who oppose it.

This brief review of the evolution of war suggests reforms

to society that may help eradicate war. If no one could make money out of the sale and manufacture of weapons, this would help. If nations cooperated rather than competed in trade, there might be less international tension. It would further help if conflicts within societies were reduced so that internal pressures to maintain coercive forces were not so strong.

Some people believe that such changes to society are a guarantee of immediate peace. But mankind has a backlog of religious, racial and political prejudices, inherited from the past 5,000 years of conflict, that will take many generations to overcome. (The war between China and Vietnam was a vivid lesson for those who believed that 'socialism will abolish war'.)

Haole store his bombs up high,
Haole store his bombs up high,
Haole store his bombs up high,
- We're all dead scared.

Hawaiian take them off again,
Hawaiian take them off again,
Hawaiian take them off again,
- We're safe once more.

Haole *is the Hawaiian word for 'white man'. In 1971, Catholic Action of Hawaii estimated that over 3,000 nuclear weapons were being stored on the island*

Nevertheless the emasculation of organizations that have a vested interest in armaments and war would be an immensely positive step for peace, quite apart from the obvious social benefits for society.

Disarmament proposals
It can be argued that the military–industrial complex is a greater

enemy of disarmament than all the misunderstandings which undoubtedly do exist between countries. Misunderstandings can be erased; fundamental support for armaments manufacture cannot. This was shown in 1955 when the Soviet Union accepted the West's proposals for disarmament in their entirety – only to find that these were then withdrawn. As a result, 'the hopeful atmosphere of that time was ... destroyed'.* This episode is of crucial importance to an understanding of the obstacles to disarmament and is worth recalling in some detail.

On 10 May 1955 the Soviet Union laid proposals before the UN Disarmament Sub-Committee which, amongst other measures, provided for armed manpower ceilings of 1,500,000, major reductions in conventional armaments and an arrangement for the abolition of 75 per cent of the stocks of nuclear and other mass-destruction weapons. They agreed to an international control organ with staffs of inspectors having unimpeded access at all times to all objects of control. The completion of all these measures was to be followed by further reductions in armaments.

The French delegate's immediate response was that 'the whole thing looks too good to be true'. The British delegate, after consultation with the government, said he was glad that the Western 'policy of patience' had 'now achieved this welcome dividend, and that the Western proposals have now been largely, and in some cases, entirely, adopted by the Soviet Union and made into its own proposals'. After listing the points of agreement, he said 'we have made an advance that I never dreamed possible'.

The US delegate, after two days' discussion with the American government, said 'we have been gratified to find that the concepts we have put forward over a considerable length of time, and which we have repeated many times during this past two months, have been accepted in a large measure by the Soviet Union'.

After months of procrastination, on 6 September the Ameri-

* Bertrand Russell, *Has Man a Future?*

can delegate dashed all hopes of agreement with: 'The United States does now place a reservation upon all of its pre-Geneva substantive positions taken in this Sub-Committee or in the Disarmament Commission or in the UN on these questions in relation to levels of armaments.' In other words all the proposals urged with vigour and persistence only three months before were withdrawn.

There is, in fact, no difficulty in devising disarmament agreements: the difficulty is to force governments to implement them. In present circumstances the military–industrial complex has far greater power and influence than the ordinary people. People of all countries want peace but are bemused and confused by propaganda. Yet Eisenhower saw that this situation cannot last: 'I think people want peace so much that one of these days governments had better get out of their way and let them have it.'

For people in Britain, the starting point must be the British government.

11. How many more?

We have made a successful start. When the [nuclear] tests are completed, as they soon will be, we shall be in the same position as the United States or Soviet Russia. We shall have made and tested the massive weapons. It will be possible then to discuss on equal terms.

Harold Macmillan, 1957

Such were the illusions. The pace of the arms race has shattered Britain's dream of equality with the superpowers. Britain is now a medium-sized European power, unrepresented at SALT (the Strategic Arms Limitation Talks). Yet the delusions of past grandeur remain.

Relative to her economic strength (measured by Gross National Product – GNP), Britain spends substantially more on armaments than comparable European countries. Relative to area, there are more nuclear bases in Britain than anywhere else in the world. This hopeless attempt at nuclear prestige affects defence strategy, military spending, the economy, foreign policy and, less directly, many other aspects of society. It is noteworthy that all major decisions on this issue have been taken without public debate or approval.

The original decision to 'go nuclear' was taken by Prime Minister Clement Attlee in the late 1940s, on the recommendation of his military advisers, without informing even the British government. It was only years later that the public were told. Since then it has proved impossible to call a halt. Even though all the original arguments for a nuclear weapons programme – such as that quoted at the head of this chapter – have proved false, the policies of successive governments have not changed.

Until about 1965 we knew why. More recently the justification has been argued behind closed doors. This secrecy is said to be for 'security reasons' but, more likely, the government fears public debate. Their case is rarely explained and, if it is, often in terms that are dated and contradictory.

'*It is a matter of political, not moral judgment*' – *Mr Denis Healey, February 1967*

(*When Mrs Healey launched Britain's second Polaris submarine, the Bishop of Chester refused to bless the vessel – but did bless the crew*)

It is bizarre to recall that one of the pledges made by the Labour Party when it won the 1964 General Election was to abandon the so-called 'independent British nuclear deterrent'. The Party's Manifesto stated firmly: 'It will not be independent and it will not be British and it will not deter ... We are not prepared to continue this endless duplication of nuclear weapons.' The essence of the 1964 pledge has been reaffirmed at subsequent Labour Party Conferences whilst the government, Labour or Conservative, has pursued the opposite policy. Indeed it was the 1964–70 Labour government that launched and blessed Britain's Polaris fleet.

In 1974 the Labour government was elected on a manifesto which promised: 'We have renounced any intention of moving towards a new generation of strategic nuclear weapons.' Nevertheless, in secret, the government authorized £1,000 million for MIRVing Polaris warheads – an 'improvement' so radical that it meant, in reality, that Britain did develop a completely new missile system. (Some members of the Cabinet claim that they were not told the nature of these 'improvements' and thought the cost would be only £24 million a year.)

The arguments for Britain's bomb are considered here in some detail since, as the first and leading minor nuclear power, the British example has influenced many other countries. Even though all the original arguments for a British nuclear weapons programme, such as that quoted at the head of this chapter, have proved false, the desire for an independent British nuclear deterrent persists and provides some justification for other countries to follow suit. It is because of these international implications that the three elements of the so-called 'independent British nuclear deterrent' must be examined from the military and political standpoint although, ultimately, the possession of nuclear weapons is a moral issue.

Independent?

Nuclear weapons are supposed to give Britain the power to pursue independent initiatives in foreign affairs. However, non-nuclear countries such as Sweden, Austria and Algeria show far greater independence in practice. By contrast Britain has adhered totally to US foreign policy, especially over issues such as the Vietnam War, European security and the SALT negotiations.

This is not surprising since the so-called independent British nuclear deterrent was acquired as a result of a deal – the 1962 Nassau agreement – in which Britain obtained Polaris 'know-how' from the US in exchange for guarantees for US bases in Britain. These bases necessitate close Anglo-American coordination, as they link the two countries together in matters of peace and war. The price of the Nassau agreement has been for Britain to give America unswerving loyalty on all issues which might lead to their use. The twin decisions of 1980 – to invite the US to station cruise missiles in the UK and to buy 'four or five' Trident submarines to replace Polaris – show that the spirit of Nassau lives on. Britain could remain a nuclear weapons power without US bases (like France) by confining its nuclear strike force to the Tornado bombers.

British?

The military case for the British nuclear force is that America is unlikely to commit nuclear suicide for the sake of Britain alone. US Secretary of State Christian Herter made this clear: 'I cannot conceive of any President engaging in an all-out nuclear war unless we are in danger of all-out nuclear destruction ourselves.'

But who would Britain fight independently with nuclear weapons? Not America or Russia – either could annihilate Britain very quickly, and the four nuclear submarines (with only one certain to be on patrol at any one time) are not a credible second-strike force against the superpowers. Nor is it conceivable that Britain would use nuclear weapons against a non-nuclear power; if she did, America or Russia might well object. That leaves China, France and perhaps India as potential candidates for a British nuclear attack.

Common sense dictates that the British nuclear submarines are credible only as *part* of the NATO nuclear striking force. Rather than admit that Britain no longer has its own credible nuclear force, the myth that the missiles are British is maintained for political reasons. There are moreover suggestions that America has retained an 'electronic key' which prevents 'British' SLBMs being fired without sanction from Washington.

Deterrent?

One thing is certain: if there is a nuclear war, Britain will be a target. East Anglia contains a greater density of nuclear bases than anywhere else in the world. The Clyde bases contain, or hold in transit, more nuclear destructive power than any other bases in Europe. These bases are said to add to our security by deterring our enemies.

It is equally likely that those bases will incite a nuclear attack. The more a potential enemy is convinced of their serious purpose, the more urgent will be his desire to eliminate the threat. Speaking in 1961, the British Foreign Secretary (later Prime Minister) Alec Douglas-Home emphasized this commitment: 'The British people are prepared if necessary to be blown

Signs of the times

to atomic dust.' Whereas countries such as Sweden and Austria may be spared from nuclear attack (though not the subsequent fall-out), in the event of war Britain will be attacked quickly to eliminate her ability to retaliate.

Thus, because of the way Britain acquired her nuclear forces, these are neither independent, nor British, nor able to deter. The Polaris fleet is a waste of money for Britain, a powerful argument for France, China, India and other near-nuclear countries to join the nuclear club and a minor yet significant complication for the SALT negotiations. Many people who are resigned to the nuclear arms race between America and Russia do not see why Britain has also to be involved.

Morality

These arguments suggest that Britain's nuclear weapons do not make political or military sense. But nuclear weapons also raise moral questions. Are there *any* circumstances in which the use, or threatened use, of nuclear weapons can be justified?

A nuclear war would bring suffering and death to millions of people throughout the world. Most would be innocent of any crime – save, perhaps, acceptance of their own government's policies. A full-scale war would severely cripple or destroy the belligerent countries – and vast numbers of non-belligerents.

It is difficult to imagine a cause or provocation so great as to justify the unleashing of such destruction upon the human race. The destruction would be so great, so purposeless and so indiscriminate that – assuming the 'good' side won – it is hard to believe that the 'good' from the war would counterbalance such unprecedented evil.

Even some supporters of nuclear weapons accept that nuclear war is totally evil. They rationalize their support on the grounds that (our) nuclear weapons exist purely to prevent war. This debating point would be valid if it were certain that the (good) nuclear bombs will never be used. But, to deter effectively, armed forces must be ready and prepared for a nuclear attack. How could these forces be kept idle in a nuclear war? Moreover people who use this argument clearly believe that our nuclear weapons are intended *solely* for deterrence. In this case, how do they justify the development of MIRVs, SRAMs, Trident and cruise missiles as these *far exceed the requirements of deterrence*?

In short, British nuclear policies are *immoral* – because they contemplate the mass murder of civilians; *suicidal* – because they invite attack; *incredible* – because they offer no hope of victory; and *provocative* – because they fuel the nuclear arms race. They are also, and incidentally, very *expensive* and so largely responsible for Britain's excessive military spending.

Approximately three fifths of British research and development and nearly two thirds of all industrial research is financed from defence funds. Around two fifths of British R & D scientists and engineers are absorbed on defence projects. It is not so much the absolute value of this waste of resources that is important (though, at more than £10,000 million per annum, this is serious enough). The misdirection of Britain's best brains on socially unproductive work has a profound significance far in excess of the monetary expenditure involved.

Britain is in a very special position. Unlike America or Russia she could renounce weapons of mass destruction without any loss of security and with great economic and political benefit. This action would be in the interests of Britain and of the world for the following reasons:

- there would be one less country able to start a nuclear war, fewer nuclear weapons around to start one accidentally, one less government to complicate negotiations for complete nuclear disarmament;
- it could encourage other people to press their governments

The dangers of leaving defence planning to 'experts'

Mary Kaldor, Fellow of the Institute for the Study of International Organization, at the University of Sussex

At a time when investment is declining, firms are collapsing and income is failing to rise, the defence sector is expanding as fast as ever. Military expenditures are rising in real terms and arms exports have exploded in size. If present trends continue, Britain could become one vast armaments factory, no longer a nation of shopkeepers but a nation of gun makers ...

It seems to me that it is time we questioned this policy and asked whether the amount and kind of military expenditures which the 'experts' say we need is really so inviolable ... The [military] situation is not as bleak as many might think. Nato spends substantially more on defence than the Warsaw Pact, and its superiority in active peacetime forces is 5,700,000 to 4,300,000. Even on the Central European front (always the scare ground in military thinking), Nato's position is not half bad. According to a recent Pentagon report, the slight Soviet superiority in manpower (now questioned) and in aircraft is offset by Nato's advantages in communication, infra-structure and the quality of equipment. The Great Russian Tank Threat is now much diminished since previous intelligence estimates apparently counted tank sheds, many of which were empty; in any case, Nato has an overwhelming advantage in anti-tank weapons which are the decisive factor in modern warfare. Finally, the Soviet naval build-up, which has agitated so many military journalists, is little more than an illusion. The Soviet Union has fewer ships than it had in 1958 – all that has changed is their deployment ...

Few people are aware that only 10 per cent of our defence budget is actually devoted to the defence of Britain. Surely something has gone wrong when a medium-rank offshore island, heavily dependent on borrowing to finance public expenditure and imports and badly in need of resources for new investment, spends so much money defending Europe, the Atlantic, and some distant dependent territories ...

(from *The Times*, October 1975)

to agree to disarm and discourage other governments who are thinking of acquiring nuclear arms;

- it would enable Britain to take independent initiatives for world-wide agreement on disarmament and on action to overcome the problems of hunger and disease.

The irrelevant bomb

It is sometimes argued that Britain's bomb does not matter one way or the other. This is a change from the days when Prime Minister Alec Douglas-Home claimed that we needed the H-bomb 'to secure our place above the salt at the negotiating table' (nothing to do with the SALT negotiations – at which Britain is not represented despite the H-bomb!). At the 1960 Labour Party Conference John Horner of the Fire Brigades Union proposed the motion to 'cease unilaterally to manufacture and test nuclear weapons and ... to prohibit the use of nuclear weapons from British territory'. He pointed out that you cannot negotiate by saying: 'Failure to agree will result in my blowing my brains out.'

But, though largely irrelevant to the SALT negotiations, the British bomb is highly relevant to the issue of nuclear proliferation. In the same speech John Horner argued:

It is said that three [nuclear powers] is better than four or five –
I put it that two is better than three. But, if possession of the bomb
has advantages for us, what right have we to declare to other nations
that they should not also possess the advantage we claim for ourselves?
. . . Indeed, if there is a single ounce of logic in the argument that some-
how there is an advantage for Britain in having the bomb, we should
be welcoming and not deploring extension of the Nuclear Club because
everybody would deter everybody else.

When the Campaign for Nuclear Disarmament (CND) was
founded in 1957, Britain was the junior member of a nuclear
club of three. It was clearly unrealistic to expect either Russia
or America to give up nuclear weapons unilaterally – that is,
without a negotiated international disarmament agreement. But
there was no pressing need for others to acquire nuclear weapons
and, indeed, France resisted the urge for many years.

The nuclear race of the also-rans began when one extra
country (Britain) joined the nuclear club. This made the French
bomb well-nigh inevitable. China, the fifth of the 'Big Five'
countries (with a permanent seat on the UN Security Council),
was then in the anomalous position of being the only non-
nuclear Big Power. Once China had the bomb, pressure grew
within India to match the Chinese threat.

Naturally our present leaders are trustworthy, but can we
be sure that the United States, Britain, the Soviet Union or
some other country will not one day be led by a madman? Prime
Minister Macmillan wrote to President Kennedy about nuclear
weapons:

If all this capacity for destruction is spread around the world in the
hands of all kinds of different characters – dictators, reactionaries,
revolutionaries, madmen – then sooner or later, and certainly I think
by the end of this century, either by error or insanity, the great crime
will be committed.

France
Domestic opposition to British nuclear weapons was watched,
with interest, from across the Channel. When it became clear

that Britain would keep its nuclear weapons, France reversed its earlier non-nuclear stand. In the face of positive discouragement from NATO allies, France built its own 'force de frappe'.

This gave France an independence not achieved by Britain. The French nuclear forces are not subject to NATO control and this is said to give France greater influence in world affairs. Domestic opposition to nuclear weapons is muted and France has no organization, like the British CND, campaigning for the unilateral renunciation of national nuclear weapons. This independence has its counterpart in aggressive commercial policies: the French sell nuclear power plants and armaments to anyone able to buy. Whenever such actions are criticized, often by US and British commentators, the French can point to the example set by the leading nuclear nations.

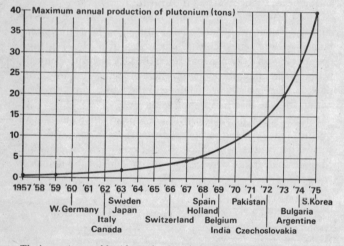

The increasing world-wide production of plutonium since 1957

The nth country

With the export of nuclear technology, it has become far easier for newcomers to obtain nuclear weapons. By 1990 the developing countries will be producing enough plutonium to make 3,000 Hiroshima-strength bombs each year. Whereas the first four nuclear nations had to develop nuclear technology themselves, other countries have been helped through the initial stages.

When China decided to become an independent nuclear nation, it precipitated a major rift in Sino–Soviet relations far more serious than that between France and the United States. The hostility was not confined to commercial issues: China and the Soviet Union have aided rival 'national liberation movements' around the world.

India, alarmed by China's nuclear forces, reversed its long-standing anti-nuclear policy and developed its own nuclear weapons. The first Indian nuclear explosion, in 1974, led to pressure in Pakistan to match the Indian threat. Nor will it end there. Pakistan's neighbour, the late Shah of Iran, warned: 'If small nations arm themselves with nuclear weapons, Iran will seek possession of them sooner than you think.' In 1979, the Ayatollah came to power and acquired control over Iranian nuclear equipment, supplied by the West.

Several other countries could make atomic bombs from domestically produced plutonium or enriched uranium. Israel and South Africa probably have done so already but have refrained from testing to avoid the international outcry.

There is little anyone or any country can do to stop proliferation continuing, as long as the main nuclear arms race is unchecked and nuclear power plants are exported indiscriminately.

Proliferation

The sheer size of the initial development costs of nuclear power has made exports inevitable. Exporting has been the only way to recoup the initial investment and make the domestic nuclear industries viable. Thus, having built the nuclear reactors primarily to make plutonium for atomic weapons, the United States, Britain and France have been obliged to sell nuclear know-how to other countries (including some potential enemies!) to recover the investment costs.

Any attempt to reverse this process can be expected to meet fierce opposition. This was shown shortly after President Carter took office, when he attempted to block further construction of plutonium-breeder reactors. Commercial pressures proved stronger than the US President's willpower, and the proposed measures, in all but name, were dropped.

There is another more fundamental reason why US efforts to halt nuclear proliferation are unlikely to succeed in their present form. With a world shortage of energy it is unreasonable to expect a poorer country to forgo the opportunity to exploit the potential of nuclear energy, especially when this is under intensive development in advanced industrial nations.

Similarly, the United States is in no position to lecture others on the dangers of nuclear weapons while leading a frenetic nuclear arms race. These problems were recognized by Jimmy Carter before his election as President.

Main events of the nuclear arms race

	1945	1950	1955	1960	1965
USA	A-bomb		H-bomb	IRBM	ICBM/ SLBM
USSR		A-bomb	H-bomb	IRBM	
UK			A-bomb	H-bomb	SLBM (from USA)
France				A-bomb	
China					A-bomb
India					
Who next?					

We Americans must be honest about the problems of proliferation of nuclear weapons ... By enjoining sovereign nations to forgo nuclear weapons, we are asking for a form of self-denial that we have not been able to accept ourselves. I believe we have little right to ask others to deny themselves such weapons for the indefinite future unless we demonstrate meaningful progress towards the goal of control, then reduction and ultimately, elimination of nuclear arsenals ... Unfortunately, the agreements reached to date have succeeded largely in changing the build-up in strategic arms from a 'quantitative' to a 'qualitative' arms race. It is time, in the SALT talks, that we complete the stage of agreeing on ceilings and get down to the centrepiece of SALT – the actual negotiation of reductions in strategic forces and measures effectively halting the race in strategic weapons technology. The world is waiting, but not necessarily for long. The longer effective arms reduction is postponed, the more likely it is that other nations will be encouraged to develop their own nuclear capability.*

Despite his encouragement for disarmament measures, under President Carter the USA attempted to deploy the neutron

*Interview for *Bulletin of Atomic Scientists*, October 1976.

1970	1975	1980	1985	?
MIRV	SRAM	Trident	Cruise/MX	?
ICBM/ SLBM	MIRV			?
			Trident/cruise	?
H-bomb	SLBM	Cruise		?
H-bomb	ICBM		SLBM?	?
	A-bomb		H-bomb?	?
		A-bomb?	H-bomb?	?

bomb, secured the agreement of Britain, West Germany and Italy to station NATO cruise missiles on their soil, commissioned the first Trident submarine and almost doubled the number of nuclear warheads pointed at the Soviet Union. Then, in 1980, Carter lost the Presidential election to a man who claimed that the USA needed to spend more to keep even further ahead in the arms race.

... Under President Reagan, however, the debate is between Right and super-Right.

This seems the case in the latest embarrassing incident in the past 24 hours in which both the White House and the State Department publicly disowned a positively apocalyptic interview on East–West relations given to the Reuters newsagency by Professor Richard Pipes, the Soviet expert on the National Security Council.

What Professor Pipes said was that detente was dead and that there was no point in negotiating with the Russians on virtually anything until it mended its ways. He argued that the US was prepared to put such pressure on the Soviet Union, on its economy and in combating its foreign policy, that the Soviet leadership would have to decide sooner or later to either reform its system, internally and externally, or 'to go to war'.

More controversially still, he said he feared that West Germany ... was susceptible to the latest Soviet peace offensive ... It was this remark, rather than the more philosophical tenor of his interview, which clearly set the State Department's alarm bells ringing ...

(from the *Financial Times*, 20 March 1981)

Britain

Britain has little influence on the main arms race between the superpowers but could still help prevent further nuclear proliferation. The most obvious step would be to leave the nuclear club, unilaterally if need be but, better still, in concert with the other minor nuclear powers. This would clear the air for the ending of the nuclear arms race through negotiation between the superpowers.

However, despite having signed the Non-Proliferation Treaty, Britain is not engaged in any negotiations for nuclear disarmament as required under Article VI. Worse still, Britain sells 'peaceful' nuclear reactor know-how and uranium to countries which have not signed the NPT. It seems that John Horner's suggestion in 1960 that Britain might welcome additional nuclear powers was remarkably near the truth.

Perhaps the greatest criticism that can be made of the nuclear arms race is its total irrelevance to the problems facing the world today.

By common consent ... the basic problems of the human race in the contemporary scene are world poverty, overpopulation and pollution. It is this situation which lies at the root of the threat of world war, by design, accident or miscalculation, which hangs over mankind. Two thirds of the world's population suffer from undernourishment or sheer starvation. Of the 100 children born in developing countries every half minute, twenty die within a year and three quarters of those who survive suffer from malnutrition and have no access to modern medical care. It is estimated that 500 million people suffer each year from disabling diseases due to lack of clean water.*

*From *The Hungry Half*, Idris Cox.

In the face of these facts people are remarkably quiescent. More is spent on armaments than on education – more in fact than the total production of all the developing countries put together. Why can't the developed industrialized countries cooperate to assist these countries?

The main reason is the serious political friction in the world which underlies the growth of nuclear armaments. If some advance could be made towards easing this tension, spending less on the deadly instruments of war, then far more resources could be channelled to assist economic growth in the developing countries.

Harold Wilson said, early in 1969,

this is the only war we seek. The war against man's ancient enemies, poverty, hunger, illiteracy and preventable disease. A war we can fight the more successfully when improved world relationships, increased trust, enable us to turn from concentration on the munitions of defence to the munitions of economic and social advance.

These are fine words. Unfortunately there is little or no evidence of any serious endeavours by successive governments to end the 'concentration on the munitions of defence'. By taking resolute action for disarmament, and in particular by opting out of the nuclear arms race, Britain could lead the world towards peace and away from 'poverty, hunger, illiteracy and preventable disease'.

12. Concerning CND

The Campaign for Nuclear Disarmament (CND) was a popular cause of the late 1950s and 1960s. Thousands flocked to its annual Easter pilgrimages from Aldermaston to Trafalgar Square. In its heyday the Labour Party was won to its programme of unilateral nuclear disarmament by Britain. Thereafter it declined. CND is now a shadow of its former self and The Bomb has ceased to be a major public concern.

The above 'quotation' is a representative amalgam of comments printed about CND in 1977 when *Overkill* first appeared. Since then there has been an upsurge of concern about nuclear weapons and a dramatic resurgence of CND. This extra chapter appears in response to the many questions asked about the Campaign – its policies, its personalities, its history and, most important of all, its future.

For the record

CND was formed in late 1957 and launched publicly on 17 February 1958 at the Central Hall, Westminster. Several overflow meetings were needed. In response to this interest a revised policy statement was issued:

The purpose of the Campaign is to press for a British initiative to reduce the nuclear peril and to stop the armaments race. We shall seek to persuade the British people that Britain must:

(a) Renounce unconditionally the use or production of nuclear weapons and refuse to allow their use by others in her defence.
(b) Use her utmost endeavour to bring about negotiations at all levels for agreement to end the armaments race and to lead to a general disarmament convention.
(c) Invite the cooperation of other nations, particularly non-nuclear powers, in her renunciation of nuclear weapons.

The founders of CND were impressive – thirteen appeared in the pages of *Who's Who*. Although they had intended CND to be a high-level pressure group, it quickly became a mass movement. The turning point was their support for a four-day march to the Atomic Weapons Research Establishment (AWRE) at Aldermaston over Easter 1958. The march was small in numbers (a few thousand at the most) yet received much publicity and sympathy. For the next few hectic years, CND headed a mass movement which spoke with many voices.

By the end of 1958 CND had nearly 300 active groups. Over Easter 1959 CND organized the second Aldermaston march. It ended with about 20,000 people at a rally in Trafalgar Square and this set the pattern of activity for more Easters. In addition to the Aldermaston marches, which at their peak may have involved 100,000 participants, local demonstrations took place all over Britain throughout the year and received enormous media coverage.

In 1960 the Labour Party conference at Scarborough passed a resolution from the Transport and General Workers Union (TGWU) specifically supporting CND's policy of unilateral nuclear disarmament for Britain. For a while it seemed that

CND would soon succeed in changing the country's nuclear policies.

This, however, was not to be. The Scarborough decision was reversed next year and internal conflicts within the Campaign (notably over the tactic of civil disobedience) began to dominate its activities. The subsequent decline that set in was not halted for a decade.

In the mid 1960s journalists were dismissing CND as a passing fashion. 'Obituaries' were written by academics and ex-activists, reinforcing myths about CND – myths which were unrecognizable to those who remained loyal to the Campaign. To redress the balance, this chapter comments on events and issues, and the development of CND over the past two decades.*

The diversity of the trends in CND is best introduced by a part historical, part analytical survey of the peace and disarmament movement before CND's formation. These earlier campaigns are worth recalling because they brought different philosophies into CND. With hindsight it is clear that all made a positive contribution but, equally, all share some responsibility for the setbacks.

Forerunners, 1945–58

What happened in 1958 was not a sudden response to a clarion call, though it is understandable that those who had only just awakened saw it that way. There had been many years of peace campaigning prior to that year. Although this prepared the way, however, the leaderships of the earlier campaigns were unable to maintain coherent mass activity. One major contribution of the newly formed CND was that it drew together old and new campaigners behind the one clear slogan: 'Ban the Bomb!'

* It must be stressed that this is a *personal* commentary. As will become clear, the campaigns of the past three decades have involved several organizations and many philosophies working in parallel, often in harmony but occasionally in conflict. In particular, during the 1958–65 period the campaign *only* came together as a whole for the Easter marches. Even the most dedicated of campaigners missed many events and, naturally, each individual responded differently to the arguments of the day.

During much of this period the USA possessed a monopoly of atomic weapons and always had an overwhelming nuclear superiority. This meant that people in Britain were able to take a semi-detached view of the nuclear issue – we were not likely to suffer from a nuclear attack and were only indirectly involved in the possible use of nuclear arms. At the height of the Cold War, in 1948, Bertrand Russell and J. B. Priestley were amongst those who backed threats to use atomic weapons on the Soviet Union – an advocacy that both regretted later when they became leading personalities in CND.

When the atomic bombs were dropped on Hiroshima and

Extracts from *Keesing's Contemporary Archives*
for 22–29 July 1950

In Great Britain the 'peace campaign' was organized by a 'British Peace Committee' under the chairmanship of Dr J. G. Crowther, the scientist, and including among its members Dr Hewlett Johnson (the Dean of Canterbury), Mr D. N. Pritt, K. C., Prof. Hyman Levy, Prof. J. D. Bernal, Dame Sybil Thorndike, Prof. J. B. S. Haldane, Prof. V. Gordon Childe and Mr J. F. Platts-Mills. A mass meeting in support of the campaign held in Holborn Hall, London, on 22 July was addressed by Ilya Ehrenburg, the Soviet writer and propagandist. Sponsors of the campaign claimed over 750,000 signatures in Britain for the Stockholm Peace Appeal:

We demand unconditional prohibition of the atomic weapon as a weapon of aggression and mass annihilation of people, and that strict international control for the implementation of this decision be established. We shall consider as a war criminal that Government which first employs the atomic weapons against any country. We call upon all people of good will throughout the world to sign the appeal.

The National Council of Labour, uniting the British Labour Party, the TUC and the Cooperative Movement, issued a state-

Nagasaki, there was public concern but no public outcry. Few had the reaction of twenty-seven-year-old Olive Gibbs (CND Chairman, 1964–7), who had to be taken from a Services Ball when she heard the news. For most people it seemed that the atomic bombs had ended a very bloody war and saved lives. Moreover, it was not until around 1950 that knowledge of the effects of radiation and radioactive fallout became widespread.

The Cold War, 1945–55
This was a bad time for peace campaigners. Meetings were attacked and individuals intimidated. Anyone who spoke up

ment on 28 June denouncing the Communist peace campaign as a 'cynical fraud' and declaring that membership of the 'British Peace Committee' was incompatible with membership of the Labour Party. The statement ran as follows (excerpts):

Following a meeting of the World Peace Conference held in Stockholm last March, the British organization and its local satellites have been busy collecting signatures for a petition calling for 'the absolute banning of atomic weapons' and 'the establishment of strict international control to ensure implementation of this measure'. No amount of propaganda can, however, alter the fact that failure to secure international control of atomic weapons has been due solely to the intransigence of the Soviet leaders. The petition now being canvassed is nothing less than a fraudulent attempt to shift the responsibility from the door of Soviet Russia where it really belongs.

Genuine peace-lovers everywhere have a clear duty to oppose Communist advocates of Soviet Russia's dangerous imperialist policy and to expose the real purpose of the so-called 'peace campaign'. To this end the National Executive of the Labour Party has declared association with the British Peace Committee and its satellites to be incompatible with membership of the Party and these bodies have now been added to the list of proscribed organizations.

'Mum! Cyril's wrote a wicked word.'

(*Giles's comment on the Cold War hysteria, 1950*)

against the anti-Soviet hysteria risked being labelled a communist or 'fellow traveller'. Opinions became polarized as never before and many peace campaigners, by inclination or simply in defiance of the unscrupulous propaganda of the Cold War, did identify themselves with Soviet foreign policy.

Today this seems an incredible posture but our recent experience of the Soviet Union has been of a superpower. Hardly anyone today remembers, even by hearsay, that the Soviet Union was once a struggling workers' state which, in 1919, was invaded by the combined armies of sixteen capitalist states. Still fewer recall that this open but undeclared war of intervention was ended by the refusal of British dockworkers, and workers of other European countries, to supply the munitions destined, in the words of Churchill, 'to strangle Bolshevism at birth'. For many on the left, not only in the Communist Party, the propaganda of 1945–55, against a weak and war-ravaged Soviet Union, was feared to be a prelude to a second war of intervention.

Yet, despite this identification with the Soviet Union, the campaigns of the British Peace Committee (BPC) were not insignificant. Tens of thousands demonstrated against NATO's plans to rearm West Germany and the BPC collected over a million signatures to the Stockholm Peace Appeal (see box on previous page). The strength of support for the BPC and the fear of being labelled pro-communist were important factors influencing the formation of CND as a separate peace organization.

The churches

Pacifist and religious groups showed their concern before the long-term hazards of nuclear explosions were widely appreciated. In 1950 several peace and religious societies cooperated in a Hiroshima Day commemoration in Trafalgar Square, attended by about 3,000 and addressed by, amongst others, the Reverend Donald Soper. In the course of the next few years numerous small meetings were held all over Britain, particularly by the Quakers but also by other religious groups and societies.

These groups realized the special moral features of nuclear warfare long before anyone else. The impossibility of waging a successful nuclear war, except perhaps as the aggressor, was quickly appreciated, challenging the concept of a 'just war'. While the BPC feared the atomic bomb as a 'capitalist weapon' to be used against 'the people', voices were already being raised in the churches against its use by anyone for any purpose.

The effect of all this discussion was highlighted early in 1957 when, against the advice of the Archbishop of Canterbury, the British Council of Churches voted to oppose the projected British nuclear tests at Christmas Island. Thus the debate over the moral implications of nuclear weapons was in full swing well before CND was formed.

Events

A number of events prior to 1958 had an influence on the formation and character of CND.

The explosion of the Soviet atomic and H-bombs and the launching of the first Soviet sputnik (Autumn 1957) dramatized the fact that America no longer had a monopoly of nuclear weaponry. This meant that Britain also would be vulnerable in a nuclear war and the 1957 and 1958 Defence White Papers acknowledged that there is no means of providing adequate protection for the people of this country against the consequences of an attack with nuclear weapons.

The trauma of Suez heightened political awareness and also made people in Britain realize that they could not count on America to support Britain unconditionally. For the first time since 1945, vast numbers of people began to think seriously about Britain's future role in the world.

The denunciation by Khruschev of the crimes of the Stalin era combined with the Hungarian events to shatter illusions about the Soviet Union. Thousands left the Communist Party while those who stayed adopted more independent attitudes towards Soviet policies. This added to the favourable climate for the launching of a non-aligned peace movement.

The scientists

As described in the first chapter, the scientists who worked for the allied A-bomb project were by no means unthinking or unaware of the implications of their work. As knowledge became widespread, scientists in Britain began to voice their concern, as individuals and through a variety of organizations – Professor Bernal, Professor Burhop, Scientists for Peace and several others. Dr Kathleen Lonsdale, a Quaker and a nuclear physicist, and Dr Alex Comfort, a pacifist and a biologist, did much to publicize the *special* features of nuclear weapons which made them more than just big bangs.

In April 1950 one hundred Cambridge scientists petitioned the government, asking that Britain should give the lead in *not* making H-bombs. From this time on, a powerful 'Atoms for Peace' movement developed in the scientific community which, in the controversies that followed, consistently proved itself to be better informed about the effects of nuclear weapons than the government's own scientific advisers.

In 1955 the Russell–Einstein manifesto (see page 27) was

issued and stimulated international links between scientists opposed to nuclear weapons. By the time the first international Pugwash conference of scientists was held (1957), the lay public was very much aware of the dangers of fallout from nuclear weapons testing.

The Hydrogen Bomb National Campaign

This was formed in April 1954 and collected over a million signatures to a petition calling for a top-level disarmament conference and for the strengthening of the United Nations. Its wording was identical to that of a Labour opposition motion in Parliament and its terms were acceptable to the government.

This initiative was backed by several Labour MPs, including Anthony Wedgwood Benn, and a number of religious leaders, including Canon L. John Collins and the Reverend Donald Soper. When the petitioning was over the campaign faltered and was later reconstituted as the Labour Hydrogen Bomb Committee.

NCANWT

The National Committee for the Abolition of Nuclear Weapons Tests was formed in February 1957 with Dr Sheila Jones and Mrs Ianthe Carswell as joint secretaries. This was not formation from 'on high' but a coordination of numerous local groups which had come into existence during the previous two years, beginning with, in March 1955, the Golders Green Campaign against Nuclear Weapons Tests.

By the end of 1955 local groups were also active in Willesden, Finchley and Hampstead, the last being chaired by Arthur Goss, a leading member of the Middlesex Society of Friends (he was later to chair the NCANWT). During 1956 the scope of activities widened, with film shows (notably *Children of Hiroshima*), meetings, deputations, letter-writing campaigns and petitions. The Cold War strait-jacket was thus already loosened during 1955–7 by the growth of nationwide nonaligned campaigning only indirectly associated with the BPC.

During 1957 the NCANWT blossomed by holding demonstrations: in May 2,000 women with black sashes and flags marched from Hyde Park to Trafalgar Square. Financial support poured in and Mrs Peggy Duff (later to become Organizing Secretary for CND) was employed full-time. By the time CND was formed, the NCANWT had over a hundred active groups. These, overnight, became CND groups when the NCANWT voluntarily merged itself, its assets and its full-time workers into the new campaign. To many people active in the NCANWT at the time, the merger was more a change of name than a new campaign. Certainly the attendance at the 'initiating' meeting for CND at the Central Hall was dominated by supporters of the NCANWT.

DAC

The Emergency Committee for Direct Action against Nuclear War (the DAC) has received more posthumous publicity than the other campaigns, mainly because of its crucial role in organizing the first Aldermaston march. Its origins have been traced back to 1952 when, in separate events, eleven people sat down outside the War Office, thirty people demonstrated outside the Aldermaston AWRE and two demonstrators lay down outside the US base at Mildenhall. At that time these methods of demonstration did not appeal to more than a few committed pacifists, among them Michael Randle, later to become Chairman of the DAC and Secretary of the Committee of 100.

The DAC itself was formed in April 1957 to raise funds for two Quakers, Harold and Sheila Steele, who hoped to halt a projected British nuclear test at Christmas Island by sailing into the danger zone. In the event the test had taken place before Harold Steele reached Japan but, despite that, the campaign was a huge success. Worldwide publicity was achieved for this highly personal style of protest which, to the more dour and political BPC, seemed merely a flamboyant and hopeless gesture.

When Harold Steele returned in November 1957 from Japan, the DAC met to discuss further projects. The idea of a four-

Little Jack Horner sat in the corner
Destroying poor Christmas Isle,
He pressed down his thumb,
   and blew up his bomb,
And said: "What a good boy am I!"

*The British used Christmas Island as a base for nuclear 'experiments'
from 1956 till 1958*

day march to Aldermaston was raised and approaches were made to other organizations for support. The NCANWT already had a group of 'direct action' enthusiasts and from these Pat Arrowsmith arrived to become the march organizer. The Aldermaston march committee was created in December 1957 and also included Hugh Jenkins (CND Chairperson 1979–81), Frank Allaun MP (Chairman of the Labour Party in 1979) and Walter Wolfgang (at that time organizer of the Labour Hydrogen Bomb Committee).

On 28 January 1958, before the inaugural meeting in Central Hall, the CND Executive decided that it would 'give its blessing to the [DAC] plans [for Aldermaston] and should publicize them, but should make clear at this stage of the Campaign they could not be very closely involved'.

CND takes over

Enough has been said by now, I hope, to demolish one myth about CND – that it was created from apathy by a small group of far-seeing personalities – a myth which had more than a faint echo in 1980 in some media treatment of the so-called 'CND revival'. The creation of CND was, in essence, a fusion of many diverse strands which had not previously succeeded in working together in a coherent campaign.

Not that the fusion occurred overnight. There were many problems. Although the NCANWT transferred all its assets and groups to CND, there was some astonishment at the refusal of the CND personalities to include prominent members of the NCANWT on the new executive (contrary to a prior understanding). Sheila Jones found herself out of tune with the new executive and left to work with the DAC. Only Arthur Goss from the NCANWT stayed with the CND.

As for the DAC, their members were held at arms' length by the device of a 'coordinating committee' which the CND executive consulted but which had no authority. The BPC, by virtue of its pro-communist reputation, was not even consulted through the coordinating committee, though some private meetings did take place.

Yet, to put this in perspective, hardly one in a hundred who welcomed CND knew of these cross-currents or, if they did know, cared. What mattered most was that the new leaders of the peace and disarmament campaign brought to it one vital ingredient that all the others lacked   charisma. For the next four to five years, CND was to dominate the media to an extent that no other protest movement has ever achieved.

The heyday, 1958–62

No-one who lived through these years can forget the sheer joy that CND brought to peace campaigning. The intimidation of the few during the Cold War gave way, within months, to the exhilaration of belonging to a *popular* movement. The songs, dances, plays and jokes of the next few years reflected

CND Executive, 1958

President: Bertrand Russell; *Vice-President:* J. B. Priestley

Chairman: Canon L. John Collins; *Vice-Chairman:* Ritchie Calder

Executive members: James Cameron, Howard Davies, Michael Foot, Arthur Goss, Kingsley Martin, J. B. Priestley, Professor J. Rotblat (resigned 1958), Mrs Sheila Jones (resigned 1958)

Coopted in 1958: Sir Richard Acland, Frank Beswick MP, Jacquetta Hawkes, Benn Levy, Lord Simon of Wythenshawe (resigned 1958), A. J. P. Taylor

Treasurer: Lord Wilmot (resigned 1958), replaced by Ted Bedford

Organizing Secretary: Peggy Duff

this exuberance and became a vital ingredient of the spirit of Britain at that time. A complete history of the CND would dwell at length on these aspects – the Campaign's image, the cultural upsurge and the interplay between the popular movement and its leading personalities. In being selective, many exciting events will have to be ignored altogether.

One general conclusion needs to be admitted at the outset: whatever else was achieved during the heyday of CND, a shift in public opinion towards unilateralism was not one of them. All the public opinion polls showed that the support for unilateral nuclear disarmament remained below 30 per cent throughout these years of intense and widespread campaigning. In retrospect, it is clear that CND was far more successful in bringing out the already converted than it was in the act of conversion.

What the Campaign did do in its heyday was make the public and the politicians much more aware of the consequences of a nuclear war. Before 1958, politicians were denying the danger of radioactive fallout. However, by 1962 politicians and most of the public thoroughly understood the scientific implications of nuclear weapons – even though, to be realistic, they never gave any serious thought to British nuclear disarmament. The more obvious changes to government attitudes between 1958 and 1962 were:

1. a genuine commitment to halt atmospheric nuclear tests;
2. acceptance that Civil Defence was a waste of money;
3. realization that war might start by accident;
4. a much greater fear of nuclear proliferation.

Every one of these points was contested by the Macmillan government when first raised by CND, so the organization may fairly take some credit for the changes. However, all were incidental to the core of the CND policy – the renunciation of British nuclear weapons. Success on these peripheral aspects may have made people at a later stage less concerned about this central issue.

Unilateralism

Unilateralism was the most significant new factor CND brought into the peace movement. It gave the Campaign a dynamic appeal to youth and students, but at first made little impact on the Labour movement and the existing peace organizations, which remained multilateralist for several years. Their reluctance to accept unilateralism was important because the United Nations Association (UNA) has always had a greater 'membership' (however measured) and, until mid 1960, the BPC had greater influence at trade union and Labour Party conferences. This situation was transformed by the breakdown of the Paris 'summit conference' on 16 May 1960.

The conference was billed to usher in a new era in international relations. For the first time since 1945 the leaders of the great powers had agreed to come together to argue through their differences. For the peace movement this was the culmination of years of campaigning for multilateral international negotiations. The Stockholm Peace Appeal (1950), the H-Bomb National Campaign (1954) and, it will be recalled, the inaugural policy statement of CND (1958) all called for an all-embracing disarmament conference to settle issues of international dispute. At last, in May 1960 in Paris, it seemed that these efforts would be rewarded.

The summit conference, however, never took place. During the preparations, in violation of a personal pledge from President Eisenhower the USA continued flying over the Soviet Union with their U-2 spy planes (page 137). The reaction of Khrushchev was emotional and the Soviet delegation refused to sit down at the conference.*

For the peace movement, the summit débacle was a real trauma. The efforts of a decade had failed and the collapse brought about heightened international tension. The multilateralists were demoralized. In the aftermath, CND's demand for a British initiative took on much greater appeal and relevance.

Scarborough

The collapse of the Paris summit was not the only significant event of that year. In April the government cancelled 'Blue Streak' – a missile that was supposed to carry the British independent nuclear 'deterrent' of the mid 1960s. It became clear that a truly independent British nuclear force was *no longer practical*. Hence, when the October Labour Party conference met in Scarborough, previous government policies were thoroughly discredited and the conference opposed further attempts by Britain to make her own 'independent' nuclear deterrent. The only astonishment at Scarborough was the vehemence of the rearguard action from the Labour leader, Hugh Gaitskell, who made support of nuclear weapons an

---

* Many theories have been advanced to explain what happened. It could well be that Eisenhower was genuinely unaware of the U-2 flights and believed that the conference was sabotaged from within his own administration. This would explain the intensity of his warning about the influence of the military–industrial complex when he stepped down as President seven months later (see page 152).

issue of confidence in his leadership. His anti-CND speech polarized the dispute and ensured that unilateral nuclear disarmament became the key demand of the peace movement in the years that followed.

After Scarborough, CND continued to grow as a popular movement. The Easter 1961 demonstration was the biggest ever and, following the resumption of nuclear tests by the USA and USSR, even the Beaverbrook press gave sympathetic coverage to marches on the two embassies. The Committee of 100 (p. 206) grew in strength and, despite the antagonism between the leadership of the two campaigns, the short-term effect, at least, was helpful to CND.

The 1961 Labour Party conference, however, overturned the Scarborough decision. A well-oiled backlash campaign, masterminded by William Rodgers, had little difficulty in defeating unilateralism. But neither then nor on any occasion since did they succeed in reversing the Labour Party (and TUC) opposition to the Polaris bases. What happened was that Labour's traditional desire for unity won the day for Gaitskell on the *principle* of not accepting unilateral nuclear disarmament, even though Labour remained opposed in practice to the *possession* of nuclear weapons.

The media naturally hailed the decision as a defeat for CND, hardly mentioning the Polaris decision. The Campaign's leadership agreed with the media's interpretation, essentially because they had argued for unilateral nuclear disarmament as a *moral issue* which had to be won as a *principle*. Instead of working to consolidate their victory on the Polaris bases (which would have meant a lot of detailed argument about dangers, costs, practicality, alternative employment, etc.), the CND leaders accepted the decisions of the 1961 conference as a shattering blow to all their hopes. They had pinned their faith on a *moral* lead from the Labour Party, and the Labour Party had failed them.

Predictably, many of the rank and file also interpreted the 1961 Labour Party conference as a defeat without hope of recovery. Some joined other political parties, some turned their back on politics, some stopped campaigning altogether; but a minority actually joined the Labour Party that year, in order to win it over to unilateralism.

'Voters' Veto' and INDEC

While the CND leadership, and many ordinary members, were working through 1958–61 to win over the Labour Party, others had already dismissed this strategy. In 1958 and 1959 the DAC was recommending campaigners not to vote for any parliamentary candidate who supported nuclear weapons:

> The DAC is not primarily interested in the return of any particular party at the next election. Is it better to have a slightly more moderate Government with a Right-wing Opposition, or a Conservative Government with dynamic and radical elements in the Opposition who are supported by an active campaign in the country?

The 'Voters' Veto' campaign was not popular with CND and generated a lot of internal heat. Then, at the time of the defeat of unilateralism at the 1961 Labour conference, the idea of CND fielding candidates at parliamentary by-elections was raised by Peggy Duff and supported by the (then) New Left (Stuart Hall, E. P. Thompson, etc.). This idea, too, proved unpopular with most CND supporters and the proposal, in the form suggested by Peggy Duff, was dropped.

Later that year a new organization was formed, the Independent Nuclear Disarmament Election Committee (INDEC), with the aim of contesting by-elections *and* general elections. Its results were predictably disastrous and there has never been much regret in CND at INDEC's passing. The immediate consequence was to create bitterness amongst members of the Campaign, primarily between the Labour supporters and opponents but also involving others.

CNDs attitude to elections and candidates became the main dispute at its 1962 Annual Conference and the policy decided then has remained in force since. The successful resolution, moved by Michael Foot, stated: 'In order to retain the character of a pressure group influencing all political parties, the campaign shall not support any one candidate.'

The Committee of 100

The DAC was essentially a small pacifist group which used civil disobedience as a tactic, along with a lot of lively ideas that forced people to think. By contrast, the Committee of 100 contained people of many persuasions and employed civil disobedience as an integral part of all its major activities. While virtually all members of the DAC became active in the Committee of 100, the support for the latter was many times greater than the former ever achieved. Soon after the Committee was formed, the DAC was closed.

The Committee of 100 was established in 1960 to oppose the 'ever-growing menace of nuclear war', using the technique of 'non-violent civil disobedience'. As is well known, the new organization was supported by the President of CND, Bertrand Russell, and opposed by Canon Collins and the majority of the CND Executive. The highly personal dispute between CND and the Committee of 100 that ensued caused a great deal of bitterness among those directly participating, though remarkably little among ordinary campaigners. The heyday of the Committee of 100 lasted for only two years, although it did continue at least in name until 1968.

The 'premature obituaries' of CND all deal in great detail with these disputes and invariably have concentrated on the personalities and ignored the issues. Civil disobedience has been an important campaign activity and newcomers to CND often want to know what its present attitude is to this tactic.

Civil disobedience can be conducted at a variety of levels. At its simplest, it can obtain publicity when a conventional protest would be ignored. The sit-down of eleven people outside the War Office on 11 January 1952 was an example. Only a minor by-law was broken, no inconvenience was caused to onlookers and the threat of fines or imprisonment was almost negligible. Nevertheless, actions of this type, even by eleven people, are far more likely to attract public attention than conventional demonstrations of eleven hundred or even eleven thousand.

It is unlikely that anyone in CND really has any objection to this sort of publicity-seeking disobedience, especially given the normal lack of media coverage for a serious topic such as nuclear disarmament. Similarly, the proposed action of Harold and Sheila Steele in 1957, to sail into the danger area of a British nuclear test, won them personally, and also the cause, worldwide sympathy. Virtually all civil disobedience conducted by the DAC was publicity-seeking.

Civil disobedience changes in character when very large numbers participate, for its effects may be obstructive. Examples

Humpty Bombty sat on a wall,
Humpty Bombty had a great fall,
None of the women, nor children nor men
Could ever be healthy and happy again.

The cartoon on this page and those on pp. 131, 169 and 199 are taken from Nursery Rhymes for a Nuclear Age *by Chris Plant and Jim Hayes, published by the ATOM Committee (Against Testing On Mururoa atoll), Suva, Fiji*

of this are numerous and by no means confined to nuclear disarmament campaigners – hunt saboteurs, motorway protesters and opponents of whaling are well known. The moral justification for employing illegal actions for nuclear disarmament was explained by Michael Randle at the trial of the leaders of the Committee of 100 in July 1962:

Randle: I believe it is important to abide by majority decisions. Except in very exceptional circumstances ... every individual must finally decide whether millions of lives are threatened by a particular act, and in that situation I think they have the right to make that decision ... There were people in Germany during the Nazi regime who were ordered to commit what have since been defined as crimes against humanity. They would have been going against the law of their country by disobeying their orders. I feel that they had a moral duty to disobey that order in that situation.

Judge: As far as I can see it means this, doesn't it, if you disagree with the law you break it?

Randle: Not in general, only in particular situations. It does not mean that every time I disagree with the law I break it. It only means in particular situations where I disagree with it, and where it is flouting human rights, I will certainly disobey it, and I feel it would be a moral obligation to disobey ... I feel that the use of nuclear weapons is always contrary to basic human rights. I cannot see any situation in which they would be justified against human beings.

'But I've been sitting down here for thirty years!'

Michael Randle is quoted at length because, in this passage for sure, he spoke for virtually everyone in CND as well as the Committee of 100. The dispute about the use of civil disobedience was not, for the rank and file campaigners, about the principle but about its effectiveness.

While the first sit-downs attracted sympathetic publicity for nuclear disarmament, subsequent acts of civil disobedience were less effective and, eventually, counter-productive. This failure was not a consequence of civil disobedience as such – it was caused by its *unwise* application. By the end of 1961 one of the leading members of the Committee wrote:

We have become a public spectacle, a group isolated from the general body of public opinion and feeling, a rowdy show to be televised and reported in the press for the interest and amusement of a majority who are not with us.

The basic mistake of the Committee of 100 was to over-estimate the popularity of their cause. Unilateral nuclear disarmament did not have majority public support and the Committee's activities merely emphasized this fact. Whereas imaginative publicity-seeking acts of civil disobedience won admiration and sympathy for the cause, the preoccupation of the Committee of 100 with the methods, rather than the message, of the campaign lost it and CND public support.

The attitude of CND towards civil disobedience has not been tested in practice recently but nowadays few members would object to imaginative non-violent acts of civil disobedience to attract publicity. With regard to obstructive action, each case has to be considered on its merits. However, to illustrate the factors to be considered, here are two not so hypothetical situations where most people in CND would support civil disobedience. The first case would be justified on the grounds of *democracy*, the second on the grounds of *emergency*:

1. Public opinion polls already (1980) show a *majority* opposed to the installation of US cruise missiles in Britain. Suppose

the government, without submitting the issue to a genuine public debate, proceeds with the planned installation. In this situation, many people in CND would join a non-violent blockade of Greenham Common and Molesworth to prevent cruise missiles entering the bases;

2. Suppose the cruise missiles are in the bases and an international crisis develops. It is known that the dispersal of the missiles would be a prelude to a nuclear war and could cause a Soviet attack. In this *emergency* situation a non-violent blockade might take place to prevent the missiles leaving the bases.

Internal changes

At first these controversies took place without a proper forum in CND for debate. The Executive took the view that they had created the Campaign and those who agreed with them should join while those who didn't could do something else. The first Annual Conference of CND was not held until March 1959 and the first fully elected Executive had to wait until 1961. During the first few years, policy shifts were made by the Executive in response to representations of CND groups, the DAC and the pressure of events.

The earliest policy change has already been mentioned – the shift of emphasis to full-blooded unilateralism in response to the feeling at the Central Hall meeting. Later, it emerged that several of the original Executive interpreted this as still allowing US nuclear bases on British territory while most, at first, wanted Britain to stay in NATO. Both these issues were resolved at the first Annual Conference in 1959, and CND has ever since been committed to the closure of *all* nuclear bases on British soil and opposed to any military alliance which is prepared to use nuclear weapons. These policy changes were not to the liking of some of the original Campaign leaders and, quietly or noisily according to temperament, they began to leave.

One other change in the structure of CND occurred in the early years – the formation of specialist groups. These were established for Scientists, Christians, Architects, Labour sup-

---

CND Executive, 1962

Chairman: Canon L. John Collins; *Vice-Chairman*: Professor Richie Calder CBE

Executive members: James Cameron, Michael Foot MP, Arthur Goss, Kingsley Martin, Jacquetta Hawkes, John Cox, Olive Gibbs, Judith Hart MP, Michael Hemmings, John Horner, Michael Mitchel Howard, J. R. Lawther, Dr Antoinette Pirie, R. Robinson, S. Silverman MP

Treasurer: Laurie Kershaw

Organizing Secretary: Peggy Duff

---

porters, Women, Youth, Students and one or two others. From 1960 onwards some of these groups were allowed representation on CND's National Council (a rather large committee that met every three months from 1961 and elected the Executive). In 1981 these were Labour, Trade Unions, Christians, Liberals, Youth and Students. Each of these organizes its events within the chosen 'constituency' and produces its own leaflets and pamphlets.

The Cuba missile crisis

Some obituaries date the decline of CND from 1960, with the formation of the Committee of 100. Others date it from 1961, with the defeat of the Scarborough unilateralist policy at the subsequent Labour Party conference. Most activists date the decline from the time that demonstrations started to become smaller. Without a doubt, the Cuba missile crisis was the watershed.

This occurred in October 1962, when President Kennedy demanded the removal from Cuba of newly installed Soviet missiles. After a week-long drama, when it seemed at times that a nuclear war was inevitable, Khrushchev agreed – to the relief of all.

As the world collected its thoughts, certain conclusions emerged. The superpowers knew it had been a close call and began to take steps to avoid such situations arising again. Various confidence-building measures (e.g. the Hotline Agreement) were agreed. Negotiations for the Partial Test Ban Treaty became much more serious. To the peace movement it seemed that the crisis had shocked governments into an appreciation of the dangers.

Other factors were involved as well, amongst them – dare it be mentioned – sheer physical and mental exhaustion after four years of intense campaigning. It is easy to see now that the next two years could have been the most important of all for intensive effort, but morale was beginning to sag and in 1963 and 1964 the last of the original leadership left. By 1964 the real Vietnam war had begun to claim more attention than the still hypothetical nuclear war CND was seeking to avoid. The decline accelerated as the Labour Party took office and failed to keep its pledge to scrap Polaris.

A tribute

CND's achievements in this period were assessed with appreciation by Michael Foot, two years after his departure from the Executive:

It may be instructive to consider for a moment what would have happened over these past six or seven years or what would be the situation now if there had been no Campaign for Nuclear Disarmament, no CND, in existence at all.

Aldermaston would denote nothing much more than a disfigured Berkshire village. The road via Reading, Maidenhead and Slough to Turnham Green would not be stamped on the minds of some thirty or forty thousand citizens of this country with its full indelible ugliness. The decadence of modern youth could not be attributed to its distaste for committing mass murder or, rather, its insistence on stressing the point so shamelessly to its elders. The Defence White Papers of 1957 and 1958 might still be considered masterly essays in strategic doctrine. Massive retaliation might still be regarded as a respectable idea. That, in case you've forgotten, is what we pledged ourselves to do to the Russians in certain circumstances and it would be wrong to make any accusation of betrayal; the pledge has never been withdrawn.

But to continue. Without CND, would the Labour Party have atrophied? Scarborough would have remained just another seaside resort. Life for Labour leaders would have been almost cushy ... The awkward, hypothetical questions are endless.

Yet even without the answers it is possible to make one modest, indisputable assertion. Without CND, the worldwide debate about the most perilous invention in history would have been less noisy, less extensive, less widespread across so many frontiers. It might, so opponents could argue, have been more clear-headed, more well-conceived, less acrimonious, less hysterical. Even if these unwarrantable claims are conceded the other test remains. Is this a debate in which everyone should join or is it one to be left to the experts, the scientists who know, the military advisers, the very few? The differing responses to that question go to the root of our democracy and our political system. This was appreciated by many who joined CND and was another reason for its appeal.

It may be that the statesmen would have worked to secure a test ban treaty with no less earnestness if there had been none of the pressure which CND helped to exert. It may be that for the six years prior to the signing of the treaty all the signatories who subsequently rejoiced at the banishment of the radiation and other horrors involved in testing were as secretly alarmed as CNDers and were merely suppressing or distorting the facts out of an excessive and misplaced consideration for the tender feelings of the public.

But again one simple assertion cannot be contested. The anti-CNDers, however sweeping or brash their protests, cannot deny that CND forcefully introduced into the debate an element which almost everybody else wanted to keep out. Others thought the argument was principally about politics or strategy. CND insisted that, whatever else the question also was, it was a *moral* one. And who will dare say that this emphasis is wrong? How debasing and dishonourable to the human species it would have been if the question of massive extermination on a scale far exceeding anything known even in Hitler's death camps had been permitted to continue being discussed without the issue of moral responsibility arising. But that is what so many people wanted and still want. CND was never guilty on that charge.

And this brings us to the most explosive point involved, CND's distinctive contribution, the demand for unilateral action by Britain. As it happened, at the first meeting when the organization was formed in February 1958, it was by no means certain that this clause would be included in CND's programme. Some of those present at the meeting argued that the case for general nuclear disarmament should be presented in more widely-embracing terms. No doubt a few worth-while public meetings could have been conducted in this style. The Archbishop of Canterbury would doubtless have bestowed his bless-ing from the outset and might even have marched from Aldermaston in such a respectable cause – if there had been any marches. No one can deny the plain fact. CND developed differently from the cam-paigns that had gone before, provoked furious enthusiasms and emnities, and made a spectacular appeal particularly to the young, precisely be-cause it did not take refuge in vague generalities, precisely because it did urge that something could be done, precisely because it did pin responsibility on our country, on us.

This is not the place to press the case. Whatever the verdict CND has already one achievement to its credit of which many of us are extremely proud. It made our country the most active and vocal in the world in attempting to arouse mankind to an awareness of the nuclear horror. Without CND, the complacency of those in power would have been even more perilous and contemptible than it was. But, of course, this is only a first, minor victory. The armour-plated smugness of our rulers is only dented. At the moment of writing the most widely accepted bromide of our statesmen (disseminated by the same people who pretend to favour general disarmament and still put forward plans allegedly designed to serve this end at Geneva) is that the balance of terror keeps the peace and can always be relied on to do so. Nuclear weapons, it seems, have conferred on suffering humanity the matchless boon of perpetual peace. No one advances this insanity with greater as-surance than [the Prime Minister]. Which is just another reason why if there was no CND in existence now, it would be necessary to invent it.

(Michael Foot, August 1964)

Decline, 1962–72

Many reasons have been advanced to explain the decline. Some are obvious:

1. After the Cuban missile crisis, and with the signing of the

Hotline agreement, it seemed that the superpowers now appreciated the danger of nuclear war and, at long last, were beginning to take steps to minimize the risks;

2. With the agreement to ban atmospheric nuclear tests (the PTBT), the immediate risks from radioactive pollution of the atmosphere were all but eliminated;

3. The non-proliferation treaty (NPT) appeared likely to restrict the numbers of countries that would acquire nuclear weapons;

4. The Vietnam war diverted the attention of peace campaigners away from nuclear weapons.

Events in Britain also conspired to make campaigning seem less worthwhile. The Nassau agreement, signed by a Conservative government in 1962 and implemented by the 1964 Labour government (despite its election pledge), meant that Britain now had a new system for nuclear weapons (Polaris) with an expected lifetime of around twenty years.

Furthermore, and partly arising from the above events, morale faltered. After over four years intense effort with no apparent success in Britain despite some easing of international tension, many campaigners were physically and emotionally exhausted. Moreover, as morale sagged the infighting amongst the leaders of the campaign became more disturbing and, by the end of 1964, all the original charismatic personalities had left. As the decline continued, media coverage became derisory and weakened morale even more.

In addition, campaigners found other outlets for their energies. Some joined political parties (there was, for example, an influx into the Young Liberals from Youth CND). Others turned their backs on party politics and became involved in environmental issues and community or cultural activities. By 1970, ex-CND activists were dotted all over the British political and apolitical landscape, bringing up families, starting communes, projects or careers.

These 'defections' were *not* caused by disenchantment with the aims of CND. People did not change their opinions about nuclear weapons or the need for Britain to get rid of them. What changed was their faith in CND as the means to achieve these aims or in the power of ordinary people to influence governments.

A recent survey (1977–8) of CND supporters suggested sixteen possible reasons why 'the Disarmament Movement failed in its major objectives beween 1958 and 1965'. Not one of the suggested 'internal explanations' won favour (e.g. too political, not moral enough, too pro-Labour, not pro-Labour enough, bad leadership, etc.). The simplest explanations proved to be the most popular:*

1. CND's campaign declined naturally, as a result of changes in circumstances *external* to the movement (82–95 per cent);
2. it failed to win the support of ordinary people (69 per cent);
3. gradually 'we have learned to live with The Bomb' (65–68 per cent);
4. the single issue of unilateral nuclear disarmament could not for long unite so many conflicting groups (62–63 per cent).

Vietnam

CND always opposed the US intervention in Vietnam. What was in dispute, and remained a problem for as long as the war lasted, was the amount of attention CND should give to the anti-war campaign. Ever since 1958, the broad appeal of the Campaign had been threatened each time it took up an additional issue or cause. This was not so noticeable when CND was growing but soon became obvious when the growth slowed.

Step by step CND had broadened its policies and narrowed its appeal, but it was not until July 1963, when it organized demonstrations against a visit of the Greek royal family, that this became evident. The Greek connection with unilateral nuclear disarmament was far from clear to supporters of CND, let alone the public.

From then on CND became more cautious about taking up

---

* From *The Protest Makers* by R. Taylor and C. Pritchard, Pergamon Press, 1980.

But, by 1962, CND was already beginning to wane. With the Test Ban Treaty, the following year, the thaw in the Cold War was already melting imperceptibly into the beginnings of 'Detente'. By the mid sixties, when I went on to university, CND and its concerns had ceased to impinge greatly upon the average radical student conscience. Mine was no exception. Our eyes turned away from the tensions between the great power blocks towards national struggles against imperialism, especially, of course, the war in Vietnam. And then, with the events of 1968, we were preoccupied with the *promise* of socialism much closer to home. In the early seventies, I wrote for far left papers ... within that milieu, we regarded CND with faint contempt, as something passé and irrelevant, a bit like a cross between the Fabians and the League Against Cruel Sports. We were concerned with the *real* issues.

All that was a long time ago. Times change, and so do one's values. Like most of those who lived through those days, I have been questioning our ideologies and trying to glimpse 'beyond the fragments' ... Today, I am convinced that the nuclear arms race issue is that upon which all other issues (and much else besides) depend. Nuclear arms menace not just the *nature* of the material conditions of our lives, but the continued existence of those conditions themselves.

(Peter Fuller, writing in *Time Out*, November 1980)

issues not directly relevant to nuclear weapons. The Vietnam war was 'conventional' so, it was argued, it did not concern the Campaign. In the first years of the US intervention, those who wanted CND to take a stand had to show that the fighting might escalate into a nuclear war!

This 'legalistic' argument masked serious divisions within CND about the nature of the war. Many on the left quickly identified themselves with the political and armed struggle of the Vietnamese. While they wanted a 'solidarity' campaign for the Vietnamese, most members were not prepared to go further than calling for an end to the US intervention. Although CND did campaign against the Vietnam war from 1965, and held quite large demonstrations on the issue during 1966 and 1967 (see Plate XXI), by 1968 a new organization – the Vietnam Solidarity Campaign (VSC) – had displaced CND in terms of mass support.

The VSC had the support of most of the left political groups, remnants of the BPC and several erstwhile CND leaders (amongst them Peggy Duff, who resigned as General Secretary in 1967 to be succeeded by Dick Nettleton). The politics of the VSC were too far left and its campaigning style too militant for most members of CND to endorse and the VSC leadership, in return, dismissed CND as 'passé and irrelevant'.

At the other extreme there *were* pacifists in CND opposed in principle to the use of armed struggle (though often sympathetic to the Vietnamese resistance) and others politically opposed to any measure which might aid the Vietnamese communists. They were not as clear as the VSC about what they wanted CND to do but often argued for solidarity with a Buddhist or pacifist third force in Vietnam.

Spanning both extremes, most members of CND were forthright in their opposition to the US intervention but did not want the Campaign to pass opinions on the internal politics of Vietnam. The policy they most favoured was British dissociation from US policy in Vietnam and support for the right of the Vietnamese people to settle their own affairs, free from foreign interference. From about 1967 this attitude found a secure home in yet another organization, eventually named the British Campaign for Peace in Vietnam (BCPV). As the VSC declined – for reasons that do not concern us here – the BCPV became the main, and eventually the only, campaigning organization specifically concerned with Vietnam.

The links between CND and the BCPV were very close. In terms of personnel they shared the Treasurer (Alistair MacDonald MP), with Dick Nettleton, Malcolm Caldwell and John Cox officers of both. The BCPV lodged in the CND office, virtually rent-free, sharing all facilities. This arrangement enabled CND to maintain its identity as a campaign concerned mainly with nuclear weapons while, simultaneously, providing substantial backing for the Vietnam campaign, which, to be frank, many of its supporters considered more important during 1966–72.

This relationship with the BCPV set a pattern for a more cooperative style of working with other organizations (previously CND had been somewhat autocratic). It also showed how to handle the problem of side issues – by working with other organizations when campaign objectives overlapped, rather than attempting to broaden CND's goals.

The Peace Convention

In 1970 CND formally ushered in the new era of cooperation, when it called together about forty peace, religious, political and trade union organizations to discuss, on an equal basis, policies and joint activities. This was the first of several similar conferences in the 1970s, which led to the creation of the World Disarmament Campaign (WDC) in 1980.

In its diminished role, CND listened more to the opinions of others and adapted its campaign tactics accordingly. Gradually contact was re-established with former CND activists, who were now busy in a variety of other organizations and working for many other causes. In the course of the next decade, a new framework for joint campaigning on nuclear disarmament began to take shape. One early example was a new approach to the trade unions.

Of workers and trade unions

In spite of the block votes cast at Labour Party and TUC conferences for nuclear disarmament, CND at first made less impression on manual workers than on professional people. As part of the general questioning of the reasons for CND's decline, its lack of success on the shop floor came under scrutiny.

It began to be appreciated that worries about job security were not swept away by trite slogans and high morality. The slogan 'One Polaris = Ten Hospitals' was no comfort to a shipyard worker employed on Polaris construction. Instead of shouting slogans at factory workers, CND began to listen to the opinions of trade unionists and respond to these fears.

The process was slow and was continued thoughout the 1970s by the Labour and trade union CND specialist groups. But as early as 1970 the annual Easter march left Crawley headed by the Trades Council banner (Plate XXII) and followed by the banners of more than half the trade union branches of the town.

Greece and Czechoslovakia

There was, however, one hiccup at the end of the 1960s. As mentioned earlier, CND had developed a keen interest in Greek politics and naturally viewed the Greek colonels' regime with great distaste. Equally, there was widespread opposition to the Soviet intervention in Czechoslovakia. It seemed a good idea in 1970 to call a demonstration against the NATO and Warsaw Pact military alliances by focussing attention on what had happened to these two countries.

The demonstration was a political fiasco and a financial disaster. The easy equation of Greece and Czechoslovakia, which was applauded enthusiastically by sympathetic audiences, did not withstand serious political scrutiny and the role of the alliances was disputed by the invited speakers from the two countries. The débâcle confirmed a growing conviction that CND should campaign primarily on the weapons issue and, moreover, concentrate on the country it knew best – Britain.

The 1970 perspective

By the turn of the 1970s, CND had less than thirty active groups, no effective regional organizations, a full-time staff of only four and debts exceeding its expected annual income.* Yet, to see matters in perspective, this still left the nuclear disarmament campaign incomparably stronger than at the time of the formation of the NCANWT. The level of activity throughout the 1960s had been higher than during the previous decade.

* By then the DAC, Committee of 100, the BPC and the VSC had ceased to exist or had no measurable support.

The real problem now was psychological. The thousands who had demonstrated for CND felt cheated. If the biggest protest movement of the century could not change government policy, what could? It was no comfort to be told that CND 'peaked' too soon, that is, two years before the first change of government since the campaign began, this being the first occasion on which a change of government policy *might* have been effected.

By the end of the decade, the wearing of the Campaign badge would be greeted by 'CND? I thought that died long ago', and it didn't help newcomers much to be told that a demonstration of several thousands was 'not like the good old days'. (In 1974, when all the full-time staff of CND were new and under twenty-five, they could shrug off the old-timers with 'Tell me about Aldermaston then, grandaddy.')

Growth, 1972–

Some time in the early 1970s the decline was halted. There are three reasons for dating the turning point in 1972:

1. The SALT-1 treaty exposed the myth that détente was automatically leading to disarmament. From then on, CND's warnings about the continued arms race were heard with greater attention;
2. The Labour Party, for the first time since the 1960 Scarborough conference, agreed on a show of hands on the *principle* of unilateral nuclear disarmament (see page 225 for text);
3. Scotland became the first CND region to reform itself and thereafter, throughout the 1970s, showed that CND could achieve wide support once again (see Plate XXIII).

The growth that followed was uneven. London and Yorkshire had effective regions by 1976; East Anglia, Oxfordshire and the West Midlands not until 1980. But the trend has been steadily upwards throughout the decade. Four aspects of the growth are worth some scrutiny: the ecology, Labour and peace movements and, last but not least, the influence of external events.

The ecology movement

The present generation of children learns at junior school that we live in a finely balanced environment which can be easily upset by a vast number of industrial activities. By contrast, when the NCANWT in 1957 warned of the risks of atmospheric strontium-90, they had to explain the air–soil–grass–cows–milk food chain to disbelieving politicians who were at that time quite ignorant of such issues.

In one sense, the present-day ecological movement, especially the opposition to nuclear power plants, is a by-product of the campaign against nuclear weapons tests. In the late 1960s, Dr Sternglass (a US scientist) claimed evidence for the deaths of 400,000 children from nuclear test explosions fallout. Two US Atomic Energy Commission (AEC) critics (Drs Gofman and Tamplin) showed that Dr Sternglass was wrong by a factor of one hundred, but they realized that their figure of 4,000 dead children was not negligible either. Their criticisms of the AEC radioactive levels started the debate about the safety of nuclear power stations *as such*. (Previous opposition to nuclear power stations had centred on their role in supplying plutonium for nuclear weapons.)

While nuclear tests were polluting the atmosphere, no-one had given much thought to low-level radiation hazards. Gofman and Tamplin transformed this situation. Since 1970 there has been world-wide opposition to nuclear plants because of the risks from radioactive emissions and industrial accidents. In Britain this movement now involves a wide variety of antinuclear groups and the Friends of the Earth, many of these being opposed to *any* activity involving radioactive substances.

CND members are divided in their attitudes towards nuclear technology. Most of the scientist members still believe there are genuine 'peaceful' uses for radioactive substances, notably in sterilization and other medicinal applications. Despite some differences of emphasis there is, however, a broad consensus

---

CND Executive, 1971

Chair: Dr John Cox; *Vice-Chair:* Mrs Olive Gibbs, Dr Malcolm Caldwell, Tony McCarthy

Executive members: Stan Banks, Lucy Behenna, Howell Bithel, Roger Dudman, Sonja Kvalheim, John Minnion, Janice Ogg, Will Parkin, Ernie Roberts, Barbara Sheehy, Nigel Young, Walter Wolfgang

Treasurer: Alistair McDonald

General Secretary: Dick Nettleton

---

opposed to the construction of more nuclear power plants in Britain and to the export of nuclear technology, especially while the nuclear arms race continues unabated and the future of the NPT is in doubt.

Thus, throughout the 1970s, there has been a considerable overlap between the policies and supporters of CND and the various organizations of the ecology movement. This has provided plenty of opportunities for joint activities though, at a national level at any rate, it has proved better for each to preserve its separate identity. CND continues to concentrate on the weapons issue, with the support of those of its members who believe in peaceful uses for nuclear energy.

The Labour movement

Contrary to the impression often suggested in the media, CND is far from being a left-wing pressure group inside the Labour Party. At times its direct influence has been almost non-existent. By 1970 its parliamentary and trade union committees had folded and Labour CND was merely a rump. The transformation of this situation was one of the first successes of the early 1970s.

As a crude measure of the problem, the sponsors' list of 1958 included over a hundred eminent artists, scientists, reverends and politicians and only two trade unionists. This omission was not rectified until 1972 when Jack Jones, Hugh Scanlon, Alan Fisher and about ten others joined the list. (By 1980 the sponsors' list included nine members of the General Council of the TUC, including its Chairman.)

One problem was that until 1970 CND had no constitutional mechanism for establishing formal relationships with other organizations. At the end of 1980, over 300 trade union branches and regions, constituency Labour parties and other bodies were affiliated to CND. These formal associations provide the Campaign's Labour and trade union committees with a sound framework to plan activities.

The nature of the activities also has changed. In the past, meetings were held simply to whip up support for CND's proposals. Since about 1975, when David Griffiths took over the main responsibility for Labour CND, the conferences and activities have been broader in scope and so have acted also as listening posts. One consequence of the new line was CND's early initiatives on redirecting resources from military projects into socially useful production, now a widely accepted approach.

CND has not formally re-established a parliamentary group but now enjoys close relations with sympathetic MPs. In 1973 the tradition was established of one of the Vice-Chairpersons being an MP (then Hugh Jenkins, latterly Jo Richardson). Since then the governments have faced much more systematic probing on defence issues, with Robin Cook, Stan Newens and Frank Allaun being particularly effective. One of the pleasing additional features of recent years has been the support given in Parliament by some members of the minority parties, notably Plaid Cymru and SNP.

The peace movement

For a newcomer to the campaign, the number of peace organizations is bewildering. In practice the situation is by no means as confusing as it might first seem.

The main objective of the United Nations Association (UNA) is to foster support for the UN and its policies. In

House of Commons, 'Early-day motion',
tabled 8 November 1972

That this House, having regard to the following passage in the
1964 Labour Party General Election manifesto:

Nor is it true that all this costly defence expenditure will
produce an 'independent deterrent'. It will not be independent and
it will not be British and it will not deter ... we are not prepared
any longer to waste the country's resources on endless duplication
of strategic nuclear weapons,

and to the 1972 Conference resolution, which reads as follows:

This Conference is convinced of the futility of a nuclear war
which would be suicidal for the human race and in view of the
present world unrest feels the time is ripe for positive action by the
British Government. The presence of American nuclear bases pre-
vents us from taking the kind of political stance which would
encourage world disarmament. There is no doubt this country
presents a sitting target. This Conference is opposed to any British
defence policy which is based on the use or threatened use of nuclear
weapons either by this country or its allies and demands the re-
moval of all nuclear bases in this country.

believes that these policies should now be implemented.

Proposed: Hugh Jenkins, Ian Mikado, Joan Lester, Judith Hart,
Barbara Castle, Frank Allaun, Lena Jeger

Supported by: Stanley Orme, Russell Kerr, John Silkin, James
Sillars, Sydney Bidwell, Norman Atkinson, Laurie Pavitt,
Alexander Wilson, Paul B. Rose, Eric S. Heffer, Will Griffiths,
Ted Fletcher, Robert Hughes, Lewis Carter-Jones, Michael
Barnes, Raphael Tuck, Peter Hardy, David Stoddard, Hugh
D. Brown, Frank McElhone, Richard Kelly, Tom Driberg,
William Wilson, Dennis Skinner, Joyce Butler, Albert Booth,
Renée Short, Norman Buchan, Neil Kinnock, Gavin Strang,
Arthur Latham, Raymond Fletcher, Julius Silverman, Eric
Deakins, Dr Edmund Marshall, James Lamond, Edward
Milne, Roy Hughes, Guy Barnett, Caerwyn Roderick, Arthur
Davidson, Neil Carmichael, Robert Woof, Leo Abse, Dr
Miller, A. W. Stallard, Kenneth Marks, Alan Beaney,
Thomas Swain, Joe Ashton, John Prescott, Robert Edwards,
W. T. Williams, Marcus Lipton, James Bennett, Tom Torney,
Maurice Orbach, William Molloy, Mr Urwin, Mr Donald
Stewart

practice, this means that it is able to publicize the many excellent resolutions on disarmament passed by the UN in recent years and, subject to certain reservations, point out the failure of governments (including our own) to comply with these decisions. Moreover, the UNA is formally committed to oppose Trident and cruise missiles in Britain.

The National Peace Council (NPC) is an 'umbrella' to which virtually every peace organization, including CND, is affiliated. It is an absolutely invaluable clearing-house for coordinating activities. Many of these organizations derive their support from religious conviction or concentrate their efforts on particular groups (doctors, scientists, women, etc.). This diversity is part of the strength of the peace movement today.

CND took the initiative in the calling of the Camden Assembly, which in January 1978 attracted a very representative 700 delegates and adopted, virtually unanimously, the declaration reprinted as an appendix to this chapter. This declaration is an authoritative summary of the policies generally accepted throughout the peace movement today.

Following the Camden Assembly, and the lobbying of the UN Special Session on Disarmament (UNSSD) that took place in May that year, a further conference was called specifically to support UN efforts to achieve multilateral disarmament. CND backed this conference, which took place in April 1980, and now cooperates closely with the World Disarmament Campaign (WDC), which was formed afterwards to work for the success of the second UNSSD in 1982.

Special mention should be made of the work amongst the churches. This has improved considerably since 1975, thanks largely to the influence of Monsignor Bruce Kent. Another key figure has been Sister Deirdre Duffy, whose order (the Sisters of Saint Joseph for Peace) have seconded her to work fulltime for disarmament since 1977. One of the most impressive sights in New York in May 1978 (at the time of the UNSSD) was a large contingent of the Sisters, in full convent regalia, marching in a great international demonstration to the United Nations headquarters.

The British Council of Churches

The following resolution was adopted by the British Council of Churches at their Autumn Assembly in 1979:

The Assembly

1. (a) welcomes the publication of the Report 'The Future of the British Nuclear Deterrent';
   (b) thanks the Working Party of the Council on Christian Approaches to Defence and Disarmament;
   (c) urges Christians to study the issues raised in the Report.

2. (a) reaffirms the conviction which the Council expressed in 1963 that nuclear weapons 'are an offence to God and a denial of His purpose for man. Only the rapid progressive reduction of these weapons, their submission to strict international control and their eventual abolition can remove this offence. No policy which does not explicitly and urgently seek to realize these aims can be acceptable to Christian conscience';
   (b) believes that the non-replacement by the UK of its present strategic deterrent (the Polaris missile system) would strengthen moves for nuclear non-proliferation, and urges Her Majesty's Government to take a decision to this effect;
   (c) invites other governments to take comparable confidence-building measures of restraint or renunciation, and encourages Christians actively to promote such steps.

'After all, the 39 articles say a Christian may take up arms in a righteous cause.'

The British peace movement has been stimulated on many occasions by similar movements in other countries. In 1975 a Japanese peace delegation came to England and Scotland and took part in CND events. The Dutch anti-neutron bomb campaign was a major spur to renewed efforts in Britain in 1977–8. CND maintains friendly bilateral campaigning relations with several foreign peace campaigns and cooperates, when appropriate, in international events.

CND also is a constituent part of the European Nuclear Disarmament campaign (END) which campaigns for a nuclear-free Europe, 'from Poland to Portugal'.* In this way CND shows that it favours multilateral measures – indeed, CND would *prefer* disarmament by mutual agreement to disarmament by Britain alone (if such agreement could be achieved more quickly than seems likely so far!).

External events

Relations between the USA and the USSR deteriorated in the late 1970s, although the atmosphere still was not as bad as during the Cold War years. The origin of this deterioration can be traced to around 1976, when NATO began to press for a 3 per cent increase in defence spending and when the Pentagon began its efforts to deploy the neutron bomb, cruise missiles, Trident and, latterly, the MX missile system.

Most NATO countries were reluctant to adopt these proposals as, at that time, the international situation was not too bad. Someone may then have recalled the words of John Foster Dulles, US Secretary of State during the Cold War:

In order to make the country bear the burden [of arms expenditure] we have to create an emotional atmosphere akin to wartime psychology. We must create the idea of a threat from without.

The Soviet replacement of her older intermediate-range missiles by SS-20s was the major excuse used to justify the NATO build-up (until December 1979). Since then, the Soviet coup in Afghanistan has been the excuse for almost everything

* The full text of the END declaration of Europe appears in *Protest and Survive*, Penguin, 1980.

– non-ratification of SALT-2, the abortive Olympic boycott, laser-beam weapons in space – the list is endless.

In Britain, it was revealed only in 1980 that the 1974–9 government had secretly spent £1,000 million on 'updating' Polaris. In the same year £5,000 million (at least) was sanctioned to replace Polaris by Trident. With most items of public expenditure being cut, Civil Defence was allocated a staggering increase of 60 per cent.

That year also saw, for the first time in a decade, a British Defence Minister (Francis Pym) wondering aloud whether we should develop our own offensive chemical weapons, while the Home Secretary (William Whitelaw) claimed:

Most houses in this country offer a reasonable degree of protection against radioactive fallout from nuclear explosions and protection can be substantially improved by a series of quite simple do-it-yourself measures.

The losing candidate in the 1980 US Presidential election, who had sanctioned the biggest-ever increase in arms spending and who had authorized the re-targeting of US and NATO missiles to make a first strike feasible, accused his opponent of seeking to resolve international disputes by military means. Also during

'I suppose it's all part of the nostalgia boom.'

1980, nuclear alerts were called more than once when Pentagon computers falsely detected Soviet nuclear attacks.

CND's response

The 'revival' of CND in 1980, like its creation in 1958, was the culmination of years of effort by hundreds of campaigners.

In 1975, after numerous unsuccessful attempts, CND was allowed to buy a copy of *The War Game*, the BBC TV film banned in 1965. In the years that followed, over a quarter of a million people saw this harrowing indictment of nuclear war. Attendances at CND's public meetings soared and, in 1977 alone, Duncan Rees (Secretary 1976–80) spoke to audiences totalling over 20,000.

At about the same time, sales of CND's publications rose and, in 1976 and 1977, *Overkill* and *On the Warpath* (for schools) achieved an estimated readership of 200,000. In September 1977 the Scottish region of CND took more than a thousand demonstrators by paddle steamer to the US base at the Holy Loch. In January 1978 the Camden Assembly was the springboard for much of the campaigning in support of the UN Special Session on Disarmament. Also in 1978, CND obtained over 250,000 signatures for its petition against the neutron bomb.

In 1979 CND's income from donations doubled and, for the first time since 1960, the number of staff employed was increased. The pace of campaigning then escalated even more, especially after the election of a new and stridently bellicose government. In late 1979 and early 1980 local groups sprang up in Oxfordshire and East Anglia around the locations proposed for cruise missile bases. In the light of all these developments, though initially with some misgivings, CND decided to call its first national demonstration since 1974.

The build-up for the October demonstration fulfilled all expectations. In Spring 1980 Edward Thompson's pamphlet *Protest and Survive* sold nearly 20,000 copies; the END Declaration broke through the media blackout; and nearly 3,000 delegates launched the World Disarmament Campaign. In

April and May some dozens of new CND groups mushroomed in Birmingham and Bristol.

On 22 June the Labour Party held its first-ever demonstration for peace, addressed (amongst others) by Michael Foot and Bruce Kent (Secretary of CND since 1980). Marches were held at Caerwent, Newbury and at several other military bases. It was clear from midsummer onwards that the national demonstration would be an outstanding success.

Still the build-up continued. The Labour Party reaffirmed its support since 1972 for unilateral nuclear disarmament and gave the proposed CND demonstration official backing. The British Council of Churches confirmed its opposition to the replacement of Polaris by Trident and the Liberal Party only just voted down a call for a non-nuclear defence policy. Newspapers were inundated with readers' letters expressing concern about the growing danger of nuclear war.

Then, on 26 October 1980, 70,000 people marched to Trafalgar Square for a 100,000-strong rally against cruise missiles and Trident and for a cut in arms spending.

CND had held many demonstrations in the past but none, not even the most successful of the first Aldermaston marches, was more significant. As one newspaper headline put it, 'CND back with a 100,000 bang'. The biggest protest movement of the century had proved it had another of the vital ingredients needed for success – stamina.

The future

The spectacular growth continued into 1981. In the course of only twelve months there was almost a tenfold increase in membership and local groups. Phil Bolsover's pamphlet on Civil Defence sold over 40,000 copies and Betty England's *Nuclear Disarmament for Britain* sold 25,000 in its first four months. Half a million signatures were obtained for CND's petition against cruise missiles and Trident and for a nuclear-free Europe. Public opinion polls confirmed the growth, with around 40 per cent backing the principle of British unilateral nuclear disarmament. It began to seem as though Britain might be rid of the nuclear menace within the time scale of this up-surge in peace campaigning.

Nevertheless, the arms race continued to accelerate and the international situation to deteriorate. As thousands flocked to CND, many of the past doubts and controversies resurfaced. Do governments take any notice of ordinary people? Would a Labour government carry out its election pledges? Will CND remain a united campaign when, as is virtually inevitable, the impetus of the new upsurge slows?

Success for CND is no more a certainty than is the survival of the human race. Yet few will dispute that the organization has gained in influence and effectiveness. Its policies have matured and its appeal has widened. As shown by this brief historical survey, there are many grounds for optimism.

The Campaign has retained most of the features that first won it mass support two decades ago. It is still, above all, a moral crusade with a simple message – nuclear weapons are totally evil. It is still a non-aligned independent peace campaign. It is also, still, a broad coalition of many shades of political and religious opinion, appealing to people from all walks of life. In addition, however, CND has learnt many important lessons. Three merit special emphasis.

Tolerance

Internal squabbles were a factor in the earlier decline. Now, thankfully, there is a greater understanding of policy differ-ences, unconventional methods of protest and of how to handle the many, sometimes antagonistic, viewpoints of its supporters. In short, CND has come to terms with the problems of being a broad coalition of diverse opinions.

These problems have been resolved in part by institutional means, by working externally with other campaigns (for ex-ample, END and WDC) and internally through specialist groups (for example, Labour, Christian and Liberal CND). More important than these procedural means, as a result of the shared experience of the past decades there is a much greater trust between individuals and groups within the Campaign. In

CND National Council, 1980

Chairperson: Hugh Jenkins; *Vice-Chairpersons:* John Cox, Olive Gibbs, Paul Oestreicher, Duncan Rees, Jo Richardson

Elected Members of National Council: Alistair Beale, Meg Beresford, Phil Bolsover, Ian Davison, Barbara Egglestone, Betty England, Mike Pentz, Paul Rogers, Joan Ruddock, Dan Smith, Roger Spiller, Ron Todd

Treasurer: Cathy Ashton

Secretary: Bruce Kent

particular, those that stayed with CND have learnt the virtue of compromise and, far from seeking to impose their views on the Campaign as a whole, take positive steps to maintain its breadth.

Relevance

The scale of the arms race makes a normal person despair – megadeaths, megatons and billions of dollars are beyond comprehension. CND has therefore had to learn to relate its policies to the everyday concerns of ordinary people.

This has had far-reaching consequences. Whereas the moral case for unilateralism used to be isolated from, or elevated above, other issues, today CND stresses the connections. The new approach shows that, for example, cuts in social services and starvation in the Third World, far from being side-issues, are caused and made worse by the nuclear arms race. By making the issues more understandable and relevant to day-to-day problems, CND attracts a wider audience and the moral case has been strengthened.

Persistence

Lack of progress has been another common cause for dis-illusion. Enthusiasm has led to disappointment and activity to exhaustion. CND shares the blame for this: in the past it was commonplace to overdramatize the dangers and to over-emphasize the value of mass demonstrations.

Today CND makes haste more slowly. Its strength lies in its hundreds of local groups, each holding dozens of small meetings, and in its links at national and local level with other organizations (trade unions, church groups, etc.). In the end, a change of public opinion depends upon every CND member talking about nuclear weapons with friends. Demonstrations remain an essential part of the Campaign's activities but they are no longer considered the sole measure of its progress.

CND has learnt also the tactical and psychological value of, from time to time, working for limited demands. 'No cruise', 'no Trident', 'cut arms spending' are realizable short-term demands from which CND may build its campaign for the complete renunciation of nuclear weapons. Success on such limited issues would encourage campaigners who might otherwise become dispirited by lack of progress on the overall objectives. This balance between long-term and short-term aims is essential if CND is to achieve steady and sustained growth.

Join CND!

At the start of the 1980s, the international situation has been deteriorating. People have become more afraid of the possibility of nuclear war than at any time in the past two decades. In this new climate of opinion, people are more disposed to listen to CND's suggestions for ending of the arms race.

The timing of the decisions to install new US missiles in Britain and to replace Polaris favour a new British initiative. It is much easier to prevent new weapons being deployed than it is to scrap weapons once they are in place. If CND fails to rid Britain of nuclear weapons in the 1980s, we will be saddled with NATO's first-strike nuclear forces until the turn of the century – assuming we last that long.

If there ever was a time to work for nuclear disarmament, it is now. The risk of nuclear war is greater, the pace of the arms race is faster and the prospects for success are brighter than ever before. Anyone who is concerned to see the human race survive into the twenty-first century should join and campaign with CND now.*

Aims

The aim of the Campaign for Nuclear Disarmament is the unilateral abandonment by Britain of nuclear weapons, nuclear bases and nuclear alliances as a prerequisite for a British foreign policy which has the worldwide abolition of nuclear, chemical and biological weapons leading to general and complete disarmament as its prime objective.

The Campaign for Nuclear Disarmament is opposed to the manufacture, stockpiling, testing, use and threatened use of nuclear, chemical and biological weapons by any country, and the policies of any country or group of countries which make nuclear war more likely, or which hinder progress towards a world without weapons of mass destruction.

(from the CND constitution)

---

* See page 245 for membership form.

Appendix

Declaration of the Camden Assembly, 1978 (excerpt)

This Assembly urges the United Nations Special Session on Disarmament to:

1. *encourage* immediate steps towards disarmament including agreements to:

   (a) cut all military expenditures, as a first step, by 5 per cent per year with half the funds saved earmarked for additional development assistance to the less developed countries

   (b) reduce stockpiles of arms by weapon producing countries and place restrictions on weapon transfers

2. *promote* treaties

   (a) banning the use of nuclear weapons

   (b) banning the use of all other weapons of mass destruction

   (c) banning production and deployment of new weapons such as the neutron bomb or cruise missiles

   (d) banning further R & D on weapons and delivery systems

   (e) reducing nuclear weapon stockpiles leading to their elimination

3. *agree* immediate measures for strengthening UN peace-keeping and peace-making capacity including:

   (a) provision of appropriate peace-keeping forces and mediating teams

   (b) methods of effective international control of agreements reached

   (c) further strengthening the UN Disarmament Centre including provision of massive public education programmes on the need for, and methods of, achieving disarmament

4. *agree* a timetable for disarmament including:
   (a) the fixing of a date for a World Disarmament Conference
   (b) the initiation of discussions for a Treaty on General and Complete Disarmament which must include the dissolution of NATO, WTO and other Regional Military Alliances

5. *recognize* unconditional conscientious objection to military service as an inalienable right and guaranteeing automatic asylum to conscientious objectors from any country not yet accepting this right.

This Assembly calls upon the British Government to support the foregoing proposals and to take initiatives of its own by announcing a timetable for:

1. immediate reductions of military spending to the level of other NATO European countries, the resources thus released to be used to meet the needs in Britain and less developed countries

2. phasing out British nuclear weapons including the non-replacement of Polaris submarines

3. closing all nuclear bases

4. refusing to participate in any strategy based on the use, or threatened use, of nuclear weapons

5. cessation of arms trading and the closure of the Defence Sales Organization starting by discontinuing further arms sales to areas of actual, or potential, conflict and witholding from governments such arms as are used for the subjection of their own people

6. the setting up of major programmes for:
   (a) converting military R & D and industries to the production of socially useful goods and services making clear that the changes produce not only more employment but better job security than 'one-off' contracts
   (b) examining non-military, including non-violent, methods of defence and/or resistance
   (c) discouraging educational assumptions that war is desirable, natural or inevitable including providing peace speakers for schools and colleges
   (d) significantly increasing the number of University Chairs for Disarmament and Peace

Book list

Hiroshima and Nagasaki

Hiroshima Diary, Michihiko Hachiya, Gollancz, 1955.
A powerful first-hand account by a Japanese doctor.

Hiroshima, John Hersey, Penguin, 1946; reissued as Penguin Modern Classic, 1972.
The experiences of six survivors. Hersey was sent to Hiroshima by the *New Yorker* magazine soon after the bomb was dropped.

Hiroshima: The Decision to Use the A-Bomb, Edwin Fogelman, Scribner's, 1964.
An examination of the political, moral and military implications.

Nagasaki: The Forgotten Bomb, F. W. Chinnock, Allen & Unwin, 1970.
A comprehensive account of the immediate circumstances of the Nagasaki bombing.

The H-bomb

Brighter than a Thousand Suns, Robert Jungk, Gollancz and Hart-Davis, 1958; Penguin, 1964.
A classic (and very readable) account of the scientists' endeavours to understand nuclear energy and their reactions to the development of the H-bomb.

The Voyage of the Lucky Dragon, Ralph Lapp, Muller, 1957; Penguin, 1958.
The story of the Japanese fishermen who were showered with fall-out from the first successful F F F explosion at Bikini in 1954.

The Bombs of Palomares, Tad Szulc, Gollancz, 1967.
An account, by the *New York Times* Madrid correspondent, of how four American H-bombs fell accidentally on to Spanish soil (see Plate XIII).

Nuclear war

On the Beach, Nevil Shute, Heinemann, 1966; Pan, 1969.

The Chrysalids, John Wyndham, Michael Joseph, 1955; Penguin, 1969.
The scientific accuracy of these two novels is dubious, but they do convey the futility of nuclear war most effectively.

Effects of the possible use of nuclear weapons and the security and economic implications for states of the acquisition and further development of these weapons, United Nations booklet, 1968.
The best scientific appraisal.

The arms race and military strategy

From Yalta to Vietnam, David Horowitz, Penguin, 1969.
A good account of the Cold War for the beginner.

On Thermonuclear War, Herman Kahn, Princeton University Press, 1960.
Anyone who believes that no one would be mad enough to start a nuclear war should read this!

Arms Control, articles from *Scientific American* collated by Herbert York, W. H. Freeman, 1973.
An excellent compendium of articles on such topics as the history of the bomb, military strategy, arms control, etc. With good illustrations.

World Armaments and Disarmament, Stockholm International Peace Research Institute (available through MIT Press), yearly.
An expensive but invaluable yearbook giving up-to-date international information.

The Arms Trade with the Third World, Stockholm International Peace Research Institute, Penguin, 1975.
A reduced version of a report prepared by SIPRI.

The Arms Bazaar, Anthony Sampson, Hodder & Stoughton, 1977.
An exposé of the arms trade.

Philosophy and policy

Has Man a Future?, Bertrand Russell, Allen & Unwin, 1961; Penguin, 1970.

The Fearful Choice, Philip Toynbee, Gollancz, 1958.
This is a wide-ranging topic, and many books could be listed. But these two should make a good starting-point.

Protest and Survive, E. P. Thompson and Dan Smith, Penguin, 1980.
A contemporary collection of essays on aspects of the problem.

The Defence of the Realm in the 1980s, Dan Smith, Croom Helm, 1980.
A detailed contemporary study of military strategy by a former Secretary of CND.

For schools

On the Warpath, John Cox, Oxford University Press (Standpoints series), 1976.
A sixty-four-page illustrated book on the subject of modern weapons and the arms race, intended to stimulate classroom discussion.

Films

The War Game (available from CND, 11 Goodwin Street, London N4; telephone 01-263 4954).
Commissioned by the BBC but never shown on television, this film simulates the effects of a nuclear attack on Britain.

Dr Strangelove (available from Columbia-Warner 16 mm. Library, 135 Wardour Street, London W1).
The famous full-length feature film.

A number of other relevant films are available from Concord Films, Nacton, near Ipswich, Suffolk, IP10 0JZ (telephone Ipswich 76012). A catalogue of the films available is obtainable from that address, price 40p (post free), with a supplement of the most recent films, price 25p. The following films might be found especially interesting:

Energy: The Nuclear Alternative
Explores what fission power is and how it works.

Mr Nixon's Secret Legacy
Journalist John Pilger visits a Minuteman base in South Dakota and presents an awesome picture of the men and women working there.

Mururoa
The story of a small group of people who attempted to stop French H-Bomb tests in the Pacific in 1973 by sailing into the test area.

The Palomares H-Bomb Incident
A Granada *World In Action* programme which examines the incident in more depth.

Glossary of terms

ABC: *atomic, biological and chemical* weapons
ABM: an *anti-ballistic missile* shoots nuclear warheads at oncoming missiles to prevent them landing on target
ALCM: an *air-launched cruise missile*
APW: *anti-personnel weapons* are designed to cause suffering to people rather than destruction of military targets
ASW: *anti-submarine warfare* involves all measures designed to locate, track and destroy hostile submarines
ballistic missile: a missile that travels on 'free-fall' trajectory after its initial launch
CBW: *chemical and biological weapons*
CEP: *circular error probability* is a measure of the accuracy of a missile. It is the radius of a circle around the target into which half the 'shots' at the target can be expected to fall
counter-city strike: retaliation against cities in response to a nuclear attack by the other side
counter-force strike: a pre-emptive attack against military forces to prevent a nuclear attack by the other side
cruise missile: a missile that can change its course either continuously or from time to time during flight
disarming strike: another term for *counter-force strike*, employed to make it sound less aggressive
ecocide: wanton destruction of the ecology of a country
first strike: any attack which takes place without waiting for the other side
force loading: numbers of nuclear warheads that are loaded on missiles, aircraft etc., and can be delivered to targets in the enemy's territory

hard target: usually a military target protected (hardened) by walls to withstand the blast overpressure (in pounds per square inch – psi) from explosions

ICBM: an *intercontinental ballistic missile* (e.g. suitable for the USA/USSR range of around 8,000 miles)

IRBM: an *intermediate-range ballistic missile* (e.g. suitable for the Europe/USSR range)

kill probability: a measure (k) of the likelihood of a nuclear warhead with yield y (in megatons) and accuracy CEP (in nautical miles) destroying a target (ignores 'hardness')

kiloton: the explosive equivalent of one thousand tons of TNT

lethality: another term for *kill probability*

LRCM: a *long-range cruise missile* is a cruise missile with the range of an ICBM.

MAD: *mutually assured destruction* means that each side in a conflict is capable of inflicting a level of damage equivalent to 'minimum deterrence' even when retaliating after a surprise attack

MARV: *manoeuvrable re-entry vehicles* are re-entry vehicles like MIRV, but with the additional facility of being able to change course (manoeuvre) during flight

megaton: the explosive equivalent of one million tons of TNT

minimum deterrence: the ability to inflict an unacceptable level of destruction upon the enemy. This is commonly supposed to be equivalent to killing about a quarter of the population and destroying half the industry

MIRV: *multiple independently-targeted re-entry vehicles* are sprayed from a single missile; each has its own guidance system and is programmed to aim at a pre-determined target

MRV: *multiple re-entry vehicles* are sprayed from a single missile but, having no guidance system, scatter randomly

neutron bomb: a nuclear bomb designed to release most of its energy in the form of radiation

nuclear warheads: these are carried by missiles or the re-entry vehicles (whether MRV, MIRV or MARV) of a missile and are equivalent to the nuclear bombs dropped from aircraft

NPT: the *Non-Proliferation Treaty* (1968) provides for non-nuclear countries to remain non-nuclear and nuclear countries to work for nuclear disarmament

overkill: the ability to destroy an enemy more than once

Polaris: a nuclear submarine with sixteen SLBMs each of which, in

1975, had three MRV warheads of 200 kilotons and a range of 2,500 miles

Poseidon: a nuclear submarine with sixteen SLBMs each of which, in 1975, had ten MIRV warheads of 50 kilotons and a range of 2,500 miles

pre-emptive strike: another term for *counter-force strike*

PTBT: the *Partial Test Ban Treaty* (1963) bans all nuclear tests above ground

SALT: the *Strategic Arms Limitation Talks* between USA and USSR are intended to satisfy the obligations of the superpowers under the NPT

second strike: retaliatory attack following a first strike

SLBM: a *submarine-launched ballistic missile* – e.g. Polaris, Poseidon and Trident (USA), Sark and Serb (USSR)

soft target: an unprotected military target (i.e., not hardened to withstand blast overpressure of 100 pounds per square inch) or a non-military target

SRAM: a *short-range attack missile*, usually air-to-surface (i.e., launched from the air to attack targets on the ground)

strategic superiority: more overkill than the other side

strategic weapons: weapons for an all-out nuclear war (e.g., ICBMs, SLBMs)

tactical weapons: weapons for a 'limited' nuclear war (generally with missile ranges of no more than 100 miles and warhead strengths below 50 kilotons)

Trident: see ULMS

ULMS: an *underwater long-range missile system* using Trident submarines which may have twenty-four SLBMs per submarine with ten MIRVed warheads and a range of over 4,500 miles

yield: the explosive strength of a nuclear bomb or warhead, usually measured in megatons

Join CND

You can join CND by sending us your membership subscription or by filling in the bankers order form overleaf

MEMBERSHIP RATES AND CATEGORIES

Adult (£6)
Student (£3)
Couples (£9)
Unwaged and Youths (£2)
ADDITIONAL LITERATURE SUBSCRIPTION (receive all our new publications) Extra £2.
All members receive Sanity at no extra charge.
Sanity only — £1.50

CHEQUES, POSTAL ORDERS, CASH

If you are sending a cheque, cash or a postal order please fill in the following:

Name:...

Address:...

....(BLOCK CAPITALS)

Please find enclosed £..................... to join CND (*tick which category*)

PLUS £2 Literature subscription (*delete if inapplicable*)

PLUS £...... additional donation (*delete if inapplicable*)

TOTAL: £ ....

Join CND

You can join CND by completing this bankers order form or by mailing your subscription. Membership rates are given overleaf.

----

bankers order form

To the manager .... Bank Ltd

(Address) ....

Name: ....(BLOCK CAPITALS)

Account Number...

Address...

....(BLOCK CAPITALS)

Please pay the Co-Operative Bank Ltd, 110 Leman Street, London E1 (Code 080308) for the account of the Campaign for Nuclear Disarmament (A/C No: 50036163) the sum of

£...

on the...day of ....

198.... and thereafter every month/Quarter/Six Months/Year (*delete as appropriate*) until countermanded by me at two months' notice.

Signed ....

Date..

DO NOT SEND THIS FORM DIRECT TO YOUR BANK, BUT RETURN IT TO: CND
11 Goodwin Street, London N4 3HQ

Index

ABM *see* missiles
A-Bombs *see* bombs, atomic
accidents *see* war
AEC (Atomic Energy Commission, USA) 36, 222
Afghanistan 228
Africa 146, 161, 163
aircraft 81
  ALCM *see* missiles
  Backfire 93
  B-1 bomber 115
  B-52 bomber 81, 120
  FB-111 bomber 81, 91
  MRCA (Multi-Role Combat Aircraft) 86, 167, 175
  SRAM missiles 81, 106, 177, 185
  U-2 spy-plane 137, 203
  Vulcan 93
Alamogordo 17–18, 33
ALCM *see* missiles
Aldermaston *see* CND
Algeria 135, 174
Allaun, Frank 199, 224, 225
Anderson, Sir John 28
APW *see* warfare
Archbishop of Canterbury 195, 214
Argentina 133, 182
arms control 128–43
arms race 59, 71, 94–116
  conventional forces 111–13
  lethality 79, 94–5
  military spending 109–10, 137
  missiles *see* missiles
  naval balance 106, 108, 179
  nuclear stockpiles 43, 44, 58, 124, 128
  nuclear warheads 93–5, 99

arms trade 164, 165
ASROC *see* warfare, ASW
ASW *see* warfare, ASW
ATOM (Against Testing on Mururoa Atoll) 131, 169, 199, 207
atom, the 28–31
atomic power *see* nuclear power
Attlee, Clement 172
Austria 174, 176

BCC *see* Christians
BCPV *see* Vietnam, anti-war activities
beams, proton/particle 90
Bethe, Hans 16, 38, 45
Benn, Tony 197
Bikini 38–43
Biological Convention *see* treaties
biological weapons *see* warfare, CBW
Blackett, P. M. S. 26
Bohr, Niels 16, 26
bombs
  atomic 29–33, 43, 75, 148, 184–5
  clean/dirty 43, 55, 56, 131
  FFF (fission-fusion-fission) 38–9, 43
  incendiary 59, 65
  neutron 56, 60, 185, 228
  strategic 38, 99, *see also* missiles
  tactical nuclear 38, 91–3, 122, 125, *see also* missiles
  thermonuclear 37–43, 71, 98, 184–185
bombing
  carpet 68
  conventional 67–70, 125

Born, Max 27
BPC *see* British Peace Committee
Brawdy 89
Brazil 133, 147
Bridgeman, P. W. 27
Britain
  policies 172–81
  *see also under appropriate subject
    headings*
British Council of Churches *see*
  Christians
British Campaign for Peace in
  Vietnam *see* Vietnam, anti-war
  activities
British Peace Committee 192–8,
  202, 220

caesium-137 25, 37, 55
Camden Assembly 226, 230, 236–7
Canada 35, 81, 148, 182
carbon-14 53–5
Carter, Jimmy 184–6, 229
CBW *see* warfare
CEP (circular error probability) 85,
  94–5, 148
chain reaction 30, 31, 37
chemical weapons *see* warfare, CBW
China 36, 59, 62, 130, 136, 169,
  181, 183
Christians
  BCC 195, 227, 231
  Christian CND 210–11, 226,
    232
Christmas Island 195, 198–9
Churchill, Sir Winston 27, 43–4
civil defence 46–7, 50–51, 56, 202
Civil disobedience *see* Committee of
  100
Clyde bases 175
CND 181, 189–235
  Aldermaston marches 189, 190,
    198, 199, 221, 231
  executive 199, 201, 211, 223, 233
  groups 190, 220, 231
  Labour CND *see* Labour movement
  origins 191–200
  organization 210–11, 219, 232–3

pacifism 168, 195, 218
policy 177, 181, 191, 198, 201, 205,
  210, 213–14, 233–5
  Scotland 221, 230
Cold War 192–4, 197, 200, 217, 228
Collins, Canon L. J. 197, 201, 206,
  211
Committee of 100 204, 206–10, 220
Cook, Robin 224
Cox, Idris 187
critical mass 31, 37
cruise missiles *see* missiles
Cuba 133, 211, 214
Cyprus 141
Czechoslovakia 15, 220

DAC 198, 199, 200
Defence White Papers 109, 112,
  124, 196, 212
deuterium 29, 37, 39
disarmament 144–53, 169–70, *see
  also* treaties
  European *see* END
  GCD 145
  multilateral 169–70
  nuclear-free zones 145–6
  unilateral *see* CND, policy
Duff, Peggy 198, 201, 205, 211, 218
Duffy, Sister Deirdre 226

early-warning systems 118–20, 141
East Anglia 122, 175, 230
ecocide 67–8, 70
ecology movements 222–3
Einstein, Albert 15, 16, 26, 27
Eisenhower, Dwight 23, 152, 154,
  167, 171, 203
electronic battlefield 69
electronic eavesdropping 141
employment 167, 168, 219
END 228, 230–32
Eniwetok 38, 41
enrichment 30, 34, 183
Europe *see* END, nuclear free zones
  and other subject headings
explosions, conventional 44

explosions, nuclear 31, 45–58
  atmospheric tests 54, 123–4, 130, 139
  blast effects 25, 45, 46, 48, 49
  detection 134–6, 139, 140, 146–7
  firestorm 49
  heat effects 25, 45, 46, 48, 49
  peaceful 35, 44, 146–7
  radiation effects 25–6, 47, 49, 52–6
  tests, frequency 44, 54, 130–34, 172
  underground tests 54, 130, 135–6, 146–7
  underwater 89

fallout 47, 49, 51–6
Fermi, Enrico 15, 16, 38
Finletter, Thomas K. 26
fission 29–35
Foot, Michael 201, 205, 211–14, 231
Forrestal, James V. 122
France 59, 62, 130–31, 136, 170, 181–2, *see also appropriate subject headings*
Fuller, Peter 217
fusion 29, 36–7

Geneva 132, 161, 170–71
Germany 15, 16, 24, 162–3, 187, 195
Gibbs, Olive 193, 211, 223, 233
Goss, Arthur 197, 200, 201, 211
Graham, General Daniel 113
Guam 106, 108

half-life 53
Halperin, Morton 125
Hawaii 41, 169
H-Bomb *see* bombs, thermonuclear
Healey, Denis 125, 173
Helsinki 123
herbicides *see* warfare, CBW
Herter, Christian 175
Hiroshima 10, 18–23, 33, 49, 55, 192, 195, 197, 238
Holland 162, 182, 228
Holy Loch 105, 108, 175, 230
Home, Sir Alec Douglas- 176, 180

Horner, John 180, 187, 211
Hungary 196

ICBM *see* missiles
incendiaries *see* bombs
India 35, 59, 133, 147–8, 184–5
Infeld, L. 27
inspection 134–42, 147, 149, 170
iodine-131 59
Iran 126, 183
Iraq–Iran war 126
IRBM *see* missiles
isotopes 29, 33
Israel 36, 133, 147, 183
Italy 182

Japan 16–28, 33, 39–43, 141, 162, 198
Japanese peace movement 228
Jenkins, Hugh 199, 224, 225, 232
Johnson, L. B. 139
Joliot-Curie, J. F. 27
Jones, Sheila 197, 200, 201

Kahn, Herman 154
Kaldor, Mary 165, 179
Kennedy, John F. 98, 106, 114, 181, 211
Kent, Bruce 226, 231
Krushchev, Nikita 98, 196, 203, 211
kill probability *see* arms race, lethality
Kissinger, Henry 14, 71, 79, 101, 103, 129
Korea 60, 182

Labour movement
  Labour CND 210–11, 220, 223–4, 232
  Labour H-Bomb committee 197, 199
  Labour Party 190, 192, 193, 199, 210, 215, 219–25, 231–2
  Scarborough conference 180, 190–191, 203–4, 213, 221, 223
  Trades Union CND 211, 220
lasers 44, 90, 229
Latin America 134

laws of war *see* war
Leggatt, Robert 95
lethality *see* arms race
Liberal CND 211, 232
Liberal Party 215, 231
Los Alamos 38
LRCM *see* missiles, cruise
Lucas Aerospace 167
Lucky Dragon 39–42, 238

MacMillan, Sir Harold 172, 181,
    202
MacNamara, Robert 96–8
Marshall Islands 38, 41
MARV *see* missiles
Mason, Roy 167
Meacham, James 111
Mead, Margaret 156
military–industrial complex 152,
    167–9
military strategy 71–4
  first-strike 58, 72–4, 102–4, 114–
    116
  flexible response 128
  minimum deterrence 98, 100, 103
  mutually assured destruction
    (MAD) 71–3, 103, 115
Minuteman *see* missiles
missiles 75, 82–3, 93–5
  ABM 77, 129
  ALCM 85
  Blue Streak 203
  cruise 12, 75, 81, 85, 90–91, 101–
    102, 116, 148–50, 152, 168, 209,
    228, 230–31
  GLCM 85
  ICBM 75, 80, 83, 99, 129, 149,
    185
  IRBM 93, 106, 184–5
  MARV 78
  Minuteman 84, 94–5, 149
  MIRV 78, 101, 104, 114, 115, 129,
    144, 174
  MRV 77
  MX 12, 81, 84, 115, 116, 128
  Pershing 85
  Pluton 93
  protection 80

SLBM *see* nuclear submarines
SRAM *see* aircraft
SS-9 94, 95
SS-20 85, 93, 101, 228
Titan 94, 95
Montgomery, Lord 122
Mountbatten, Lord 13, 124, 126
MRCA *see* aircraft
Mururoa *see* ATOM
Muller, H. J. 27
Mustard gas *see* CBW
MX *see* missiles

Nagasaki 10, 24–6, 33, 192, 238
napalm *see* bombs, incendiary
Nassau agreement 174–5, 215
National Peace Council (NPC) 226
NATO (North Atlantic Treaty
    Organization) 109, 111, 125–6,
    175, 179, 210, 220
NCANWT 197–9, 200, 220, 222
Nettleton, Dick 218, 223
Newens, Stan 224
News Chronicle 28
Nimrod 92
Nixon, Richard 62, 99, 104, 126,
    129
Noel-Baker, Philip 14, 128, 134
NPT *see* treaties *and* nuclear
    proliferation
nuclear-free zones 146
nuclear power 31–5, 222–3
nuclear proliferation 35, 147–8,
    181–6
nuclear submarines 104, 107
  detection of 89
  Polaris/Poseidon 77, 86, 88, 94–5,
    100, 108, 174–5, 204, 227
  SLBM 75, 82, 86, 94–5, 99, 105,
    108, 129, 149, 175
  Trident/ULMS 86–8, 106, 108,
    115–16, 175, 186, 228, 231
nuclear tests *see* explosions, nuclear
nuclear waste 33, 222–3
Nuremburg tribunal *see* war, laws of

Okinawa 141
Oppenheimer, J. Robert 15, 38

Orford Ness 141
OTH *see* early-warning
Overkill 11, 12, 14, 101, 189, 230

pacifism *see* CND
Pauling, Linus 27
Pentz, Michael 13, 233
Phosgene 61
pikadon 22, 24, 40
Pipes, Professor 186
plowshares 28, 44
plutonium 30, 33–5, 39, 43, 44, 60, 148, 182–3
Powell, C. F. 27
Powers, Francis Gary 137
Presidential Directive (PD 59) 116
Priestley, J. B. 192, 201
Protect and Survive 46–7, 50–51, 56
proton beam 90
public opinion polls 201, 209, 231
Pugwash Movement 27, 145, 197

Quakers 195, 196

radiation, radioactivity 25, 26, 39–43, 47–56, 77
radiation sickness 52
radioactive fallout *see* fallout
Randle, Michael 198, 207–9
Reagan, Ronald 186, 229
Rees, Duncan 230, 233
Richardson, Jo 224, 233
Rodgers, William 204
Roman Empire 158, 159
Roosevelt, Franklin D. 15, 16
Rotblat, Joseph 11, 16, 26, 27, 39, 201
Rusk, Dean 117
Russell, Bertrand 27, 170, 192, 196, 201, 206

SALT 12, 99, 104, 128–34, 141–9, 172, 185, 221, 229
satellite observation 137–40, 142
Scarborough *see* Labour movement
Schlesinger, James 73–4
scientists 185, 196, 210, 222

sensors 69–70, 88–9
Silkin, John 225
SIPRI 12, 54, 91, 109, 117, 164, 239
Soper, Rev. Donald 195, 197
South Africa 147, 183
Spain 182
Sprint *see* missiles, ABM
sputnik 195
SS-9 *see* missiles
SS-20 *see* missiles
Stalin, Joseph 18
Steele, Harold and Sheila 198, 207
Steele, Jonathan 13, 121
Stockholm Peace Appeal 192–5, 203
strontium-90 25, 53, 55, 222
Suez 196
summit conference 202, 203
surveillance
  underwater 89
  spy photography 137
Sweden 174, 176, 182
Switzerland 182
Szilard, Leo 15, 16, 17, 26

tanks 113
Teller, Edward 38
Thompson, Edward (E.P.) 205, 230, 240
Titan *see* missiles
TNW *see* missiles
Tornado *see* aircraft, MRCA
treaties 132–3
  BW convention 62, 128, 132–4
  CTBT (Comprehensive Test Ban) 132–4, 146–7
  GCD (General and Complete Disarmament) 145–6
  Hotline 122–3, 211, 215
  NPT (Non-Proliferation) 133, 147–8, 186, 215
  PTBT (Partial Test Ban) 130–32, 135, 211–17
  SALT *see* SALT
  Threshold 131–3, 136
tritium 29, 37
Truman, Harry S. 38
Turkey 140

underground nuclear tests *see* explosions, nuclear
United Nations   144, 150, 170, 171, 238
  Association (UNA)   202, 224, 226
  Special Session on Disarmament (UNSSD)   150–51, 226, 230
uranium   15, 29, 30, 34, 183
USA *see under appropriate subject heading*
USSR *see under appropriate subject heading*

verification *see* inspection
Vietnam
  war   60, 67–9, 102, 169
  anti-war activities   212, 215–19

Waldheim, Kurt   146
Walker, Walter   104–6
war
  accidental   117–24, 202
  laws of   14, 59, 61, 65–6, 161, 208
  limited/small   60, 70, 125, 163
  toys   155

War Game, The   230, 240
warfare   154–64
  APW (anti-personnel)   64–66, 161
  ASW (anti-submarine)   12, 88–90, 185
  CBW (chemical and biological)   61, 62–4, 67–8, 229
  communal   158
  conventional   69, 88
  electronic   69, 88
  national   160–62
  nuclear   45–58
  professional   158
Warnke, Paul   12
Warsaw Pact   109, 113, 179, 220
WDC   219, 227, 230, 232
weapons *see* bombs, missiles, nuclear submarines, warfare
Westmoreland, William   69
Wilson, Sir Harold   188
World Disarmament Campaign *see* WDC

Yukawa, Hideki   27

Zuckerman, Lord   150, 166

More About Penguins and Pelicans

For further information about books available from Penguins please write to Dept EP, Penguin Books Ltd, Harmondsworth, Middlesex UB7 0DA.

In the U.S.A.: For a complete list of books available from Penguins in the United States write to Dept CS, Penguin Books, 625 Madison Avenue, New York, New York 10022.

In Canada: For a complete list of books available from Penguins in Canada write to Penguin Books Canada Ltd, 2801 John Street, Markham, Ontario L3R 1B4.

In Australia: For a complete list of books available from Penguins in Australia write to the Marketing Department, Penguin Books Australia Ltd, P.O. Box 257, Ringwood, Victoria 3134.